Soldiers of the Cross

Soldiers of the Cross

The African American Journey from Slavery to the Promised Land

Rev. Charlie White and the First South Carolina Volunteers at Hilton Head, South Carolina

John Allen White Jr

ISBN: 0692531599
ISBN 13: 9780692531594
Library of Congress Control Number: 2016901268
CreateSpace Independent Publishing Platform
North Charleston, South Carolina

Contents

Preface

M‌Y PERSPECTIVE OF African American liberation evolved over a twenty year period. Shortly after the release of the movie *Glory* over twenty years ago, I researched black Civil War history and slavery. I was shocked by the amount of history in existence that, although readily available, was completely unabsorbed or unowned by African Americans. This perplexed me for many years. An African American once asked me a simple question that I struggled for twenty years to answer. The question was "Why do we need to know the history that you are revealing?" My answer was clear: "Because it is the truth." But I didn't feel that my answer was adequate. I was not connecting with the African American community. I felt that it was vital that African Americans learn the truth about their history, but I struggled to explain why and convince my audience that it was necessary. After all, if the history that I revealed was not supported by the NAACP and black leaders such as Jesse Jackson, then why should anyone listen to an engineer who studied black history as a hobby?

Respect for one's identity can only be taught by learning the correct history. Respect was traditionally won on the battlefield. When one's history is controlled by another, respect can be lost by hiding or changing history. A poor picture of what we were can negatively impact what we can do in the future.

Malcolm X tried to correct the poor self-image of African Americans by teaching an antiestablishment view of African American history. He discovered, however, that African Americans were skeptical of historical information that came from outside of the establishment. Malcolm X said in his autobiography, "You have to be very careful introducing the truth to the black man, who has never previously heard the truth about himself. The black brother is so brainwashed that he may reject the truth when he first hears it. You have to drop a little bit on him at a time, and wait a while to let that sink in before advancing to the next step."

African American history and identity as well are based on the premise of victimization. It is hard to argue that slaves were not victims, but it is also easy to conclude they had no self-reliance. That is the problem with being victims: we are not expected to improve our condition or have high expectations. It is these low expectations that haunt African Americans. It is these low expectations that keep people from trying to find the truth of their history and accepting what is given to them.

President Barack Obama does not consider himself to be a victim, and he sees his potential as unlimited. However, Obama has no slave blood in him, a fact that is seldom mentioned. He was raised by white people, and his father was an African. He may have experienced racism, but it did not harm or restrict his identity. It is significant that America's first black president has no slave blood and appears to not carry the burden of slavery.

It is possible for victims to be transformed to victors, but it requires an act of faith. One must believe that he or she is a victor, although circumstances may suggest otherwise. I have recently become a fan of Joel Osteen. He has a very powerful message and a very large following. He often uses the words "victim" and "victor." He convinces people that they are not victims but victors, no matter what the circumstances are. Joel believes that God sees all his children as victors; we just need to believe.

I have taught black slavery and Civil War history to a wide range of people, from executives to prisoners and from children to seniors. My determination intensified after I shared this history with two Flint native black history scholars,

Dr. George Moss and Katheryn Hunter-Williams. Shortly after discovering this material, I was given an opportunity to share my research with the listening audience of a Flint, Michigan, gospel-music radio station called WFLT. I spoke for over an hour and anticipated feedback from the Flint community. Only one person called the station for more information, a college teacher named Jim Campbell. Jim asked me to speak at his black-history class at Mott Community College, which I was eager to do. I attended Mott College for three years before transferring to the engineering school at the University of Michigan. I was surprised to see that Jim was white and teaching a black-history class. I spoke to Jim's history class on several occasions for close to two hours each time. I enjoyed speaking to Jim's captive audience, and he invited me to speak to another captive audience at the Thumb Correctional Facility in Lapeer, Michigan. Jim had been a prison volunteer for some time and had established relationships with many inmates serving there. Jim was not only a teacher in prison, but he was also a friend to the prisoners. He was interested in the lives and well-being of the inmates even after they were released from prison. On several occasions, I met with him for lunch, and a prisoner who had recently been released joined us. That released prisoner remains to be a very dear friend of mine.

I had this idea of teaching black history with presentations, plays, and reenactments. The idea was to use black history as a tool for making the lives of people better. Jim agreed to help me and serve on the board of the Gospel Army Black History Group from its beginning. We were given grants by the Charles Steward Mott Foundation, even though they did not normally support educational programs. They did, however, recognize the exclusion of black Civil War history from American history and approved our grant. We were also supported by several grants from the Community Foundation of Greater Flint.

We taught this history at schools, prisons, and at a reproduction of a nineteenth-century village called Crossroads Village. Jim's most compelling role, however, was portraying John Brown at his trial and hanging. Jim wrote his own script and said what he thought John Brown would say:

> I pity the poor in bondage, that have none to help them;
> that is why I am here—not to gratify any personal animosity,
> revenge, or vindictive spirit.
> It is my sympathy with the oppressed and wronged, that are as good as you, and as precious in the sight of
> God. You may dispose of me easily, but this question is still to be settled—the Negro question—the end
> of that is not yet.
> Now if it is deemed necessary that I should forfeit my life for the furtherance of the ends of justice, and mingle
> my blood further with the blood of my children and with the blood of millions in this slaved country whose rights
> are disregarded by wicked, cruel, and unjust enactments, I say, let it be done. Let it be done, let it be done.

On his way to the gallows, Jim would stop to kiss a black child, according to John Brown's legend. Jim did this well because he had John Brown's soul. Working with Jim was like reliving history with John Brown.

I was also moved by another member of our group named Major Grays. Major would tell a story of a little slave woman who dared to pray in a slave-trading yard under risk of flogging. The trading yard was supervised by a man named Major Long. It was reported by a slave that they prayed and were questioned by the overseer. She voluntarily confessed that she prayed, while others remained silent. Major Long allowed the woman to be sold with her family intact because of respect for her bravery.

I felt this was an important story, and Major Grays did as well. Even when performing in harsh weather conditions in front of small audiences, Major would faithfully describe the power of this pious woman's faith. Even while he was dying, he walked unaided to the rocking chair, where he told his narrative. Following Jim's and Major's deaths, I questioned my purpose. Both Jim and Major were irreplaceable. I felt unworthy of leading such classy people, and I questioned our ability to influence the African American community.

Fig. 1. The Gospel Army Black History Group

Although I have only mentioned two, there were many hardworking, dedicated people that helped me with the Gospel Army Black History Group. Special thanks go to Pat Gray our director and Lou Penton our program producer. My wife Nancy wife was always by my side with my two son's Christopher and Sean White. My son's started re-enacting when they were about 12 years old. Confederate re-enactor Bill Adams introduced us to re-enacting. Bill's support gave me a positive attitude towards Confederate re-enactors which I maintain today. I am very thankful to the many Confederate reenactors who helped us honor black Civil War soldiers. It would have been impossible to reenact black Civil War battles without their help. In the Gospel Army collage picture above, a Confederate Civil War reenactment group salutes black Civil War reenactors as they march past them. Mutual respect is what my efforts are all about.

I would also like to express my gratitude to the white re-enactors of the Eighth Michigan. They taught me Civil War arms use and battle tactics. I so much loved marching with the Cumberland Guard and singing their marching song. Their support gave me the opportunity to train young black reenactment groups and participate in major Civil War battle reenactments.

I recruited Flint Northwestern High School students for the 102nd USCT Co. C Civil War re-enactment group. At the core of the group were RaMon Guines, Dana Milton, Yahel Scott and Edward Ward. LeRoy Martin sharpened our re-enacting skills. I would also like to mention my best buddy Curtis Thompson who became a re-enactor as well and accompanied Lou Penton and I too many battle re-enactments. I would especially like thank my dear friend Dr. Larry Reynolds who introduced me to re-enacting in the 102nd Michigan USCT.

Information about the history and participants of the Gospel Army can be found on our website: http://www.thegospelarmy.com/.

Transformation from victim to victor requires determination because determination is an important characteristic of victors. A popular preacher named Bishop T. D. Jake once said that a man wanted to speak at his mega church. The bishop replied that he had not earned that right. Once the man was shunned, hated, cursed, beaten, knocked down, and then got back up and climbed to his spot on the mountain, he would have earned the right to speak at his church. What the bishop said sounds harsh, but I think the point he was making was this: we all face hardships and challenges, but what we need to know is how we overcome tribulations. This is best learned by people who have withstood the test of hardship.

The greatest glory in living lies not in never falling, but in rising every time we fall.
—Nelson Mandela

As we study real African American history, we will discover values that improve our lives as well as the lives of others.
—John A. White Jr.

Introduction

I WAS A research engineer and Civil War re-enactor for over twenty years. My passion for research expanded beyond my engineering career to African American history and I founded the Gospel Army Black History Group. Much of my training is in engineering which is based on facts and mathematics developed from proofs. History on the other hand is story telling that is based on the perspective of the story teller. I discovered that much of African American history was told from the perspective of people that supported or was indifferent to slavery. African American identity was created from this southern traditional perspective which was used to support racial discrimination.

I also discovered that the African American perspective of liberation did exist, it was told by a little known man of the times, William Wells Brown. In 1866 Brown wrote *The Negro in the American Rebellion* one year after the end of the Civil War and shortly after writing the first African American history book "*The Black Man: His Antecedents, His Genius, and His Achievements* (1863)". I was sure that I could not do justice to a topic that was well addressed by this accomplished writer, historian and orator. However, Brown was unknown to many and his books were over looked. Although I am not a historian or writer, I used my passion for research and my technical skills to address this oversight. My focus was not on teaching common knowledge history, traditional historians are much better at that task. My focus is on uncovering lost history that should be common knowledge American History. I developed a perspective of African American slave liberation that used the words of contemporary African American's and abolitionist to represent their perspective.

Slavery and slave liberation is best described by former slaves, "If you want Negro History, you will have to get it from somebody who wore the shoe." Primary historical sources such as the slave narratives, the works of William Wells Brown, periodicals, letters, memoirs and paintings are used here to uncover lost history. I argue that American History that does not fully include the actions taken by African Americans to win their own freedom is incomplete and has an adverse effect on African American identity. The *power of God* and prayer were the only powers possessed by slaves. The *Invisible Steal-away to Jesus Prayer Movement* was illegal in the South with penalty of flogging but the movement inspired the abolitionists and ignited the Civil War. When the opportunity was available for liberated blacks to fight for freedom, Colored Troops had a significant impact on the Union victory. Black troops demonstrated a willingness and ability to capture deadly confederate fortifications which helped President Lincoln's win reelection over an anti-emancipation opponent. People that are commonly viewed as victims are redefined as victors.

CHAPTER 1

African Slave Identity

"Our fathers were brought here slaves because they were captured in war,
and in hand to hand fights, too."

The Bushmen, Adam, and Eve

RELIGION PLAYS A significant role in the lives of Africans and is a major part of African identity. The belief in the power of God started in Africa, the homeland of the human race. According to the Journey of Man DNA study, the Bushmen or San (which means "settlers" in Nama) of South Africa are thought to be the first descendants of the human race, and all other races are their descendants. In other words, the biblical character Eve resembled a Bushman.[1]

All humans of all races can be differentiated by thirteen genetic markers on the Y chromosome. European ancestors left Africa in the second wave around thirty thousand years ago. Their trail led to Syria and then northwest to the Balkans. From the Balkans, they traveled to Central Asia, where they split into several groups. One of these groups, characterized by marker M174, traveled east to Europe. The other twelve markers, such as skin color, reflect adaptation to climate as humans occupied various environments around the world. Europeans have the genetic markers of the Bushmen as well as M174.

I went to visit a remote Bushmen village called Nhoma in northwest Namibia Africa in the summer of 2014. Facial features of all human races can be seen in their faces. Note that their skin complexion in not much different than mine. However, the source of their skin color is 100 percent Bushmen while mine is a mixture of West African and European. Also note that I am a lot taller than the Bushmen. The Bushmen were hunter-gatherers and did not participate in large-scale warfare. This fact suggests that humans are basically peace-loving creatures. Large-scale wars accompanied large civilizations.

In 1886, Andrew Lang published a book called *Myth, Rituals, and Religion.* Lang's book suggests that all religions share common elements, including a belief in a power that Lang says "makes for righteousness in this world and the next, and a mythical element." Lang obtained his information from early explorers and missionaries such as Dr. David Livingstone. Livingstone was a Scottish missionary and among the first white men to explore Africa. From 1840 to 1873, he explored Africa from the Cape to the Equator and from the Atlantic Ocean to the Indian Ocean. Livingstone observed the religious practice of people such as the Bushmen long before they were in contact with white men. He concluded that their reliance on prayer and the power of God was similar to his own. He said, "*They spoke in the same way of the direct influence exercised by God in giving rain to the answer of prayers of the rainmakers, and in granting deliverance in times of danger, as they do now, before they ever heard of white men.*" Since all humans are descendants of people that

---

1 Spenser Wells, *Journey of Man: A Genetic Odyssey* (Princeton University Press), 2002, 56–8.

resemble Bushmen, it is assumed that reliance on prayer and the power of God was passed down from our early common ancestors. This would explain why the practice of prayer and belief in God is shared by all people all over the world.

Fig. 2. Nhoma Village Bushmen and the author, 2014

Slave Trade among African Tribes

By the eighteenth century, thirty thousand slaves a year passed through the Elmina (West Africa) slave port alone. These slaves spoke many different languages or tongues. In the book *Historical and Cultural Atlas of African Americans,* Molefi K. Asante and Mark T. Mattson [2] describe the African origin of American slaves. A few of the many African American seed tribes are: Nok, Ghana, Sundiata, Timbuktu, Sankore, Nsibidi, Benin, Uthman dan Fodio, Gao, Jenne, Ouagadougou, Segu, Dogon, Touba, Keita, Mali, Shango, Oshun, Ogun, Kumasi and Agades. There are thousands of other names of tribes in the western region of Africa.

---

2 Molefi K. Asante and Mark T. Mattson, *Historical and Cultural Atlas of African Americans* (Macmillan Publishing Company), New York, NY, 1992, 6-8.

Tribal Warfare

England outlawed slavery by the 1800s; however, Africa was addicted to slavery's wealth and continued the practice until modern times. Many Africans were not ready to let go of the slave trade and lower their lifestyle. Although most East African slavers were Arab, most West African slavers were black. It should be noted that most African Americans are of West African descent. Many slaves were taken by war between competing West African tribes. For example, an article that appeared in an Indiana and Maryland newspaper in 1847 described the execution of two thousand slaves by a warring black tribe. This incident occurred at a slave port called Gallineous on Ascension Island in the Atlantic Ocean between Africa and South America. Gallineos appears to be a West African port. Since many black West African tribes were slavers, it is assumed these slavers were black tribesmen. The article speaks for itself.

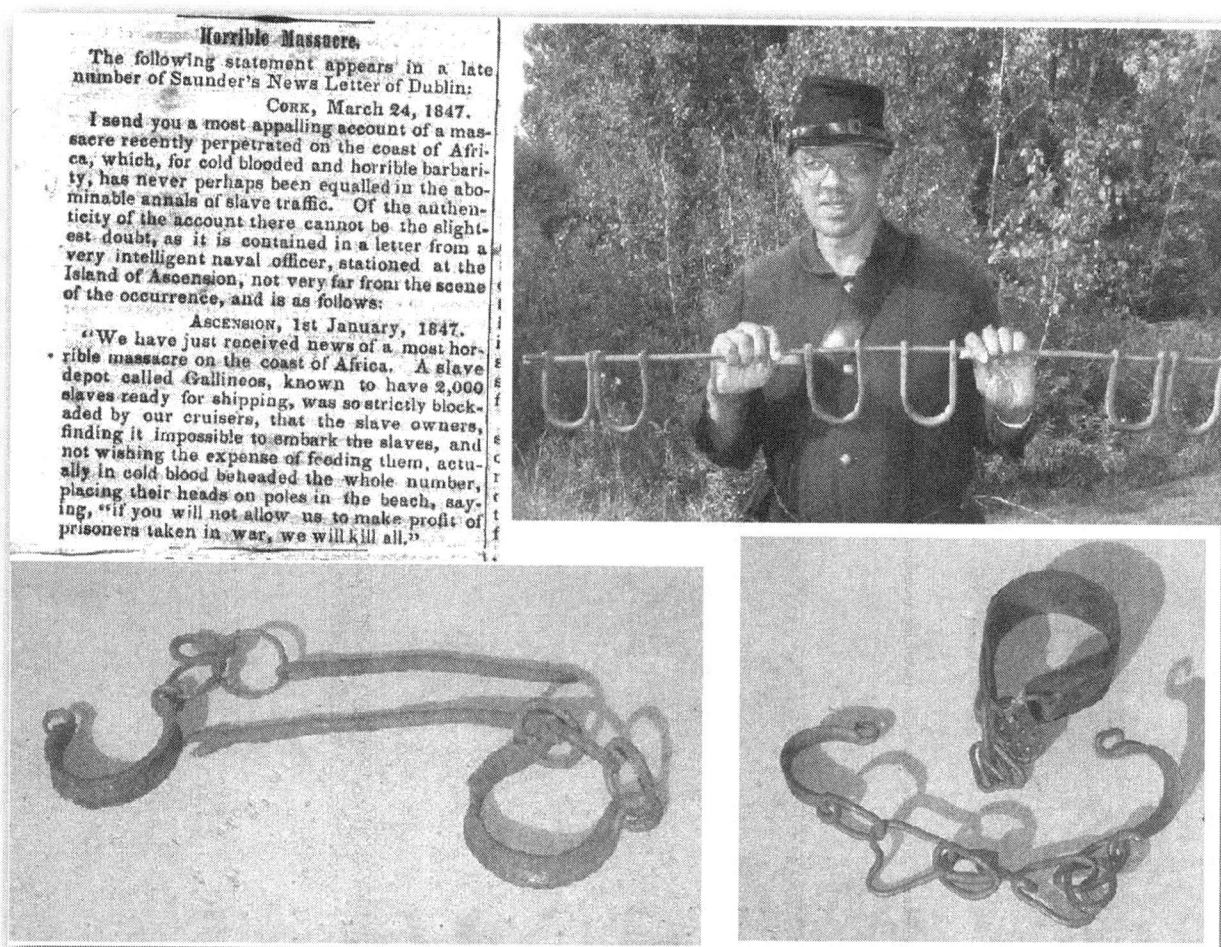

Fig. 3. Top: "Horrible Massacre" (*Washington Republican*, Salem, Indiana, Friday, May 21, 1847, and *Carroll County Democrat* (Maryland), April 29, 1847 and Slave Ship Shackles
Bottom: Slave Shackles and Collar

Traditionally, African American slaves were viewed as victims of capitalistic white slave traders. This belief supports an identity of dependency and lack of personal responsibility. When people deny responsibility for their predicament, they also lack the belief that they can change it. Blacks played a large part in supporting the slavery system. For example, a free black man from New Orleans said to General Butler, "General, we come from a fighting race. Our fathers were brought here slaves because they were captured in war, and in hand to hand fights, too. We are willing to fight. Pardon me, General, but the only cowardly blood we have got in our veins is the white blood." Not only did this man take responsibility for his people's enslavement, but he also took responsibility for winning their freedom. He became an officer in the first black Union regiment and led his men in the first major battle. Accepting responsibility for one's position is a major step toward healing.

CHAPTER 2

African American Identity Persecution

"I ain't no nigger, I's a Negro, and I'm Miss Liza Mixon."

The Slave Narratives

IN ORDER TO understand the N-word, we must understand the people who wore that label. Slaves were not allowed to read or write, but their lives were captured in the slave narratives. Only the white perspective on slavery was well known at that time. When Harriet Beecher Stowe revealed the black perspective in her book *Uncle Tom's Cabin*, antislavery sentiment increased significantly. Still, white Southerners hid the ugly aspects of slavery in the closet to support the slavery system.

Unfortunately, little historical material about slavery or the Civil War is written for black audiences. Much of this material is difficult to find, so I am including in this book primary historical documentation. I will review each document and discuss the influence the material can have on our daily lives.

Black universities such as Fisk University of Tennessee and Southern University of Louisiana were the first to see a need to document American slave history in 1929. At this time, former slaves were in their seventies, and it was important to get their perspectives on slavery before they passed away.

During the Depression, over fifteen million people were unemployed. President Franklin Roosevelt responded with a project called the New Deal for economic recovery and social reform. The Work Progress Administration or WPA was established to aid unemployment during the Great Depression. Between 1936 and 1938, the WPA Federal Writers' Project (FWP) sent out-of-work writers in seventeen states to interview ordinary people in order to write down their life stories. Over two thousand interviews were made and compiled into seventeen volumes of *Slave Narratives: A Folk History of Slavery in the United States from Interviews with Former Slaves*. My favorite source of the slave narratives is *Bullwhip Days: The Slaves Remember*, edited by J. Mellon. Mr. Reed, a former slave, explains in the book's introduction why the interviews are so important:

> If you want Negro History, you will have to get it from somebody who wore the shoe, and by and by, from one to the other, you will get a book.

Review of the slave narratives reveals a constant and exclusive use of the word "nigger" by former slaves to describe themselves. This is a turnoff for most people. It is hard to respect people who refer to themselves as niggers or expect them to have anything to contribute to well-educated people. We judge people, however, through the eyes of the American establishment.

Slaves were taught to not talk about slavery. Songs were altered to not appear to criticize the system.

'Lots of old slaves close the door before they tell the truth about their days of slavery. When the door is open, they tell how kind their masters were and how rosy it all was. You can't blame them for this, because they had plenty of early discipline, making them cautious about saying anything uncomplimentary about their masters."[3]
---MARTIN JACKSON
Bull Whip Days Page225

An Analysis of the N-Word

African American identity is unique to the extent that a label for identity, the N-word is an insult. The creation of this insult is the result of slave identity persecution. Identity persecution is the act of controlling someone's identity for self-interest, in this case to support slavery. Slave identity receives little respect from the American establishment. A popular impression of slaves is that of servants portrayed in the classic movie *Gone with the Wind*. Slaves are considered helpless victims with no control of their lives or future, lacking the crucial American values of liberty and purpose. A lack of ancestral respect can lead to a lack of self-respect and respect for others. Generations of African American youth are expected to carry this ancestral shame, with little preparation or support.

When Europeans first came in contact with the dark-skinned people of Africa, English speaking people used the Latin term *niger*,[4] which means "shining black," to name them. I acquired an old German map of the people of Africa that divided the continent into three sections. The top section was called "Arab," the bottom section was called "Bushmen," and the large middle section was called "Neger." I was puzzled by the word "Neger," so I asked a European colleague if he knew the word's meaning. He said promptly, "Black." *Neger* means "black" in German and it is capitalized to be used as a proper noun. The American English word "nigger" simply came from the Latin name *Niger* however it is not capitalized or it is used as a common noun. The Spanish version of the word for black African is *Negro,* and the French version is *Negre.*

The British appear to be responsible for creating the N-word but not responsible for using it as a racial slur. Oddly, the *English Dialect Dictionary*[5] does not define a nigger as a black person at all but as "a hard worker; adept." The British referred to African slaves or "Niger's" as hard workers absent of racial inferiority. They appear to have created the common noun *"nigger"* to describe any hard worker of any race. However, racism was used to justify American slavery and slave identity was property so their name was used as a common noun instead of proper noun. The derogatory aspects of the N-word are an American creation that was probably derived to support American slavery racism.

The American Heritage Dictionary of the English Language, however, defines a "nigger" as "a Negro or member of any dark-skinned people." This is an offensive term used derogatorily. Similarly, the modern Webster's definition of "nigger" is "a negro; in vulgar derision or depreciation. It is usually intended and interpreted as highly insulting and vulgar."

---

3 Martin Jackson, Bull Whip Days, p225

4 Wiktionary, *niger,* http://en.wiktionary.org/wiki/niger.

5 Joseph Wright, *The English Dialect Dictionary Being The Complete Vocabulary Of All Dialect Works Still In Use, Or Known To Have Been In Use During The Last Two Hundred Years* (New York: G. P. Putnam's Sons, 1905).

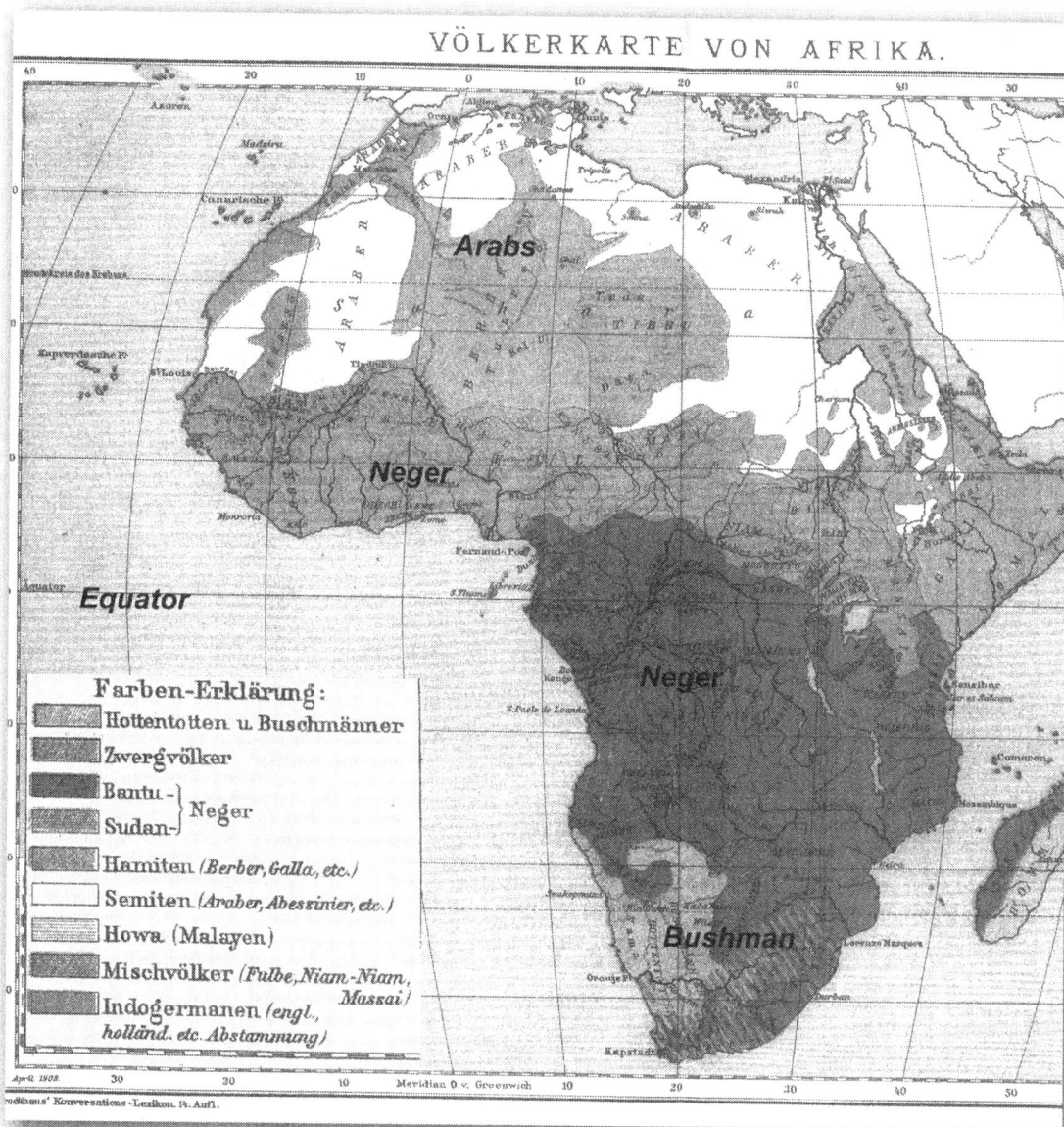

Fig. 4. 1908 German map of Africa

In other words, "Niger" is like "Negro" because they refer to a dark-skinned African, but "nigger" is an insult. Note that the word "Niger" sounds like "nigger," except to the American establishment, the meaning is different. In other words, a black American slave is defined by the American establishment as inferior, demonic, or evil. The Spanish version of slavery was far more humane than the American version of slavery. Spanish slaves were treated with more respect, so their name "Negro" became a more respectable version of "Niger," which eventually was removed from the English language.

The word "coolie" is similar to the word "niger" in that it also became an offensive term used to refer to a race of people. "Coolie" is a racial slur toward people of Asian descent. The word originally referred to Asian laborers. Apparently, nonwhite, poor laborers were frowned upon in the American system; thus their name, "coolie," became derogatory like "niger."

Slave Dehumanization; Identity Degradation and Humiliation

The origin of the N-word is slavery, and it was a label given to the American slave. Racism was used to justify slavery, and racism was identity persecution. The Jane Elliot Experiment[6] clearly describes the destructive effects of racism on identity. Jane Elliot was an elementary teacher in Iowa. The day after Martin Luther King's assassination, she divided her class into a brown-eyed group and a blued-eyed group, treating each as though they were superior and inferior for a day. The group labeled superior was rewarded by praise for achievements and were given extra privileges such as allowed to sit at the front of the room. The group labeled inferior was blamed for failure and criticized; they had to sit in the back of the room. When the inferior group was allowed to be superior on the following day they showed significantly more compassion to the inferior group. Results revealed that racism effectively destroyed healthy identity and replaced it with low self-esteem. The superior group was program to excel and the inferior group was programed to fail. African American identity was persecuted to the extent that their identity became a derogatory word, which adversely affects the performance of black youth.

Why does the American establishment have such low regard for slaves? The persecution of victims is a right won by victors on the battlefield. American manhood is based on the courage and purpose of victors; those that lacked these traits, such as victims, were not respected. American establishment heritage is Western civilization. The Western theory of slavery can be traced back to Aristotle (382–322 BC). In his book *Politics*, he said, "Humanity is divided into two: the masters and the slaves; or, if one prefers it, the Greeks and the Barbarians, those who have the right to command; and those who are born to obey." Slavery was practiced all over the world for centuries. Slaves were captured in war, and when at war, we demonize and vilify our enemy. We want to hate our enemies, not love them, so differences, such as race, have always been emphasized and similarities minimized. It is difficult to destroy or hurt people we like. Racism was used during the years of the slave trade to justify the dehumanization of slaves. It was impossible to implement slavery humanely and maintain its profitability. Mental bondage was essential to bind the minds of the slave so that hands and feet were free to work.

At the heart of the slaves' apparent inferiority as judged by the American establishment was the perceived inferiority of slaves on the battlefield.

Fig. 5. "Dark Artillery," *Frank Leslie's Illustrated*, October 5, 1861

---

6 Wikipedia, *Jane Elliot,* http://en.wikipedia.org/wiki/Jane_Elliott.

This cartoon was published in *Frank Leslie's Illustrated* on October 5, 1861. This cartoon reflected the views of the American establishment at the beginning of the Civil War. Northern Civil War officers and soldiers shared this view.

The American establishment propagated its views of slaves through the media. Supporters of slavery used newspapers and magazines to promote the idea that blacks were happy as slaves and uninterested in freedom. This value of not wanting freedom was considered by the establishment to certainly be un-American. The media portrayed black men as cowards with no principles who were unwilling to fight for their freedom. A proslavery newspaper published this article following the Fort Donelson battle, which occurred February 16, 1862. William Wells Brown collected many articles during the war and published them in the first African American Civil War history book, *The Negro in the American Rebellion.* Brown wrote:

" Proslavery newspaper correspondents from the North, in the Western and Southern departments, still continued to report to their journals that the slaves would not fight if an opportunity was offered to them. Many of these were ridiculously amusing. The following is a sample

"I noticed upon the hurricane-deck, to-day, an elderly negro, with a very philosophical and retrospective cast of' countenance, squatted upon his bundle, toasting his shins against the chimney, and apparently plunged into a state of profound meditation. Finding by inquiry that he belonged to the North Illinois, one of the most gallantly behaved and heavily-losing regiments at the Fort-Donelson battle, and part of which was aboard, I began to interrogate him upon the subject. His philosophy was so much in the Falstaffian vein that I will give his views in his own words, as near as my memory serves me: -

" ' Were you in the fight ? '
" ' Had a little taste of it, sa.'
" ' Stood your ground, did you ? '
" ' No, sa ; I runs.'
" ' Run at the first fire, did you ? '
" ' Yes, sa. ; and would ha' run soona had I know'd it war comin'.'
" ' Why, that wasn't very creditable to your courage.'
" ' Dat isn't in my line, sa ; cookin's my perfeshun.'
" ' Well, but have you no regard for your reputation ? '
" ' Refutation's nuffin by the side ob life.'
"'Do you consider your life worth more than other people's ? '
" ' It's worth more to me, sa.'
" ' Then you must value it very highly.'
" Yes, sa, 'I does ; more dan all dis wuld ; more dan a million of dollars, sa : for what would dat be Wuf to a man wid de bref out of him. Self-perserbashum am de fust l'bm wid me.'
" ' But why should you act upon a different rule from other men ? '
" ' Because different men set different values upon dar lives : mine is not in de market.'

" ' But if' you lost it, you would have the satisfaction
of knowing that you died for your country.'
" ' What satisfaction would dat be to me when de
power ob feelin' was gone ? '
" ' Then patriotism and honor are nothing to you ? '
" Nuffin whatever, sa: I regard dem as among de
vanities ; and den de gobernment don't know me ; I hab
no rights ; may be sold like old hoss any day, and dat's
all.'
" 'If our old soldiers were like you, traitors might
have broken up the Government without resistance.'
"'Yes, sa; dar would hab been no help for it. I
wouldn't put my life in de scale 'ginst any gobernment
dat ever existed; for no gobernment could replace de
loss to me.'
"'Do you think any of your company would have
missed you if' you had been killed ? '
" ' May be not, sa; a dead white man ain't much to
dese sogors, let lone a dead nigga; but I'd n missed
myself, and dat was de pint wid me.'
" It is safe to say that the dusky corpse of that African
will never darken the field of carnage."[7]

The black soldier portrayed in this article had a well-developed philosophy that was self-centered. He valued his life more than he valued such things as honor, duty, or self-respect. He had no purpose but to save himself. He ran from a battle, not because he was scared like most soldiers, but because it was the most logical action to take, considering the circumstances. He had "no dog in this fight." The author claimed that the black soldier was part of a Northern Illinois regiment. Black troops, however, were not mustered into Illinois regiments until 1864, two years after the article was published. These types of characterizations were so commonly used that blacks today easily believe that typical black soldiers were like the one described in the article. Most blacks lived in the South, where black characterizations were common in published literature and black heroism was censored.

Beatings were an inhumane method of controlling slave behavior. Beatings were a reminder to slaves that they were property and had no rights, which significantly degraded slave identity. The following narratives speak for themselves.

"Befo' I's a 'ield hand, dis nigger never gits whupped, 'cept for dis: Massa use me for huntin', and use me for de gun rest. When him have de long shot, I bends over and puts de hands on de knees, and Massa puts his gun on my back for to git de good aim. What him kills I runs and fotches, and I carries de game for him.

All dat not so bad, but when Massa shoots de duck in de water and I has to fotch it out, dat give me de worriment. De fust time off he tells me to go in de pond, I's skeert, powe'ful skeert. I takes off de shirt and pants, but dere I stands. I steps in de water, den back 'gain, and 'gain. Massa am gittin' mad. He say, "Swim

---

7 Brown, *The Negro in the American Rebellion*, 127.

in dere and git dat duck. " I says, "Yes, sar, Massa, " but I won't go in dat water till Massa hit me some licks. I couldn't never git use' to bein' de water dog for de ducks."[8]
John Finnely

" Nawsuh, he warn't good to none of us niggers. All de niggers roun' dar hated to be bought by him, 'kaze he wuz so mean. When he wuz too tired to whup us, he had de overseer do it, and de overseer wuz meaner dan de massa. But, Mister, de peoples wuz de same as dey is now. Dere wuz good uns and bad uns. I jus' happened to belong to a bad un. One day, I remembers my brother, January, wut cotched ober seein' a gal on de next plantation. He had a pass, but de time on it done gib out. Well, suh, when de massa found out dat he wuz a hour late, he got as mad as a hive of bees. So when brother January he come home, de massa took down his long mule skinner and tied him wid a rope to a pine tree. He strip his shirt off and said, "Now, nigger, I'm goin' to teach you some sense."

Wid dat, he started layin' on de lashes. January was a big, fine-lookin' nigger, de finest I ever seed. He wuz jus' four years older dan me, an' when de massa begin a-beatin' him, January neber said a word. De massa got madder and madder, kaze he could't make January holler.

"What's de matter wid you, nigger!" he say. "Don't it hurt?" January he neber said nothin', and de massa keep a-beatin' till little streams of blood started flowin' down January's chest, but he neber holler. His lips wuz a-quiverin', and his body wuz a-shakin', but his mouf it neber open; and all de while, I sat on my mammy's and pappy's steps a-cryin'. De niggers wuz all gathered about, and iome uv 'em couldn't stand it; dey hadda go inside deir cabins. Atter uhile, January, he couldn't stand it no longer hisself, and he say in a hoarse, loud whisper, "Massa! Massa! Have mercy on' dis poor nigger. "[9]
--William Colbert

It was essential that the slave except his fate. The slave was brain washed into believing that his ancestors were wild in Africa and he therefore needs a master to care for him in this new land.

"Ole Missus and young Missus told the little slave children that the stork brought the white babies to their mothers, but that the slave children were all hatched out from buzzards' eggs. And we believed it was true. ""[10]
--Katie Sutton

'We hadn't been brung over an' made slaves, us an' us chillun dat cing educated an' civilized would be naked savages back in Africa, now.'[11]
Tony Cox

Liberated African American Identity: I Ain't No Nigger

Slaves used the word "nigger" correctly, but as they merged into the American establishment, the word had a dual meaning. This is because the American establishment used the word "nigger" to assert dominance over blacks. The derogatory aspects of the N-word were based on racism.

---

8 John Finnely, Bull Whip Days, p238
9 *William Colbert*, Bull Whip Days, p420
10 Katie Sutton, Bull Whip Days, p39
11 Tony cox, Bull Whip Days, p50

As blacks displayed their fighting ability on the battlefield, myths of black inferiority were shattered. The power of the N-word was frequently abused, but this black soldier for example, went from being a victim to a victor, and the word had no power. A white captain in the USCT tried to sneak out of camp without authorization. He was stopped and questioned by a black USCT on guard. The captain tried to dominate the guard by saying that he would "shoot you, you damned nigger." The black corporal replied " that he was not a "nigger" but "a Federal soldier and wear the Federal uniform. I have taken the same oath that you have,""[12]. The captain was court-martialed and dismissed from the service.

Since the English word for black, "nigger," meant slave, an untarnished name for black Africans was borrowed from the Spanish—the word "Negro." Slaves were property; they had no last names, and their first names were commonly replaced by the N-word by their white owners. As slaves were liberated by the Union army, they were no longer property and took the last name of the previous owner. Since the N-word was reserved for American black slaves, the Spanish word for black, "Negro," was given to free or respected blacks. Eliza Evan described in her narrative her attempted transformation from disrespected property or nigger to respectable Negro.

> "One time, some Yankee soldiers stopped and started talking to me. One asked me what my name was. I say, "Liza," and he say, "Liza who?" I thought a minute and I shook my head, "Jest Liza. I ain't got no other name. "
>
> He say, "Who live up yonder in dat big house!" I say, "Mr. John Mixon. " He say, "You are Liza Mixon. " Den he say, "Do anybody ever call you 'nigger'?" And I say, "Yes, Sir. " He say, "Next time anybody. call you 'nigger, ' you tell 'em dat you is a Negro and your name is Miss Liza Mixon. " The more I thought of that, the more I liked it, and I made up my mind to do jest what he told me to.
>
> My job was minding the calves, while the cows was being milked. One evening, I was minding the calves and Old Master come along. He say, "What you doin', nigger?" say real pert like, "I ain't no nigger, I's a Negro, and I'm Miss Liza Mixon. " Old Master sho' was Surprised, and he picks up a switch and starts at me.
>
> Law', but I was skeered! I hadn't never had no whipping, so I run fast as I can to Grandma Gracie. I hid behind her, and she say, "what's the matter wid you, child?" And I say, Master John gwine whip me." And she say, "What you done?" And I say, "Nothing." She say she know better, and 'bout that time Master John got there. He say, "Gracie, dat little nigger sassed me. "She say Lawsie, child, what does ail you?" I told them what the Yankee soldier told me to say, and Grandma Gracie took my dress and lifted it over my head and pins my hands inside, and Lawsie, how she whipped me and I dassen't holler loud either. I jest said dat to de wrong person, didn't I?"[13]

African American Use of the N-Word

As I look back over the many years that I taught this material, a visit with a Flint Sunday-school class stands out. Flint was the birthplace of General Motors. Many folks from the South were recruited to work on the automotive assembly lines. Over the past thirty years, plants closed and poverty increased. Flint was known to have the highest rate of killings of any city its size in the nation. Many people, including blacks, have left Flint seeking the American dream in the

---

12 Glatthaar, *Forged in Battle*, 90.
13 Eliza Evens, *Bullwhip Days*, 341.

suburbs. I have had a number of coworkers refer to areas in Flint as places that they avoid. Still, I have gone into these areas to teach black Civil War history and enjoyed being there.

I worked with many prison inmates from Flint. Their families resided there, and I became acquainted with several of these families and frequently visited them. I noted that the mother of an inmate—let's call her Inmates' Mama—frequently used the N-word to describe black people. I wanted to understand how she used the N-word, so I asked Mama if Dr. Martin Luther King Jr. was a nigger. She replied no. I then pointed to a black kid playing on the sidewalk in front of her house and asked, "Is he a nigger?" She answered yes without hesitation. I don't think that she was trying to be disrespectful or hated black kids. She was only voicing her interpretation of our society's or establishment's view of black kids. Take the Trayvon Martin case, for example; many white people felt that killing Trayvon was justified because they viewed him as a threat. Martin Luther King Jr. is respected by everyone, but that black kid on the street may only be cherished by his mother. Not much good is expected of the black kid on the street as well as Inmates' Mamas kids or herself. Inmates' Mama appeared to have an alcohol problem, but she was a beautiful person. She just needed someone to tell her that she was not a nigger.

I discovered that this nigger identity of black children was prevalent throughout Inmates' Mama's neighborhood. I was given the opportunity to talk with a group of Sunday-school kids at a local church about black Civil War history. The kids in the class ranged in age from five to about ten years old. I asked them the question, "What is a nigger?" The answer came quickly and enthusiastically: "Us; we are niggers." The word "nigger" was their identity, but if we look that word up in the dictionary, it is described as an insult. Many Americans see a nigger as a person with low expectations and having little purpose but to "get over" or "get by." How do you tell kids that their identity is not respected by Americans or other people in the world? These children have inherited the shame of slavery, which results in no purpose, low expectations, low self-esteem, and low self-respect. These low expectations are far below their capability, so drug abuse often accelerates the failure process. Lack of self-respect leads to disrespect of others and violence. Black youth are expected to carry the burden of slavery but are not prepared by their teachers. I was there to teach them the truth about their identity, and that is what I did.

This is not the first time that I encountered this issue. I had too many very dear friends that died early of drug abuse. These people were very close to me, and I cherished their friendship. I noticed, however, that they lacked one important characteristic: a sense of purpose for their lives. My best friend's dad told me when I was a college student that I would one day lose my friend because he was going nowhere. We had been together all our lives; we met in kindergarten when we were four years old. Ricky's dad was right; Ricky committed suicide a few years later. I felt that my purpose was to make his life and death important.

My Liberation

Typical of young African American males of my generation, I was ashamed of slavery. In America, pride of one's identity was based upon love of freedom and the willingness to die protecting that freedom. African Americans were taught that their ancestors did practically nothing to gain their freedom largely because slavery was not that bad. The South argued that slavery was the natural state of blacks and that slavery represented their best interest. We were taught that slaves were liberated by President Lincoln and the Union army. There was a lack of African American Civil War history that supported slave victimization and a lack of personal responsibility. Identity is defined by history, so African American identity is largely shame.

I was a product of my environment; we are what we are taught. However, the truth can set you free; my mind was liberated by the truth. For ten years, I lived next door to a black Civil War re-enactor named Alvin Pinckney.

I often saw him dressed like a Civil War soldier on Saturday mornings. He said he was part of a Union artillery Civil War reenactment group. The group was white, but he said blacks had fought in the Civil War as well. *Noble,* I thought, *but delusional.* I had never heard of blacks fighting in the Civil War. I had seen thousands of Civil War soldiers in movies and on TV, but I had never seen black Civil War soldiers. Blacks were always portrayed as servants or laborers by the media, and unfortunately, that's how we learn a lot of American history. It was a well-established fact that blacks were freed by Abraham Lincoln and white Civil War soldiers because slaves were helpless victims. For ten years, I watched Alvin leave for Civil War reenactments on summer mornings, thinking he was fooling himself.

Fig. 6. *The Storming of Fort Wagner,* Lithograph by Louis Kurz and Alexander Allison, 1890

Several years after returning to Flint, Michigan, from Columbus, Ohio, I saw the movie *Glory.* I thought of Alvin as I watched the black men storm Fort Wagner. The movie supported Alvin's claims; maybe I was wrong. Once the movie appeared at local rental stores, I was embarrassed by the lack of interest in it. There were always plenty of available copies of *Glory* to rent, when, at the same time, competing movies were in short supply. The movie went on sale in the discount rack, but there were no takers, even after the price was cut in half.

The black soldiers who stormed Fort Wagner deserved more respect, and I needed to make a retribution for my ignorance and lack of faith in them. I had a conscience planted in my brain by my father. Although he commonly used the N-word to refer to blacks, he had an unending dedication to his ancestors. Every year, he attended the home coming of a church his grandfather, Charlie White, ministered at in Holly Grove, Arkansas. He supports our ancestral cemetery that is across the street from the church.

I made a plan to create a painting of black troops storming Fort Wagner. First, I sought to find a Civil War battle image and then have an artist friend replace white Union faces with black faces. At a bookstore outlet, I found the perfect book, *Great Battles of the Civil War*, by Martin Graham and George Skoch. The book contained prints of Civil War battles that were painted and published in 1880s by Louis Kurz and Alexander Allison.

I was in for a life-altering shock. The battle of Fort Wagner, which I had planned to create, had already been painted and published in 1890. On top of that, I discovered that there were other battles that included other black units, such as the battle of Olustee, Fort Pillow Massacre, and the Battle of Nashville. I thought there was only one black Civil War regiment when there were actually over 130 black regiments. I also thought that the black regiment only fought in two battles. With a little more research, I discovered that black regiments actually fought in more than four hundred battles. This was a mystery to me; why was black Civil War history hidden from me, or why didn't I look for it? With every step, Alvin appeared right, and I was wrong.

But how wrong was I? A trip to the Flint Public Library would surely prove that this information was hidden and my ignorance was justified. But no such luck; a book written by a former slave, one year after the Civil War, was easy to find. I didn't even need the aid of a librarian. The book was written by William Wells Brown and was called *The Negro in the American Rebellion*. Brown collected material during the Civil War that he felt would be important to blacks. The story of Big Bob is a good example of the type of material Brown collected. Big Bob was a slave preacher forced into Confederate labor with his followers. He overpowered his guard, put on a Confederate uniform, and marched his slaves to the Union line. The Union requested that he become a guerilla fighter, attacking Confederate targets behind Confederate lines.

In his book, Brown also included information about the religious sentiment of the men, which was not shown in the movie *Glory*. Apparently, the Fifty-Fourth Massachusetts carried a Christian banner. Brown wrote, "This is the first Christian banner that has gone into our war. By a strange, and yet not strange, providence, God has mistic this despised race the bearers of his standard. They are thus the real leaders of the nation."[14]

I was not, however, alone in my ignorance about Brown. Although the book was in plain sight, it had only been checked out seven times in ten years. I was not alone.

I wanted my own copy of the book, so I tried to obtain a copy at a bookstore. After describing the book to the salesperson, she replied, "This should be a classic." However, no copies had been ordered in ten years, so copies were no longer available. While browsing through a section of Civil War books, a book called *Bullwhip Days: The Slaves Remember* came to my attention. I immediately passed it by because I had been taught that slaves can contribute nothing of value. Despite my reluctance, something told me to pick the book up. My father had known former slaves and had a great deal of respect for them; they had purposeful lives. My great-grandmother (Clara White) was a former slave, and she frequently babysat him. They could not read or write, but they built schools, he often said, so that their descendants would learn to read. The book was a compilation of slave narratives, gathered through interviews of slaves who were part of the Work Progress Administration (WPA) program in the 1930s. Black universities had wanted to document the slave experience before all surviving ex-slaves were dead. The first narrative was that of Mary Reynolds, taken when she was one hundred years old. Mary was blind at the time of the interview, probably from glaucoma. The eye disease is very aggressive in African Americans and a leading cause of blindness. My mother, two of her brothers, and her mother went blind from the disease, and I have it as well. Each day that I can see is a gift from God. I skimmed the first page out of curiosity, to prove to myself that she had nothing worthwhile to contribute. For the third time, I was wrong again—however, big time, this time.

My curiosity was ignited by my discovery of black Civil War soldiers and the slave narratives. For many years, I researched both African American slavery and black Civil War history. I discovered that the American history that I was taught in school omitted many aspects of slave life as well as omitting practically all black Civil War history. History is written for an audience, and the primary goal of the author is to make money. A large audience is the southern public,

---

14 William Wells Brown, *The Negro in the American Rebellion* (n.p.: Lee & Shepard, 1866), 153.

which also has a significant influence on African American history. The southern white audience believed their Civil War cause was noble and blacks were better off as slaves. This southern perspective is what I was taught in school.

There is also an important question that needs to be answered: why is there so little support of slave history among African Americans? We have been all taught that slaves were victims that needed to be rescued and all that victims can possibly gain is justice. African American purpose is therefore limited to acquiring justice, which is self-centered. However, if African Americans saw slaves as victors, effort would be directed toward respecting and learning from slaves such as the study of the slave narratives.

Chains were used to hold the bodies of slaves in bondage, and Jim Crow was used to shackle the minds of African Americas. With the truth and help of Jesus, It is possible to turn these victims into victors. Jesus believed that "the truth shall set you free" (John 8:32).

CHAPTER 3

The Color of African American Slavery

"Miss Sara's maw died and they brung Miss Sara to suck with me. It's a thing we ain't never forgot."

William Wells Brown

WILLIAM WELLS BROWN was the first writer to reveal the intimacy between white slave masters and their black slaves. Brown's father was white, and his mother was a black slave. Brown wrote the first African American novel, which was called *Clotel; or, the President's Daughter*;[15] however, he was in England at that time. It was rumored that Thomas Jefferson fathered several children with his slave Sally Hemings. Wikipedia says, "A 1998 DNA study confirmed a match between the Jefferson male line and Eston Hemings's direct male descendant.[16] Based on this and the body of historic evidence, most Jeffersonian scholars have come to accept that Jefferson did father Hemings's children in a long relationship."

My favorite book on the Civil War is called *The Negro in the American Rebellion* by William Wells Brown. This book fascinated me because it was written by a "man of the times" and a former slave. While living in St. Louis as a slave, Brown worked for Lovejoy, another abolitionist. He escaped from his owner in St. Louis and became a conductor on the Underground Railroad as well as a great antislavery orator.

Brown wrote the first African American history books and documented the part blacks played in the Civil War. Brown wrote *The Black Man: His Antecedents, His Genius, and His Achievements* in 1863 and *The Negro in the American Rebellion* in 1867. Brown's view of the Civil War was unique. He admitted that he was neither historian nor writer; however, modern editors disagree. His work is highly respected. He included articles and letters in his book that he collected during the Civil War. Unfortunately, there was a fire at his publisher's warehouse, and many of Brown's books were destroyed. I am certain that few if any copies of his book existed in the South or at least in southern black classrooms, since very few African Americans have ever heard of William Wells Brown.

Slave Wet Nurses

Slave women routinely nursed and raised the children of their owners. The intimacy of nursing created strong emotional bonds between slaves and the children of slave owners. It was also an established practice that the children of slave owners be separated from the black children. It was important to the slave owners that their children grow up dominant

---

15 William Wells Brown, *Clotel; or, The President's Daughter: A Narrative of Slave Life in the United States*, 1853, ed. Robert Levine (Boston: Bedford, 2000).

16 Wikipedia, *Clotel*, http://en.wikipedia.org/wiki/Clotel.

and unattached to slaves. This did not always occur, however. For example, although Mary Reynolds was thought of as a "nigger gal" by her owner, Mary's love made the difference between life and death for the daughter of Mary's owner.

"I was born same time as Miss Sara Kilpatrick. Dr. Kilpatrick's first wife and my maw come to their time right together. Miss Sara's maw died and they brung Miss Sara to suck with me. It's a thing we ain't never forgot. My maw's name was Sallie and Miss Sara allus looked with kindness on my maw."

"We sucked till we was a fair size and played together, which wasn't no common thing. None the other li'l niggers played with the white chillun. But Miss Sara loved me so good. "I was jus' bout big nough to start playin' with a broom to go bout sweepin' up and not even half doin' it when Dr. Kilpatrick sold me. They was a old white man in Trinity and his wife died and he didn't have chick or child or slave or nothin'. Massa sold me cheap, cause he didn't want Miss Sara to play with no nigger young'un. That old man bought me a big doll and went off and left me all day, with the door open. I jus' sot on the floor and played with that doll. I used to cry. He'd come home and give me somethin' to eat and then go to bed, and I slep' on the foot of the bed with him. I was scart all the time in the dark. He never did close the door. "

"Miss Sara pined and sickened. Massa done what he could, but they wasn't no peartness in her. She got sicker and sicker, and massa brung nother doctor. He say, You li'l gal is grievin' the life out her body and she sho' gwine die iffen you don't do somethin' bout it.' Miss Sara says over and over, I wants Mary.' Massa say to the doctor, That a li'l nigger young'un I done sold.' The doctor tells him he better git me back iffen he wants to save the life of his child. Dr. Kilpatrick has to give a big plenty more to git me back than what he sold me for, but Miss Sara plumps up right off and grows into fine health. "Then massa marries a rich lady from Mississippi and they has chillun for company to Miss Sara and seem like for a time she forgits me."[17]
Mary Reynolds

Poor Whites

Slaves were not the only people held in low regard. Poor whites were often treated poorly. My wife, Nancy White, had an aunt named Laura Clark from Washington County, Kentucky. She lived to be one hundred years old, and I met her for the first time a month before her one-hundredth birthday. I enjoy listening to people like her, and I was particularly interested in finding out what life was like for her in the old days. She was born many years after the end of slavery, but she experienced a lot of southern culture. She said that there was one incident that puzzled her throughout her life. Back in the old days, the turn of the twentieth century, black people lived separately from white people in rural Kentucky, but people were not separated economically. The well-off and poor whites lived in the same neighborhoods. Once there was a young, poor white family with a very sick baby. Aunt Laura said, "You know, those poor white folks walked right past all those other white people all the way out to my house to ask for help. I don't understand why they did that after all these years." She said she did the best she could to help them. A picture of Aunt Laura and Nancy are included in the right bottom corner of the *Introduction* collage.

When we are scared or hurt, we seek protection and love. Poor whites were judged as unsuccessful and not having what it takes to prosper. The poor whites with a sick baby felt that they could find better help among poor blacks than rich whites. The Rachel Cruze narrative, below, sheds a little light on Aunt Laura's experience.

---

17 Mary Reynolds, narrative in Mellon, *Bullwhip Days, 15–23,* and *The American Slave,* vol. 5: 236–246.

Rachel Cruze was the daughter of a slave and a slave owner. Miss Nancy was her white grandmother, and she owned many slaves. Miss Nancy loved Rachel, but since Rachel was half black, she would not inherit any of Miss Nancy's property. Rachel's observations appear to support those of my wife's aunt:

"Do you know, the pore white folks of the South mostly had a harder time than the colored folks, under slavery, because the other white folks did not want them around. Many pore white folks would have starved if it had not been for slaves who stole food from their masters to feed the white folks."

Rachel Cruze went on to describe how her own grandmother did not want her to get physically close to the poor whites in her neighborhood:

"Fanny Oldsby was one of the pore whites who lived near Mis' Nancy, and Mis' Nancy would sometimes give her sewing to do, but she had to take it home to do it. Mis' Nancy wouldn't have her around the place. I used to get pretty lonesome sometimes because there wasn't a child of my age to play with. Fanny Oldsby had a little girl who came with her sometimes, but do you think Mis' Nancy would let me play with her? No, ma'am. I'd no more than sit down close to the little girl than I'd hear, ' Rachel, you come here this minute.' And, when I would go to her, Mis' Nancy would say, 'Don't you sit near her. Why, she'll bite you and she'll get your head full of lice.' The pore child would look at me and I'd look at her, but I didn't want her to bite me, so I didn't get close to her."[18]
Rachel Cruze

Another ex-slave narrative that appeared in *Bullwhip Days* corroborated this view that blacks and poor whites were on somewhat equal footing in the period after the Civil War:

"The white folks rode to church and the darkies walked, as many of the poor white folks did. We looked upon the poor white folks as our equals. They mixed with us and helped us to envy our masters. They looked upon our master as we did."[19]
Squire Dowd

---

18 Rachel Cruze, narrative in Mellon, *Bullwhip Days*, 209.
19 Squire Dowd, narrative in Mellon, *Bullwhip Days*, 136.

CHAPTER 4

Trib'lation: 'Things Past Tellin'

"Death would be preferable to the living death of the cotton fields"

Hopelessness

SLAVERY EXISTED ALL over the world. The Catholic form practiced in Spain permitted slaves to marry their masters; however, the Protestant version practiced in the United States was the cruelest form. Slavery was particularly cruel in the Delta cotton fields, where it was big business. Rachel Cruze describes how young black men that were taken to the Delta to be sold chose death over life in the cotton fields. When there was no hope, death could quickly follow, as pointed out in this narrative:

"As they walked together, they talked about their future, and they all agreed that death would be preferable to the living death of the cotton fields. And they decided that the first time they had to ferry across a river with the nigger trader, they would walk onto the Ferryboat and keep right on walking till they had walked off the other end. At the end of Dr. Sneed's farm was a ferry to carry people over to the Macabee farm on the other side, and when the nigger trader drove those slaves onto the ferry, that is exactly what they did: they all walked 'off into the deep of the river at the other end. If there was any among them who was lukewarm he was shoved in by the ones behind him."[20]
Rachel Cruze

Beatings

The beatings appeared to one of the worst aspects of slavery; they dehumanized the slave as well as the slaver. Slaves were frequently beat for poor or no reasons, which made their lives seem not worth living.

"Slavery was the worst days was ever seed in the world. They was things past tellin', but I got the scars on my old body to show to this day. I seed worse than what happened to me. I seed them put the men and women in the stock with they hands screwed down through holes in the board and they feets tied together and they naked behinds to the world. Solomon the [sic] overseer beat them with a big whip and massa look on. The niggers better not stop in the fields when they hear them yellin'. They cut the flesh

---

20 Mellon, *Bullwhip Days*, 213.

most to the bones and some they was when they taken them out of stock and put them on the beds, they never got up again.

"Seems like after I got bigger, I member' more'n more niggers run away. They's most al us cotched. Massa used to hire out his niggers for wage hands. One time he hired me and a nigger boy, Turner, to work for some ornery white trash name of Kidd. One day Turner goes off and don't come back. Old man Kidd say I knowed bout it, and he tied my wrists together and stripped me. He hanged me by the wrists from a limb on a tree and spraddled my legs around the trunk and tied my feet together. Then he beat me. He beat me worser than I ever been beat before and I faints dead away. When I come to I'm in bed. I didn't care so much iffen I died.

"I didn't know bout the passin of time, but Miss Sara come to me. Some white folks done git word to her. Mr. Kidd tries to talk hisself out of it, but Miss Sara fotches me home when I'm well enough to move. She took me in a cart and my maw takes care of me. Massa looks me over good and says I'll git well, but I'm ruint for breedin' chillun"[21]
Mary Reynolds

Slavery was composed of great contradictions. On one hand Blacks were considered inferior by white's but at the same time white's reserved the most intimate act that a mother has with her child. Black women commonly breast fed white children. It was an emotional an intimate experience for both wet nurse and child. It is not natural for humans to dehumanize others. In the following narrative a boy is taught to dehumanize the woman that breast fed him when e was a baby.

"My mother, she didn't work in the field. She worked at a loom. She worked so long and so often that once she went to sleep at the loom. Her masters boy saw her and told his mother. His mother told him to take a whip and wear her out. He took a stick and went out to beat her awake. He beat my mother till she woke up. When she woke up, she took a pole out of the loom and beat him nearly to death with it. He hollered, "Don't beat me no more, and I won't let 'em whip you." She said, "I'm goin' to kill you. These black titties sucked you, and then you come out here to beat me." And when she left him, he wasn't able to walk.

And that was the last I seen of her until after Freedom. She went out and got an old cow that she used to milk--Dolly, she called it. She rode away from the plantation, because she knew they would kill her, if she stayed."[22]
--Ellen Cragin

Cruelty hardens the heart and tends to make one unable to see the truth. It is difficult to treat people inhumanely and not lose ones humanity. In this narrative the slave master discovers that she has less humanity than her slave.

"The last whipping Old Mis' give me she tied me to a tree and oh, my Lord!--she whipped me that day. That was the wors' whipping I ever got in my life. I cried and bucked and hollered, until I couldn't. I give up for dead, and she wouldp't stop. I stop crying and said to her, "Old Mis', if I were you and you were me, I

---

21 Mellon, *Bullwhip Days.*
22 *Ellen Cragin, Bullwhip Days, pg238*

wouldn'd beat you this way. " That struck Old Mis's heart, and she let me go, and she did not have the heart to beat me anymore."[23]
-- Sarah Douclas

Nigger Dogs and Patrollers

A white friend who lived in a predominately black neighborhood once asked me, "Why are black people so afraid of dogs?" He had fairly large but gentle dogs that often sent black people running in terror. Dogs were often bred in the South to literally eat people. These were called "nigger dogs," and they were used by plantation patrollers to keep slaves frightened to leave the plantation.

"Aunt Cheyney was jus' out of bed with a sucklin' baby one time, and she run away. Some say that was nother baby of massa's breedin'. She dont' come to the house to nurse her baby, so they misses her and old Solomon gits the nigger hounds and takes her trail. They gits near her and she grabs a limb and tries to heist herself in a tree, but them dogs grab her and pull her down. The men hollers them onto her, and the dogs tore her naked and et the breasts plumb off her body. She got well and lived to be a old woman, but nother woman has to suck her baby and she ain't got no sign of breasts no more."[24]
Mary Reynolds

"They'd send for a man that had hounds to track you, if you run away. They'd run you and bay you, and a white man would ride up there and say, "If you hit one of them hounds, I'll blow your brains out. " He'd say "your damn brains. " Them hounds would worry you and bite you and have you bloody as a beef, but you dassen't to hit one of them. They would tell you to stand still and put your hands over your privates. I don't guess they'd have killed you, but you believe they would. They wouldn't try to keep the hounds off you; They would set them on you to see them bite you. Five or six or seven hounds bitin' you oa every side, and a man settin' on a horse holding a doubled shotgun on you."[25]
Henry Waldon

"My mother was smart and apt, and Old Mis' took her for a house servant. One day, she got mad about something what happened at the big house, so she runned off. When she couldn't be found, they hunted her with dogs. Them dogs went right straight to the ditch where my mother was hid, and before the men could get to them, they had torn most of her clothes off her and had bitten her all over. When they brought her in, she was a sight to see all covered with blood and dirt. Old Mis' flew into a rage, and she told those men not to never again hunt nobody on her place with dogs."[26]
Evie Herrin

---

23 Mellon, *Bullwhip Days*, pg244
24 Mellon, *Bullwhip Days*.
25 Henry Waldon, in Mellon, *Bullwhip Days, 300.*
26 Evie Herrin, in Mellon, *Bullwhip Days, 3.*

THE BLOODHOUND BUSINESS.

Fig. 7. Top: The Bloodhound Business (Library of Congress)
Bottom: Slave hiding in a tree, trapped by armed whites on horseback;
dogs surrounding tree (Library of Congress)

Slave Auctions

Fig. 8. Top: The Front of a Slave Auction House in New Orleans Before the Auction, Harper's Weekly, Jan. 24, 1863, p. 61. These slaves were probably house servants. Field slaves were sold in the trading yard across the river.
Bottom: Marker on New Orleans building indicates that it was once a Slave Exchange

The helplessness of black male slaves to protect their families was devastating to their identity. Slaves had no rights to protect relationships with their children or their spouse. The pain of split families was inherited by the descendants of slaves. The pain of slave auctions is best described by former slaves. The following is a description of a slave auction.

Fig. 9. Bibb describes this scene of family praying, being whipped then auctioned

"After the men were all sold they then sold the women and children. They ordered the first woman to lay down her child and mount the auction block; she refused to give up her little one and clung to it as long as she could, while the cruel lash was applied to her back for disobedience . . . . There was each speculator with his hand-cuffs to bind his victims after the sale; . . . the Christian portion of the slaves asked permission to kneel in prayer on the ground before they were separated"[27]
Henry Bibb

The most painful experience of American slavery was the buying and selling of slaves.

"I had a brother, Jim, who wuz sold ter dress young Missus fer her weddin'. De tree am still standin' whar I set under an' watche em sell Jim. I sat dar an' I cry an' cry, specially when dey puts de chains on him an' carries him off. An' I ain't neber felt so lonesome in my whole life. I ain't never hyar from Jim since, an' I wonder now, sometimes, iffen he's still livin."[28]
Ben Johnson

---

27 Henry Bibb, *Narrative of the life and adventures of Henry Bibb, an American slave*, 199–200.
28 *Ben Johnson, Bullwhip Days, The Slaves Remember, page 292*

CHAPTER 5

We Are Climbing Jacob's Ladder

"De preachers 'ud exhort us dat us was de chillun o' Israel in de wilderness an' de Lawd done sent us to take dis lan' o' milk an' honey."

We Are Climbing Jacob's Ladder

SLAVES WERE NOT allowed to read or write, but their lives are recorded in their spirituals. Although they had no education, God gave them sacred songs along with a sacred way of singing them as a means of preserving their culture. They expressed their feeling in their songs and eventually changed music around the world. Dinah Cunningham attributes the magic of their spirituals to their love for the Lord.

"They say that we can carry the song better than the white folks. Well, maybe we do love the Lord just a little bit better, and what's in our mouth is in our hearts."[29]
Dinah Cunningham

"Sometimes somebody would start humming an old hymn, and then the next=door neighbor would pick it up. In this way it would finally get around to every house, and the music started."[30]
Reverend Green

A program called *The Civil War*, produced by Ken Burns, was aired on PBS several years ago. When blacks were mentioned, the spiritual "We Are Climbing Jacob's Ladder"[31] was sung by Dr. Bernice Johnson Reagon and played in the background. The effect was powerful. It appeared to add purpose to the Union cause in the Civil War, and it added purpose to African American identity as well. Historian David Cecelski said this hymn was popular among African American slaves at the onset of the Civil War. Wikipedia says, "The spiritual saw a parallel in the ladder's steps representing the upcoming exiles of the Jews with the tribulations of American slavery with both to be ended by example of God's covenant to Jacob."

---

29 Dinah Cunningham, narrative in Mellon, *Bullwhip Days, p. 187.*
30 Albert J. Raboteau, *Slave Religion: The "Invisible Institution" in the Antebellum South* (Oxford University Press, 1978) 220.
31 YouTube, *"We Are Climbing Jacob's Ladder"*, https://www.youtube.com/watch?v=D8NVo7oqNdM.

We are climbing Jacob's ladder
We are climbing Jacob's ladder
We are climbing Jacob's ladder
Soldiers of the cross

Every round goes, higher, higher
Every round goes, higher, higher
Every round goes, higher, higher
Soldiers of the cross

Children do you want your freedom
Children do you want your freedom
Children do you want your freedom
Soldiers of the cross

Sinner do you love my Jesus
Sinner do you love my Jesus
Sinner do you love my Jesus
Soldiers of the cross

If you love him, why not serve him
If you love him, why not serve him
If you love him, why not serve him
Soldiers of the cross

Do you, think Ill, make a soldier
Do you, think Ill, make a soldier
Do you, think Ill, make a soldier
Soldiers of the cross

We are climbing Jacob's ladder
Rise, Shine, give God the glory
Rise, Shine, give God the glory
Soldiers of the cross

The African American gospel-music tradition preserves the important elements of religious slave life. A song performed by John P. Kee reveals how religious faith helps to deliver people from the valley of tribulation to the fulfilment of the Promised Land. The song is called "Lily in the Valley."[32] The song contains the rhythms of Africa and says someone found hope, God, love, peace, and joy in the valley.

---

32 YouTube, "*There's A Lily In the Valley | John P Kee & VIP Seminar Mass Choir*", https://www.youtube.com/watch?v=MxlpAnpqrRE

Biblical Identity

Charlie Davenport, an ex-slave who contributed a narrative to the book *Bullwhip Days,* says that niggers are the "Children of Israel."

"Us niggers didn't have no secret mettin's. All us had was church meetin's in Arbors woods. De preachers 'ud exhort us dat us was de chillun o' Israel in de wilderness an' de Lawd done sent us to take dis lan' o' milk an' honey."[33]
Charlie Davenport

'I've heard 'em pray for freedom. I thought it was foolishness, then but the old-time folks always felt they was to be free. It must have been something 'vealed unto 'em. Back then, if they'd catch you writing, they would break you if they ha I to cut off your finger, but still the old-time folks knew they would he free. It must have beer 'vealed unto 'em."[34]
-- Anonymous

The reference of identity to the Children of Israel was widespread. This identity was shared by both slaves and black Civil War soldiers. White officers who fought with them were considered to be part of their biblical history as well. A black soldier in the Twenty-Ninth Illinois USCT gave the following note to the widow of a fallen white officer:

" Allow me to say, that although a Colored man, a private in the 29th, I found in Colonel Bross a friend, one in whom every member of the regiment placed the utmost confidence, for, and with whom, each one would help defend the country to the end...He was loved by everyone, because he was a friend to every one. Weep not for him who was one of God's chosen ones, who tried to deliver his people out of Egypt."[35]

W G Kiphant was a Union army chaplain with the Tenth Iowa Veterans. Kiphant worked with the freemen in Decatur, Alabama, and observed their religious traditions.

" There is no part of the Bible with which they are so familiar as the story of the deliverance of the children of Israel. Moses is the ideal of all that is high, and noble, and perfect, in man. I think they have been accustomed to regard Christ not so much in the light of a spiritual Deliverer, as that of a second Moses who would eventually lead them out of their prison-house of bondage."[36]

Slaves not only identified with the Children of Israel but actually took on their identity. In the book *Trabelin' on the Slave Journey to an Afro-Baptist Faith,* historian Mechal Sobel described the transition from the slaves' African faith to that of the Afro-American Christian faith. Sobel was not an American and had a somewhat objective and remote view of the African American experience. She was not part of the American establishment. Sobel claimed that although slaves lost their identity when enslaved, they found a new identity in the Bible. They believed they were the Children

---

33 Charlie Davenport, narrative in Mellon, 377.
34 Anonymous, narrative in Mellon, 190
35 Glatthaar, *Forged in Battle,* 97.
36 Albert J. Raboteau, *Slave Religion: The "Invisible Institution "in the Antebellum South* (Oxford University Press, 1978) 311.

of Israel. Sobel wrote: " *Bible history—the history of Israel, of the Hebrew slaves and their redemption—became the black Baptist's sacred past.*" [37] They believed as the African's believed that following death they would go home to Heaven where they would find their ancestors waiting and they would not have to cry any more.

Revelation 7:14

In his song "Revolution," gospel-music artist Kirk Franklin brought to my attention that the source of the Children of Israel Identity may have been Chapter 7 of the book of Revelation. In Mary Reynolds's narrative in *Bullwhip Days*, she recalls that the slaves prayed for the end of tribulation. The word "tribulation" is not a common term used in American speech, but it does appear in the Bible. Why would a former slave use it? A search in the Bible for the term *"tribulation"* reveals that it appears only in the book of Revelation 7:14:

> *"These are they which came out of great tribulation, and have washed their robes, and made them white in the blood of the Lamb."*

This possibly could be a source of the slaves' obsession with the Bible and the Children of Israel identity. This passage talks about things predicted to come and offers hope for those who are experiencing tribulation. This passage also describes the Children of Israel, who had a plight that was very similar to their own, and they "came out of great tribulation."

> *"After this I saw four angels standing at the four corners of the earth, holding back the four winds of the earth, that no wind might blow on earth or sea or against any tree.*
>
> *[2] Then I saw another angel ascend from the rising of the sun, with the seal of the living God, and he called with a loud voice to the four angels who had been given power to harm earth and sea,*
> *[3] saying, "Do not harm the earth or the sea or the trees, till we have sealed the servants of our God upon their foreheads."*
> *[4] And I heard the number of the sealed, a hundred and forty-four thousand sealed, out of every tribe of the sons of Israel,*
> *[5] twelve thousand sealed out of the tribe of Judah, twelve thousand of the tribe of Reuben, twelve thousand of the tribe of Gad,*
> *[6] twelve thousand of the tribe of Asher, twelve thousand of the tribe of Naph'tali, twelve thousand of the tribe of Manas'seh,*
> *[7] twelve thousand of the tribe of Simeon, twelve thousand of the tribe of Levi, twelve thousand of the tribe of Is'sachar,*
> *[8] twelve thousand of the tribe of Zeb'ulun, twelve thousand of the tribe of Joseph, twelve thousand sealed out of the tribe of Benjamin.*
> *[9] After this I looked, and behold, a great multitude which no man could number, from every nation, from all tribes and peoples and tongues, standing before the throne and before the Lamb, clothed in white robes, with palm branches in hands"* (Rev. 7:2–9).
> *Revelation 7:2–9*

---

37 Sobel, Mechal. *Trabelin' on the Slave Journey to an Afro-Baptist Faith*, Princeton University Press, Princeton, New Jersey, 1988, 125.

This passage goes on to refer to the "lamb" a number of times. I believe the lamb is a symbol for the innocent and that the "blood of the lamb" would represent the blood of the innocent.

> *"[10] and crying out with a loud voice, "Salvation belongs to our God who sits upon the throne, and to the Lamb!"*
>
> *[11] And all the angels stood round the throne and round the elders and the four living creatures, and they fell on their faces before the throne and worshiped God,*
>
> *[12] saying, "Amen! Blessing and glory and wisdom and thanksgiving and honor and power and might be to our God for ever and ever! Amen."*
>
> *[13] Then one of the elders addressed me, saying, "Who are these, clothed in white robes, and whence have they come?"*
>
> *[14] I said to him, "Sir, you know." And he said to me, "These are they who have come out of the great tribulation; they have washed their robes and made them white in the blood of the Lamb."*
>
> *Revelation 7:10–14*

It is apparent in the next three verses why the slaves would want to be the Children of Israel. These verses predict that the Children of Tribulation would be led out of bondage to the Promised Land.

> *[15] Therefore are they before the throne of God,*
> *and serve him day and night within his temple;*
> *and he who sits upon the throne will shelter them with his*
> *presence.*
> *[16] They shall hunger no more, neither thirst any more;*
> *the sun shall not strike them, nor any scorching heat.*
> *[17] For the Lamb in the midst of the throne will be their shepherd,*
> *and he will guide them to springs of living water;*
> *and God will wipe away every tear from their eyes."*
> *Revelation 7:15–17*

The Promised Land

The promised land has a special meaning to African Americans; this is a vigil often mentioned by Dr. Martin Luther King Jr. In Dr. King's last speech in Memphis, Tennessee, he said, *"I just want to do God's will. And He's allowed me to go up to the mountain. And I've looked over. And I've seen the Promised Land."*

The Promised Land is another name for the Land of Israel, promised by their God to the sons of Abraham, according to the Hebrew Bible. After the Israelis left Egypt, they believed that the Land of Canaan was the Promised Land, but they could not take it from the Canaanites immediately. They wandered in the desert for forty years before they were strong enough to conquer the Canaanites. At this point in time, there was probably not a universal God, or he would be protecting the Canaanites as well, unless God favored those that follow him best. It should also be mentioned that a black tribe of Jews called the *Lemba* claim to be direct descendants of the Children of Israel and have DNA results that support their claim.

This concept of tribes conquering and enslaving one another was common all over the world. The belief that their God sanctioned these conquests must have been universal and a part of human behavior. This behavior has also been observed in chimpanzees. I watched a video of the BBC natural history epic *Planet Earth* (https://www.youtube.com/watch?v=a7XuXi3mqYM) that showed a group of chimpanzees attacking a neighboring group to acquire their feeding grounds. An increase in chimpanzee population creates a need for more food. During times of scarcely available food, warfare between neighboring chimpanzees can become a matter of survival. A study at the University of Michigan suggests that warfare has evolved to be a part of chimpanzee behavior.[38] One can conclude that the idea of improving human living conditions by warfare can be traced back far into human evolution. Does God sanction warfare to improve the lives of people? This is an important observation and will be discussed in a following book.

The Promised Land was a goal—a dream—and it gave blacks a sense of purpose. Equal justice was a promise from God. During the civil rights struggle of 1970, I attended Flint Junior College. Blacks often congregated to listen to spokesmen of the college's Black Student Union. A young spokesman could electrify the black crowd simply by calling them children. William Wells Brown described a similar occurrence:

"It was quite evident, through the exercises of' the day and night, that the negroes regard the condition of the Israelites in Egypt as typical of their own condition in slavery; and the allusion to Moses, Pharaoh, the Egyptian lark-masters, and the unhappy condition of the captive Israelites, were continuous; and any reference to the triumphant escape of the Israelites across the Red Sea, and the destruction of their pursuing masters was certain to bring out a strong " Amen!"[39]
W. W. Brown

38 John C. Mitani, David P. Watts, and Sylvia J. Amsler, "Lethal intergroup aggression leads to territorial expansion in wild chimpanzees," *Current Biology* 20, no. 12(2010): R507–R508, doi: 10.1016/j.cub.2010.04.021.

39 Brown, *The Negro in the American Rebellion*, 112.

CHAPTER 6

The Steal Away to Jesus Prayer Movement: "We prays for the end of Trib'lation"

"Dey hab big holes out in de fiel's dey git down in and pray. Dey done dat way 'cause de white folks didn' want 'em to pray. Dey uster pray for freedom."

Steal Away to Jesus: The Invisible Institution

Fig. 10. "Contraband Camp at City Point" depicting an evening prayer meeting

It is a common belief that slave religion or Christianity was practiced in the balcony of the slave master's church. At these types of services slaves were reminded to serve their masters on earth before serving God. Although slaves were uneducated, they were not stupid. This doctrine offered them no hope and encouraged them to accept their condition. When no action is taken to improve our lives, we are faced with hopelessness, which leads to depression. Depression often results in poor judgment and a lack of patience, and the existing condition is often worsened. Prayer nurtures hope by allowing us to take action in a hopeless situation. Prayer allowed slaves to petition to a power that they did not possess. Prayer gave them faith, courage, and determination. They were then able to make the best use of their resources and circumstance.

The Slave Narratives suggest that slave prayer meetings were a common practice throughout the South. Apparently, slave owners saw these prayer meetings as a threat. It was unlawful for blacks to assemble in prayer groups in the South without a white person being present. This was considered a national-security issue, and the punishment for illegal prayer meetings was flogging. I found no exception to this rule in the slave narratives; slave prayer meetings were not allowed on any plantations.

Although slave prayer meetings were illegal they continued to occur. Ellen Butler said that slaves were not allowed to pray because they prayed for freedom.

"Marster neber 'low he slaves to go to chu'ch. Dey hab big holes out in de fiel's dey git down in and pray. Dey done dat way 'cause de white folks didn' want 'em to pray. Dey uster pray for freedom."[40]
Ellen Butler

Slaves, however, had a practice of "stealing away" to the woods to have their religious services. At these services, they usually prayed for freedom, and this is why these meetings were outlawed. Albert J. Raboteau is a Henry W. Putnam Professor of Religion at Princeton University. In his book *Slave Religion: The "Invisible Institution" in the Antebellum South*, referrers to this slave prayer meeting practice as the Invisible Institution. This invisible institution appears to be a slave *movement* or *prayer movement* and is frequently described by the voice of the slaves.

"When de niggers go round singin' "Steal Away to Jesus,' dat mean dere gwine be a "ligious meetin' dat night. De masters...didn't like dem 'ligious meetin's so us natcherly slips off at night, down in de bottoms or somewhere. Sometimes us sing and pray all night...Meetings back there meant more than they do now. Then every body's heart was in tune, and when they called on God they made heaven ring. It was more than just Sunday meeting and then no godliness for a week. They would steal off to the fields and in the thickets and there...they called on God out of heavy hearts." [41]

""We used to steal off to de woods and have church, like de spirit moved us--sing and pray to our own liking and soul satisfaction and we sure did have good meetings, honey-baptize in de river, like God said. We had dem spirit-filled meetings at night on de bank of de river, and God met us dere. We was quiet 'nuf so de white folks didn't know we was dere, and what a glorious time We did have in de Lord."[42]
Susan Rhodes

---

40 Ellen Butler, in Mellon, *Bullwhip Days*, 190.
41 Albert J. Raboteau, *Slave Religion: The "Invisible Institution" in the Antebellum South* (Oxford University Press, 1978) 213–217.
42 Susan Rhodes, in Mellon, *Bullwhip Days*, 194.

'Steal a-way, steal_ a-way'
steal_ a-way to Je-sus!
steal_ a-way,
steal_ a-way home,_
I ain't got long to stay here.
Steal_ a-way, steal_ a-way,
steal_ a-way to Je - sus!
steal_ a-way home,_
I ain't got long to stay here.
My Lord, He calls me, He calls me by the thun - der,
The trum - pet sounds with - in a my soul,
I ain't got long to stay here.[43]

Plantations used guards and overseers to keep slaves in their cabins at night. Guards were called patrollers, and overseers were called nigger drivers. Mary Reynolds referred to Solomon as a nigger driver.

"We was scart of Solomon and his whip, though, and he didn't like frolickin'. He didn't like for us niggers to pray, either. We never heared of no church, but us have prayin' in the cabins. We'd set on the floor and pray with our heads down low and sing low, but if Solomon heared he'd come and beat on the wall with the stock of his whip. He'd say, I'll come in there and tear the hide off you backs.' But some the old niggers tell us we got to pray to Gawd that he don't think different of the blacks and the whites. I know that Solomon is burnin' in hell today, and it pleasures me to know it."[44]

Slaves would "steal away" to pray in the woods, which was a very sacred act. Slaves literally risked their lives along with the lives of their families to attend these prayer meetings, which made their spirituality the center of their lives. Mary Reynolds describes a secret prayer meeting in the woods and how they relied on the *"power of God"* for safety:

"Once my maw and paw taken me and Katherine after night to slip to nother place to a prayin' and singin'. A nigger man with white beard told us a day am comin' when niggers only be slaves of Gawd."[45]

"We prays for the end of Trib'lation and the end of beatin's and for shoes that fit our feet. We prayed that us niggers could have all we wanted to eat and special for fresh meat. Some the old ones say we have to bear all, cause that all we can do. Some say they was glad to the time they's dead, cause they'd rather rot in the ground than have the beatin's. What I hated most was when they'd beat me and I didn't know what they beat me for, and I hated they strippin' me naked as the day I was born.

When we's comin' back from that prayin', I thunk I heared the nigger dogs and somebody on horseback. I say, Maw, its them nigger hounds and they'll eat us up.' You could hear them old hounds and sluts abayin'. Maw listens and say, Sho nough, them dogs am running' and Gawd help us!' Then she and paw talk and they take us to a fence corner and stands us up gainst the rails and say don't move and if anyone comes near, don't breathe loud. They went to the woods, so the hounds chase them and not git us. Me and Katherine stand there, holdin' hands, shakin' so we can hardly stand. We hears the hounds come nearer, but we don't

---

43 J. W. Johnson and J. R. Johnson, *American Negro Spirituals*, 114–5.
44 Mellon, *Bullwhip Days, 19.*
45 Mellon, *Bullwhip Days, 19.*

34

move. They goes after paw and maw, but they circles round to the cabins and gits in. Maw say its the power of Gawd."[46]
Mary Reynolds

The following are exerts from the slave narratives titled "ON THE SECRET RELIGIOUS MEETINGS OF ENSLAVED PERSONS."[47]

""A Negro preacher delivered sermons on the plantation. Services being held in the church used by whites after their services on Sunday. The preacher must always act as a peacemaker and mouthpiece for the master, so they were told to be subservient to their masters in order to enter the Kingdom of God. But the slaves held secret meetings and had praying grounds where they met a few at a time to pray for better things."
Harriet Gresham, born a slave in 1838 in South Carolina, as reported by her interviewer, ca. 1935

"Sometimes we would, unbeknown to our master, assemble in a cabin and sings songs and spirituals. Our favorite spirituals were—Bringin' in de sheaves, De stars am shinin' for us all, Hear de Angels callin', and The Debil has no place here. The singing was usually to the accompaniment of a Jew's harp and fiddle, or banjo."
Dennis Simms, born a slave in Maryland in 1841, as transcribed by his interviewer, 1937

"De black folks gits off down in de bottom and shouts and sings and prays. Dey gits in de ring dance. It am jes' a kind of shuffle, den it git faster and faster and dey gits warmed up and moans and shouts and claps and dances. Some gits 'xhausted and drops out and de ring gits closer. Sometimes dey sings and shouts all night, but come break of day, de nigger got to git to he cabin. Old Marse got to tell dem de tasks of de day."
Silvia King, born in Morocco and enslaved in Texas, as transcribed by her interviewer, ca. 1936

"Tom Ashbie's [plantation owner] father went to one of the cabins late at night, the slaves were having a secret prayer meeting. He heard one slave ask God to change the heart of his master and deliver him from slavery so that he may enjoy freedom. Before the next day the man disappeared . . . When old man Ashbie died, just before he died he told the white Baptist minister, that he had killed Zeek for praying and that he was going to hell."
Rev. Silas Jackson, born a slave in 1846 or 1847 in Virginia, as transcribed by his interviewer, 1937

"[The plantation owner] would not permit them to hold religious meetings or any other kinds of meetings, but they frequently met in secret to conduct religious services. When they were caught, the 'instigators'—known or suspected—were severely flogged. Charlotte recalls how her oldest brother was whipped to death for taking part in one of the religious ceremonies. This cruel act halted the secret religious services."
Charlotte Martin, born a slave in 1854 in Florida, as reported by her interviewer, 1936

---

46 Mellon, *Bullwhip Days*, p19.
47 http://nationalhumanitiescenter.org/tserve/nineteen/nkeyinfo/aarsecretmeetings.htm.

"On Sundays the slaves were permitted to have a religious meeting of their own. This usually took place in the backyard or in a building dedicated for this purpose. They sang spirituals which gave vent to their true feelings. Many of these songs are sung today. There was one person who did the preaching. His sermon was always built according to the master's instructions which were that slaves must always remember that they belonged to their masters and were intended to lead a life of loyal servitude. None of the slaves believed this, although they pretended to believe because of the presence of the white overseer. If this overseer was absent sometimes and the preacher varied in the text of his sermon, that is, if he preached exactly what he thought and felt, he was given a sound whipping."

William Ward, born a slave in the early 1830s in Georgia, as reported by her interviewer, ca. 1936

Jesus the Protector

It was a tradition in Africa for people to petition ancestors in heaven for guidance and protection. Jesus Christ became the slaves' personal protector, and he took the place of the living dead or ancestors who resided in heaven. Families were frequently broken up during slavery days. Family members were frequently sold before death, which weakened the bond between the living and their dead ancestors. For example, in a letter to a friend, the author wrote, *"I once heard a slave trader say; he had sold a woman who had nine children, but gotten in awful wedlock by nine different husbands, having been sold all that many times, and married in each place she went."*[48] The slaves replaced the ancestor role with Jesus, who was far more consistent and reliable. The bond or relationship between the slave and Jesus tended to be an intimate one. Sobel describes the replacement of the role of dead ancestors with Jesus as follows:

"Jesus became the rock and the salvation of the black man. The role the living dead had played in being concerned for their kin was taken over by Jesus, who was a far more reliable spirit."[49]

The black man felt that the living dead loved them, which was key to trust, their protection, and guidance. When we look at the Jesus's Sermon on the Mount (Matt. 5), we can see that Jesus viewed slaves not as victims but victors. It did not matter that they owned nothing, not even themselves or their families. It did not matter what the world thought of them or why they were hated. It did not matter that they had to pray in holes in cotton fields. Jesus appeared to love them as they were and wanted them to have a better life. When slaves are viewed as only victims, there is a lack of trust in this sermon. However, when there is a strong belief in this sermon, then slaves must be viewed as victors and supporters of the truth of the Gospel. Jesus was persecuted for his righteous beliefs and teachings. He was whipped and humiliated. Following his death, he became the greatest martyr in history. His crucifixion and resurrection is the ultimate example of transformation from victim to victor. According to Jesus' promise, victors would be blessed if they believed in him:

[3] *Blessed are the poor in spirit, for theirs is the kingdom of heaven.*
[4] *Blessed are those who mourn, for they will be comforted.*
[5] *Blessed are the meek, for they will inherit the earth.*
[6] *Blessed are those who hunger and thirst for righteousness, for they will be filled.*[50]

---

48 Glatthaar, *Forged in Battle.90.*
49 Sobel, *Trabelin' on the Slave Journey to an Afro-Baptist Faith*, 125.
50 Matt. 5 2–6.

"Slaves of God"

Revelations 7:14 suggests that in the Promised Land, which is God's temple, slaves must serve God *"night and day"* or become *slaves of God*. In Mary Reynolds's narrative, she describes how a slave with a white beard said *"a day am comin' when niggers only be slaves of Gawd."* [51] The man with the white beard speaks as if during slavery, slaves slaved for their owners but slaved for God as well. Therefore, in the Promised Land, they would still be slaves, but they would slave for the one that sits on the throne, or God. But what does it mean to slave for God? Slaves accepted Jesus as the son of God, so serving Jesus would be serving God. According to Jesus, Matthew 5, a slave of God would be righteous, merciful, and peacemaking.

[7] *Blessed are the merciful, for they will be shown mercy.*
[8] *Blessed are the pure in heart, for they will see God.*
[9] *Blessed are the peacemakers, for they will be called sons of God.*
[10] *Blessed are those who are persecuted because of righteousness, for theirs is the kingdom of heaven*
[11] *Blessed are you when people insult you, persecute you and falsely say all kinds of evil against you because of me. Rejoice and be glad, because great is your reward in heaven, for in the same way they persecuted the prophets who were before you.*[52]

Slaving for God required dialog with God or prayer; therefore, slaves prayed for freedom a lot. Although the American establishment's definition of "nigger" is vulgar, the slave definition of the word was different; it simply meant "African American slave." To William Moore, a "nigger" is someone who spends most of his life praying and serving the one that sits on the throne.

"Some, like niggers, just got to pray, half their life is in prayin'. Some nigger take turn with 'nuther nigger to watch to see if Marse Tom any wheres 'bout, and that they circle themselves 'bout on the floor in the cabins and pray. They get to moanin' low and gentle, 'Someday, someday, someday this yoke going to be lifted off'n our shoulders, someday, someday, someday.'" [53]
William Moore

People live for the moment, but they also have the gift of living in the future. We can plan for the future by building great monuments that take decades to finish. The downside to that gift is fear of the future when we have no control of future events. Hopelessness can lead to certain death. The slaves did not need an identity as much as they needed hope. Many of them found hope through religion—the harder their lives were, the more religious they became. Slaves were powerless, so they learned to seek the power of God through prayer.

"I was a religious child, in those days, and I'm religious now, too, but colored folks just naturally had more religion back there, before the Civil War."[54]
Rachel Reed

---

51 Mellon, *Bullwhip Days*, 19.
52 Matt. 5:7–11.
53 William Moore, narrative in Mellon, *Bullwhip Days*, 330.
54 Rachel Reed, narrative in Mellon, *Bullwhip Days*, xx.

CHAPTER 7

Persecution of the Steal Away to Jesus Prayer Movement

"Be it therefore enacted, That all meetings or assemblies of Slaves, Free Negroes or Mulattoes, at any Meeting Houses, or any other place or places in the night under any pretence whatever, shall be deemed and considered, as an unlawful assembly"

Nat Turner's Rebellion

IN 1831 NAT Turner led a slave rebellion that led to the deaths of sixty men, women, and children. Turner was very religious; he could read and write as well. Recall that the Bible says the Israelites had to conquer the Canaanites before they occupied the Promised Land. Identification of slave identity with the identity of the Children of Israel suggests that American slavers would require conquering as well. It was believed that Nat Turner's rebellion had roots in slave religion. As a result of Turner's rebellion, laws were passed restricting blacks from learning to read or write or participating in black prayer meetings.

""The Turner insurrection is so connected with the economic revolution which enthroned cotton that it marks an epoch in the history of the slave. A wave of legislation passed over the South prohibiting the slaves from learning to read and write, forbidding Negroes to preach, and interfering with Negro religious meetings. Virginia declared, in 1831, that neither slaves or free Negroes might preach, nor could they attend religious services at night without permission. In North Carolina slaves and free Negroes were forbidden to preach, exhort or teach "in any prayer-meeting or other association for worship where slaves of different families are collected together" on penalty of not more than thirty-nine lashes. Maryland and Georgia had similar laws. The Mississippi law of 1831 said: It is "unlawful for any slave, free Negro, or mulatto to preach the gospel" upon pain of receiving thirty-nine lashes upon the naked back of the presumptuous preacher. If a Negro received written permission from his master he might preach to the Negroes in his immediate neighborhood, providing six respectable white men, owners of slaves, were present" In Alabama, the law of 1832 prohibited the assembling of more than five male slaves at any place off the plantation which they belonged, but nothing in the act was to be considered as forbidding attendance at places of public worship held by white persons. No slave or free person of color was permitted to "preach, exhort, or harrangue any slave or slaves, or free persons of color, except in the presence of five respectable slaveholders or unless the person preaching was licensed by some regular body of professing Christians in the neighborhood, to whose society or church the Negroes addressed properly belonged."[55]

Fig. 11. Eastman Johnson, *The Lord is My Shepherd*, 1863 (Smithsonian American Art Museum)

Slave owners feared that slaves would learn to read the Bible. Perhaps they saw slaves finding hope in the Bible and they were establishing a biblical identity. An effort that lifted slave identity was a threat to slavery. One of the ex-slaves interviewed for *Bullwhip Days* related how her uncle Bull learned to read and was severely punished for it.

---

55 William Edward Burghardt Du Bois, *The Negro Church: Report of a Social Study Made Under the Direction of Atlanta University; Together with the Proceedings of the Eighth Conference for the Study of the Negro Problems, Held at Atlanta University, May 26th, 1903* (Atlanta University Press, 1903).

"Dere wuz Uncle George Bull. He could read and write, and, chile, de white folks didn't lak no nigger what could read and write. Old man Carr's wife, Mis' Jane, uster teach us Sunday school, but she did not 'low us to tech a book wid us hands. So dey uster jes' take Uncle George Bull and beat him fur nothin'. Dey would beat him, and take him to de lake, and put him on a log, and shev him in de lake, but he always swimmed out. When dey didn't do dat, dey would beat him till de blood run outen him, and den t'row him in de ditch in de field, and kivver him up wid dirt, head an ears, and den stick a stick up at his haid. I wuz a water toter and have stood and seen 'em do him dat way more'n once, and I stood and looked at 'em till dey went 'way to de other rows, and den I grabbed de dirt offen him, and he'd bresh de dirt off and say, "T'ank yo'," git his hoe, and go on back to work. Dey beat him lak dat, and he didn' do a thin' to git dat sort uf treatment."[56]
—Margrett Nickerson

Unlawful Prayer Meetings

It was a common practice for African Americans to assemble at night for prayer meetings. Praying for freedom was the execution of the only power that slaves had. This act is well documented in historical material but appears to be absent in American History, this maybe a result of censorship. America was founded upon the principle of religious freedom and African American religious persecution was an indictment against the institution of slavery.

Laws were also passed throughout the South prohibiting blacks from holding religious meetings without whites being present. The penalty for breaking the law was flogging. However, laws prohibiting black prayer meetings were actually enacted twenty-five years before Turner's rebellion. The 1804 excerpt from the *New York Herald* below describes African American prayer meetings in the South as being considered a national-security risk.

"The following bill, we understand is before the legislature of Virginia.

An act to amend an act, to reduce into one, the several acts concerning Slaves, Free Negroes and Mulattoes.

Where as it is represented to the General Assembly, that it is a common practice in many places within the Commonwealth, for Slaves, Free Negroes or Mulattoes, to <u>assemble in considerable numbers at Meeting Houses, and places of Religious Worship, in the night</u>, which may have a tendency to promote conspiracy and insurrection.

Be it therefore enacted, That all meetings or assemblies of Slaves, Free Negroes or Mulattoes, at any Meeting Houses, or any other place or places in the night under any pretence whatever, shall be deemed and considered, as an unlawful assembly. And that it shall be the duty of any Magistrate of the County or Corporation, where such assembly shall be, either from his own knowledge or from the information of others, of such unlawful assembly or meeting, to issue his warrant, directed to any sworn officer or officers, authorizing him or them to enter the house or houses where such unlawful meeting are, for the purpose of apprehending or dispersing the Slaves, Free Negroes and Mulattoes, and <u>to inflict corporal punishment on the offender or offenders, at his discretion, not exceeding twenty lashes.</u>

And be it further enacted, That the said officer or officers, shall have power to summon any person to aid and assist in the execution of any warrant or warrants directed to him or them, for the purposes aforesaid, who on refusal, shall be subject to a fine, at the discretion of the magistrate, not exceeding ten dollars.

All acts, or parts of acts, coming within the preview of this act, and is hereby repealed.

This act shall be in force, from and after the passing thereof.

---

56 Mellon, *Bullwhip Days*, 199.

[This gentle reader, is emphatically the State of Liberty and equality------the liberty of whipping the blacks for attending religious evening lectures.]
NEW YORK HERALD
SATURDAY, JANUARY 28, 1804"[57]

Following is an image of the article that was published in the *New York Herald*:

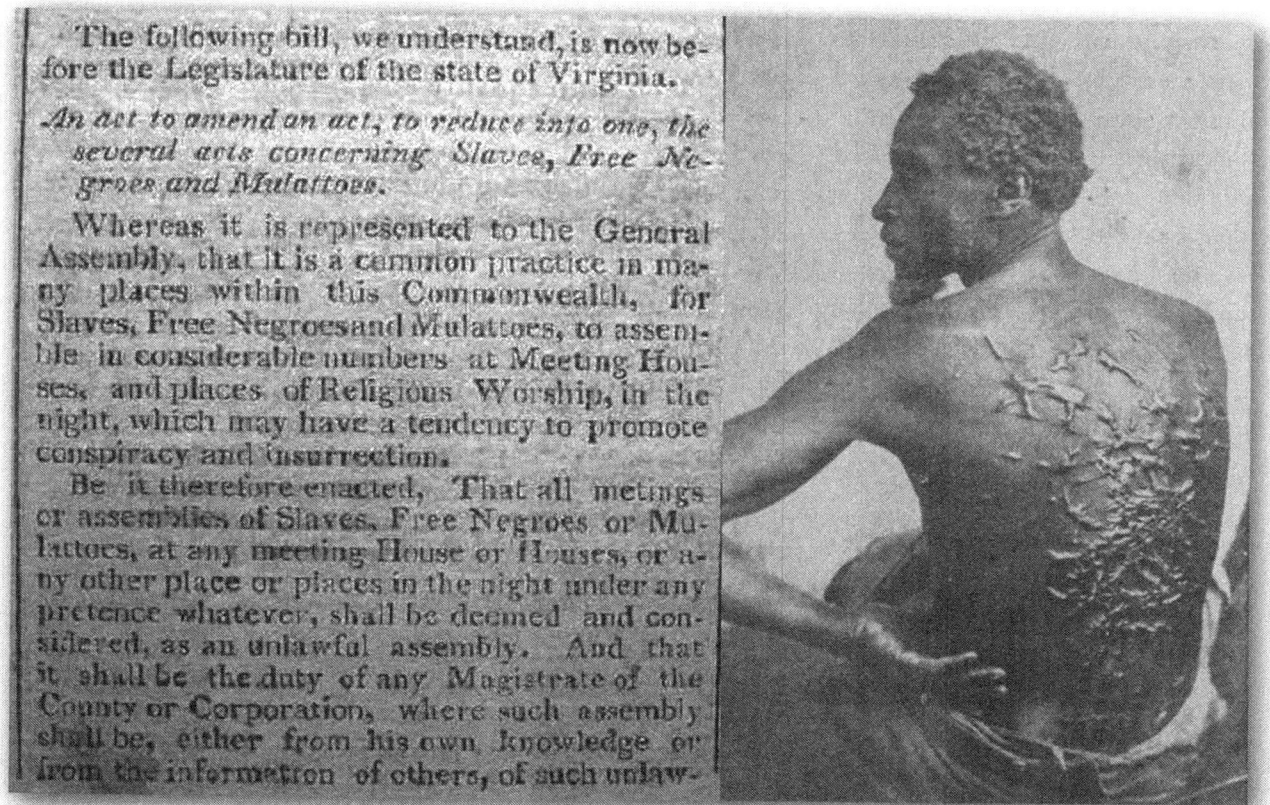

Fig. 12. *New York Herald,* Saturday, January 28, 1804 and Civil War CDV of Gordon (slave) at the Baton Rouge Union camp during his medical examination, National Portrait Gallery, Smithsonian Institution, March 1863

Blood of the Lamb—Blessed Are Those Who Are Persecuted for Righteousness

My interpretation of the blood of the lamb is that the expression represents the sacrifice of the innocent. If Negroes were caught in a prayer meeting, the punishment was flogging with a whip, such as the cat-o'-nine-tails. These whippings lacerated the slaves' bodies, causing bleeding and scarring. The blood probably stained their clothing. This narrative describes slaves who were whipped for praying; note the bleeding caused by the whip. The blood of the innocent probably soaked their clothes.

"Marse Carter had a had a house gal by de name uf Frances, an' she had wait on de white folks all day long, an' when night wud come, he made her slip out 'mongst de slaves an' see what dey wuz doin' an' talkin' 'bout.

---

57 *New York Herald,* January 28, 1804.

My mammy wus livin' wid 'nudder man, named Joe, an' one night Joe an' my Mammy an' some more slaves wuz down on deir knees prayin' fur de good Lord to sot dem free, an' Frances wus slippin' round de corner uf de house an' heard what dey wus sayin'. An' she goes back to de house an ' tells de old marse, an ' he sent de oberseer down dar an ' brung ebery one uf dem to de stake, an' tied dem, an' whipped dem so hard dat blood come from some uf dems backs."[58]
July Halfen

Slaves were ashamed of their abuse and did not share their stories with their descendants; this is likely a result of censorship as well. Experiences of faith were passed down instead by removing the slavery components from stories. An example of this is the song "*Child's Blood (Precious Lord)*" by The Pilgrim Jubilees, a traditional old-fashioned gospel group. "*Child's Blood*"[59] was a combination of a story and the Thomas Dorsey song "Precious Lord." The story is about a little girl who sat on the steps of her front porch and listened to a church service not too far away. Her father forbade her from going to church and told her that she didn't need it. One day she slipped away and went to church, and she found Jesus. She was excited about it and told her father what happened. Her father picked up a stick and beat the little girl until she was covered with blood. When her mother came home and found her covered with blood, she asked, "*Why did he do this?*" The little girl replied that she had found Jesus. The little girl then told her mother to do her a favor. She said, "*Wrap up these bloody clothes. I want to show Jesus how I bled for him.*" The mother said that she was curious and wanted to know what song they sang in church. The little girl looked up, stared, and said "*Precious Lord, Please take my hand…and lead me on*"

Components of this story are strange. First, the girl was beaten with a stick by her father until her clothes were soaked with blood. A stick beating would not have lacerated the girl's skin enough to have soaked her shirt with blood without killing her. However, clothing was easily soaked with blood following flogging by a whip or cat-o'-nine-tails. Second, it would be extraordinary for a father to beat his child for going to church. On the other hand, "stealing away" to slave prayer meetings was illegal and subject to flogging. If we replaced the father with the slave owner, replaced the church with a slave prayer meeting, and replaced the stick with a whip, then we would have a typical slave narrative.

Slave narratives, however, were not directly assimilated into African American culture, but slave experiences exist today in a coded form. This story suggests that the suffering from flogging related to prayer was a demonstration of the slaves' love and commitment to Jesus. It was not important as to who administered the punishment in this case but it was essential that love and dependence on the Lord prevail. The little girl's blood was the blood of the innocent or the blood of the lamb. The song Precious Lord petitions the Lord for support of the innocent during times of distress and persecution. The decoupling of slave experiences from slave teachings eventually led to deterioration of the message and subsequent loss of African American ancestral guidance.

Prayer in a Slave-Trading Yard

Sometimes it appears that God will not answer our prayers and that the situation is hopeless. It is difficult to love a God who appears not to love us. The slaves' faith was tested in the trader yard. For example, here is a story about a slave who possessed the faith in God to shed her blood for him and her prayers were answered. She accomplished in a trader yard what Christ's apostles had difficulty doing.

---

58 July Halfen, narrative in Mellon, *Bullwhip Days*, 196.
59 Youtube, *Child's Blood - Pilgrim Jubilee Singers*, "*In Revival*", https://www.youtube.com/watch?v=G8-bseNu9ek.

"We ain't been in New Orleans very long till Mr. Abram took sick and die, and we is taken to the trader yard to be sold. I reckon I musta been 'bout six or mebbe seven year old, at the time.

Major Long was the one who owned the trader yard where we was put, and I guess We was kept there 'bout a week, 'fore my sister Mary was sold away from us.

One morning, our family is all kinda huddled up together in a cornet of the yard away from the rest, and 'long comes Major Long carrying his bullwhip in his hand, with another man. He makes Mary stand up and says to the man with him, "Here's jes' the girl you want for a nurse girl.

Mama begs Major Long not to separate us folks, and hugged Mary and Jane and me to her. The major and the man with him talks a while, and then the major come over to where we are and pulled Mary away from Mama and he and the man took her off. "twan't till after Freedom that we ever saw her again.

Man, man, folks what didn't go through slavery ain't got no idea what it was. I reckon there musta been a hundred colored folks in that trader yard, and the dirt and smell was terrible, terrible. I was jes' a little chap, like I've told you, but I can remember that place like it happened yesterday-- husbands sold away from wives, and children taken awav from mothers. A trader, them days, didn't think no more of selling a baby or little child away from its mother than takinp a little calf away from a cow.

I rec'lec', the night after Mary is sold away from us, the colored folks in the trader yard hold prayer meeting. Mama was very religious-very religious--and it ever a soul went to Heaven, hers did. Seems like Major Long was gone that evening, and Mama and some more of the folks in the yard got together for a praying time. Didn't do no singing, 'cause that would have 'tracted attention, and the major didn't 'low no meetings. But someone saw the folks prayin and told him the next morning, and he come out in the yard with a cat-o'-nine-tails and rounds everybody up. Then, he said, "You niggers what was praying last night, step out here. "

None come out, though, 'cept Mama, 'cause they was 'fraid they was going to get whipped Major said to Mama, "Well, you are the only truthful one in the yard, and I won't whip you, 'cause you have been truthful. I'll see if I can keep you and your man and your other children together and not see you separate." Mama jes' fell on her knees and thanked the good Lord right in front of the major, and he never touched her with his whip.

Twan't but a little while till he comes back and says for us to get our bundles and come with him. We didn't know where we was going, but any place was better'n that trader yard. Jes' to get away from that place was a blessing from the good Lord.

The Major kept his word to Mama and sell us to Mr. Dan Sullivan, and he takes us up, to Alexandria in a wagon."[60]
Stephen Williams

It was the faith of Mrs. Williams and Mary Reynolds that motivated me to start writing this book twenty years ago. There are many people that feel that they don't need God but they were never a slave in a slave trading yard. Her son mentioned that she was a very religious woman. She relied on her faith to carry her through the tribulations of slavery and God supported her each time. But this time it was questionable if God had left her as Jesus questioned God when he hung on the cross. Her child was taken from her; it was planned that she would lose the rest of her family the next day. The slave trading yard was filthy, she was forbid from praying and she was labeled a nigger. However, we are reminded by Jesus that blessed are the poor in spirit, those who mourn, the meek, the merciful, the pure in heart, the righteous and those prosecuted for being righteous. Jesus made a promise in his Gospel that if we continued to believe in his words we will be victors not victims, independent of whom we are or where we are.

---

60 Stephen Williams, narrative in Mellon, *Bullwhip Days*, 290.

I have often wondered what thoughts went through the mother's mind the night before the auction that made her pray risking flogging the next day. I believe she felt "no ways tired" and refused to believe that God had not brought her this far just to leave her. The spiritual "I don't feel no ways tired", best describes her feelings. The spiritual was modified by Curtis Burrel, became a gospel hymn and made a hit by Rev. James Cleveland.[61] When we see Mrs. Williams as a victor, then victory is possible for anyone in any situation.

Calling on the Lord

American slaves frequently called on Jesus in times of trouble and apparently continued the practice long after slavery ended. Recall that the Lord took the place of ancestors in heaven and was called upon in times of need.

Jesus held the place of protector in the slave's life. It is possible that the slaves practiced an African tradition of calling out the name of their spiritual protector that resided in heaven in time of need. The Bible says, *"Everyone who calls on the name of the Lord will be saved"* (Rom. 10:13). Apparently slave masters and overseers were not comfortable with slaves calling on the Lord while they were whipping them so the slave was forbidden in this case from "calling on the Lord."

"Dey wouldn't allow 'em to call on de Lord when dey were whippin' 'em, but dey let 'em say, 'Oh, pray! Oh, pray, Marster!' Dey would say, 'Are you goin' to work? Are you goin' visitin' widout a pass? Are you goin' to run away?' Dese is de things dey would ax him, when dey wuz whippin' him."[62]
Alex Woods

Although they could not always call the Lord's name, the Lord understood and was not easily fooled. Note that in the following narrative, William Moore was from Limestone County, Texas, while Alex Woods was from Raleigh, North Carolina. The long distance between them suggests that saying "pray" instead of "Lord" was not an isolated practice during whippings.

"One day, I am down in the hog pen riling the hogs and teasing them like any yearling boy will do, when I hear a loud agony screaming up to the house. I can't make out who 'tis. I'm curious and I start up to the house and I hear, "Pray Marse Tom. Pray, Marse Tom." But still I can't tell who 'tis. When I get up close I see Marse Tom got my mammy tied to a tree with hir clothes pulled down and he is laying it on her with a bullwhip and de blood is running down her eyes and off her back. I goes crazy. I say, "Stop, Marse Tom," and he swings the whip and it don't reach me good, but it cuts just the same. I sees Miss Mary standing in the cook house door. I run aryund crazy like, and I see a big rock and I take it and I throw it and it ketches Marse Tom in the skull and he goes down like a poled ox."[63]
William Moore

Amy Spain's Hanging; Bless the Lord

In most cases, slaves were the largest portion of slave owner's wealth. Bad slaves were either whipped or sold but seldom killed. When blacks became free, their value was reduced significantly. Lynching was used as a means of controlling blacks with terror. In March 1865, a month prior to the end of the Civil War, Sherman's troops were camped outside of town of Darlington, South Carolina. As General Sherman marched to the sea, slaves were freed, and Southern white losses were significant. There

61 Youtube, Reverend James Cleveland-I Don't Feel No Ways Tired, https://www.youtube.com/watch?v=_Cw75v2uqts.
62 Alex Woods, narrative in Mellon, *Bullwhip Days,* 244.
63 William Moore, narrative in Mellon, *Bullwhip Days,* 332.

was little damage done to Darlington, however. According to *Harper's Weekly*, September 30, 1865, seventeen-year-old Amy Spain was lynched for thanking the Lord for her freedom. She was described as a martyr, which is a victor, not a victim.

There is further explanation for the hanging posted by B. Ricardo Brown, PhD, at http://node801.blogspot.com/2009/05/hanging-of-amy-spain.html, on May 24, 2009, that is somewhat of a southern view. Darlington's *New Era* newspaper disputed the *Harper's Weekly* article. Brown suggests that Amy's claim to freedom was premature and that she took household goods that belong to her master. This may have been the official Darlington reason for her hanging, but she was probably lynched for celebrating her freedom and used as an example for other slaves.

"One of the martyrs of the cause which gave freedom to her race was that of a colored woman named Amy Spain, who was a resident of the town of Darlington, situated in a rich cotton-growing district of South Carolina. At the time a portion of the Union army occupied the town of Darlington she expressed her satisfaction by clasping her hands and exclaiming, "Bless the Lord the Yankees have come!" She could not restrain her emotions. The long night of darkness which had bound her in slavery was about to break away. It was impossible to repress the exuberance of her feelings; and although powerless to aid the advancing deliverers of her caste, or to injure her oppressors, the simple expression of satisfaction at the event sealed her doom. Amy Spain died in the cause of freedom. A section of Sherman's cavalry occupied the town, and without doing any damage passed through. Not an insult nor an unkind word was said to any of the women of that town. The men had, with guilty consciences, fled; but on their return, with their traditional chivalry, they seized upon poor Army, and ignominiously hung her to a sycamore-tree standing in front of the court-house, underneath which stood the block from which was monthly exhibited the slave chattels that were struck down by the auctioneer's hammer to the highest bidder.

Amy Spain heroically heard her sentence, and from her prison bars declared she was prepared to die. She defied her persecutors; and as she ascended the scaffold declared she was going to a place where she would receive a crown of glory. She was rudely interrupted by an oath from one of her executioners. To the eternal disgrace of Darlington her execution was acquiesced in and witnessed by most of the citizens of the town. Amy was launched into eternity, and the "chivalric Southern gentlemen" of Darlington had fully established their bravery by making war upon a defenseless African woman. She sleeps quietly, with others of her race, near the beautiful village. No memorial marks her grave, but after-ages will remember this martyr of liberty. Her persecutors will pass away and be forgotten, but Amy Spain's name is now hallowed among the Africans, who, emancipated and free, dare, with the starry folds of the flag of the free floating over them, speak her name with holy reverence."[64]

The online encyclopedia Wikipedia has Amy's story a bit turned around: http://en.wikipedia.org/wiki/Darlington,_South_Carolina. Wikipedia says, "In 1865, Federal troops passed through Darlington and hanged a former slave on the Public Square for insurrection." *Harper's Weekly* portrays Amy as a martyr dying for freedom and thanking the Lord. On the other hand, southern history portrays Amy as a slave hung by the Yankees. This is an example of how African American identity is controlled with history. However, with the advent of the Information Age of online computing, there is no excuse for ignorance.

Uncle Tom Identity

"Uncle Tom" is a term that resonates in the African American community to label blacks that act in the best interest of whites at the expense of blacks. The term may have come from a character in the book *Uncle Tom's Cabin*, written by Harriet Beecher Stowe in 1851. The book was instrumental in shifting the American public opinion in the North

---

64 "Hanging of Amy Spain," *Harper's Weekly*, September 30, 1865, 613.

against slavery. According to History.com (http://www.history.com/this-day-in-history/uncle-toms-cabin-is-published), when Harriet met President Lincoln in 1862 he said, "*So this is the little lady who made this big war.*" The character Uncle Tom, however, was not a traitor to black folks and slaves. This is an example of how African American identity is altered by proslavery Southerners. In 1851 most black folks resided in the South, where the book was not well accepted and black folks could not read and write. Uncle Tom was looked down on by Southern whites because he put slavery in a negative light. Slaves looked down on him as well but for different reasons. Uncle Tom was viewed as a house servant. House slaves or servants sometimes were more loyal to their owners than their families in the fields. Some servants forgot where they came from and were self-serving. Not all house servants were disloyal to field slaves. My great-great-grandmother Clara and her father were both house servants. My father said that Clara was a very loving person to everyone.

Fig. 13. Amy was hung in March 1865 for saying, "Bless the Lord, the Yankees have come," *Harper's Weekly*, September 30, 1865

Black prayer meetings were not allowed because they prayed for freedom. The so-called "house gal" described by July Halfen in the previous narrative exposed a black prayer meeting to her owners. As a result, the accused slaves were flogged. It is easy to imagine how the behavior of the servant could create a great deal of resentment among black field slaves. It is not that Uncle Toms are friendly or fraternize with whites; it is their betrayal to the black community that angers blacks. Americans view blacks as black people then Americans. This fact generates a level of kinship or loyalty among blacks which decreases as with black prosperity. If not for many blacks and whites that fought for civil rights, blacks would not enjoy the prosperity that they enjoy today. Uncle Toms threaten the small amount of black loyalty and compassion that remains.

CHAPTER 8

Blessed Are the Merciful

"He knew no method of getting money which had so direct a tendency to efface the moral sense, to rob the heart of every gentle and humane disposition and to harden it like steel."

Sinner, Do You Love My Jesus?

THE AMERICAN ESTABLISHMENT is Christian. Most slave owners were likewise Christians and bound to Christian law. The teachings of Jesus, however, warn against choosing money over righteousness. Jesus warned against this tendency of man to seek wealth over everything. He said, *"No one can slave for two masters; for either he will hate the one and love the other, or he will stick to the one and despise the other. You cannot slave for God and for riches."*[65] Jesus also believed that we should love our enemies. *"But I say unto you, Love your enemies, bless them that curse you, do good to them that hate you, and pray for them which despitefully use you, and persecute you."*[66]

Cruelty was a necessary part of slavery. There was a zero-tolerance policy toward slave disobedience. The only argument racists could make for treating blacks cruelly was that Jesus was a racist and was referring to only loving white people. Racists had to make a choice between slaving for God and loving slaves or slaving for money and having hard hearts.

John Newton Found Amazing Grace

African slave trade was like oil today—big business, and it made many countries wealthy. Slave trade in England was big business, and initially the church supported it. England, however, was a Christian country, so racism was essential to support the slave trade. It was this dehumanization, though, that destroyed the slave trade. A preacher named John Newton was one of the first clergymen to attack slavery after becoming a "changed man." John Newton was a slave trader in the mid-1700s. He had considered his trade to be honorable, as did most Europeans of the time. Slavery required a great deal of brutality, first to capture the slaves then to control them for service. He shared in the common practice of sexually abusing slave women for his own sexual satisfaction. He used torture devices such as thumbscrews to control them. It was common for opposing armies to treat their foes brutally but the brutality was justified by national security interest. Slavery however did not represent national security interest but personal interest. Slaves were traded for financial gain and used for sexual satisfaction. Newton justified his actions by believing that the establishment condoned slavery along with its brutality. John Pollock researched the life of John Newton and describes Newton's observations of the dehumanization of slavery. "The Slave Trade was for gain and in 1745 not a pen nor a tongue had questioned or condemned it." In his old age Newton testified to a Committee of the Privy Council that he

---

65 Matt. 6:24.
66 Matt. 5:44.

knew of no method of making money that "efface the moral sense, to rob the heart of every gentle and humane disposition and to harden it like steel."[67]

John Newton changed as his love for Jesus grew, and as it did, he found slavery to grow increasingly distasteful. Newton found himself selling his soul for profit. Eventually, he became a preacher and one of the first abolitionists to fight slavery and racism in England. As his love for Christ grew stronger, he found less of a need to place himself above others, until eventually he was as humble as the slave. Historians have criticized Newton, citing his long life as a slave trader. We have a tendency to judge people without looking at the details of their lives. Few people would show their respect for black slaves by refusing prestigious honors as Newton did. Newton was offered an honorary Doctor of Divinity by The University of New Jersey. Newton refused the honor stating that "'the dreary coast of Africa had been his university' and he would never accept any diploma 'except from the poor blacks.'"[68]

John Newton is not remembered as a slave trader or as an abolitionist, but he is known for composing one of the most popular hymns written. Newton revealed his transformation from slave trader to soldier of the cross in a song that he wrote called *"Amazing Grace."*

Tenderhearted Maser Newman

Slavery was no place for the tenderhearted. Master Newman was tenderhearted; he could feel the pain of some else's suffering. He watched the whipping of a slave, but he felt powerless since it was not in the position to interfere. As a result he joined the ranks of the brokenhearted.

"Maser Newman was a slow easy-goin' sort of a man who took everything as it comes, takin' bad and good luck jest alak. He say not ter worry 'bout bad luck, 'cause worryin' won't do no good, and it would do you a lot of harm. He hardly ever did get mad, but when he did, you bettah leave him alone.

Maser Newman was tender-hearted, too. I know because 'bout de maddest I ever seen him was one evenin' when he comes in from one of de neighbor slave owners, and he sho' was mad; he was jest shakin'. Missus Jane-dat was his wife-went out ter his horse when he rode up, 'cause she could tell dat sumpin' was wrong, and she said, "Nath, what in de world is wrong?" And he begin tellin' her 'bout seem' dis feller whip one of his slaves unmercifully, and de slave beggin' him ter stop, and dis man laughin' and cussin'. Dis man keeps on whippin' him, and Maser Newman got on his horse and come home ter keep from jumpin' on him. I didn't hear all he was sayin'-I was afraid ter let Maser Newman see me listenin' ter what he was saying, while he was mad-but I heard enough ter tell dat it was 'bout dis man beatin' one his slaves nearly ter death"[69]
Mollie Dawson

Alex Stephens, Vice President of the Confederacy

Alexander H. Stephens was the vice president of the Confederacy during the Civil War. President Lincoln respected Stephens for his efforts to avoid the Civil War and to find a peaceful resolution to the conflict over slavery. Stephens was a moderate, unlike the president of the Confederacy, Jefferson Davis, who wanted to fight to the death. Stephens

---

67 John Pollock, *Amazing Grace* (Harper & Row, 1981) 51.
68 John Pollock, *Amazing Grace* (Harper & Row, 1981) 173.
69 Mollie Dawson, *Bullwhip Days*, 421.

had a humanitarian view of slavery. He saw slaves as people whose rights to respect were more important than the slave owners' desire for profits.

Publicly, however, Stephens was a racist; in his famous Cornerstone Speech he said, "Our new Government is founded upon exactly the opposite ideas; its foundations are laid, its cornerstone rests, upon the great truth that the negro is not equal to the white man; that slavery, subordination to the superior race, is his natural and normal condition."[70]

The best testimony to Stephens's humanity came from the narrative of one of the slaves he had owned that was recorded years after she became free. Georgia Baker's narrative was recorded during the Depression, when she was living in dilapidated housing and had little to eat. She recalled that Stephens had treated his slaves as family. They were fed and dressed well, had comfortable living quarters, and were treated with respect. Georgia Baker's narrative was the first one published in *Bullwhip Days*, and her experience supported the *Gone with the Wind* romantic version of slavery. Alex Stephens's love for his slaves was measured by Georgia Baker's love for her owner.

The ideal slavery experience of Georgia Baker promoted slavery, while Mary Reynolds's experience condemned slavery. Note that Georgia Baker does not describe her religious life nor the role that prayer had in her life. Her religious faith was not essential to her happiness or survival. On the other hand, Mary's religious faith played a very important role in her life. Her father risked the lives of her family to worship in the woods.

"Wher was I born? Why I was born on de plantation of a great man. It was Marse Alec Stephens' plantation 'bout a mile and a half from Crawfordville, in Taliaferro County, Georgia. Mary and Grandison Tilly was my ma and pa. Ma was cook up at de big house and she died when I was jus' a little gal. Pa was a field hand, and he belonged to Marse Britt Tilly."

"De long log houses what us lived in was called "shotgun" houses 'cause dey had three rooms, one behind de other in a row lak de barrel of a shotgun. All de chillun slept in one end room and de grown folks slept in de other end room. De kitchen whar us cooked and et was de middle room."

"Now dete you is axin' 'bout dat somepin'-t'-eat us had dem days! Oh, yessum! Marse Alec had plenty for his slaves to eat. Dere was meat, bread, collard greens, snap beans, taters, peas, all sorts of dried fruit, and just lots of milk and butter. Marse Alec had twelve cows and dat's what I learned to love milk so good. De same Uncle Jim what made our beds made our wooden bowls what dey kept filled wid bread and milk for de chillun all day You might want to call dat place whar Marse Alec had our vegetables raised a gyarden, but it looked more lak a big field to me, it was so big. You jus' ought to have seed dat dere fireplace whar dey cooked all us had to eat. It was one sho'-'nuf big somepin', all hill of pots, skillets, and ovens. Dey warn t never 'lowed to git hill of smut neither. Dey had to be cleant and shined up atter evvy meal, and dey sho' was pretty hangin' dat in dat big old fireplace."

"Marse Alec warn't home much of de time, but when he was dat he used to walk down to de cabins and laugh and talk to his niggers. He used to sing a song for de slave chillun dat run somepin' lak dis:

Walk light ladies,
De cake's all dough,
You needn't mind de weather,
If de wind don't blow.

---

70 Wikipedia, *Alexander H. Stephens*, http://en.wikipedia.org/wiki/Alexander_Stephens.

Us didn't know when he was a-singin' dat tune to us chillun dat when us growed up us would be cake-walkin' to de same song.*

George and Mack was de hunters. When dey went huntin' dey brought back jus' evvything: possums, rabbits, coons, squirrels, birds, and wild turkeys. Yessum, wild turkeys is some sort of birds, I reckon, but when us talked about birds to eat, us meant part'idges. Some folkses calls 'em quails. De fishes us had in summertime was a sight to see. Us sho' et good, dem days. Now us jus' eats what-some-ever us can git."[71]
Georgia Baker

Miss Sally's Redemption

Fanny Cannady described in her narrative how hardhearted Master Jordan tried to make his gentle, sweet, tender-hearted daughter's heart tough, ugly, and twisted like his. Master Jordan had zero tolerance for slave disobedience. He dehumanized slaves which eventual dehumanized himself. Miss Sally would have to make a choice between having her tender heart broken or standing up for righteousness.

"I wuz skeered of Marse Jordan, an' all of de grown niggahs wuz too 'cept Leonard an' Burrus Allen. Dem niggahs wuzn' skeered of nothin'. If de debil hese'f had come an' shook er stick at dem dey'd hit him back. Leonard wuz er big black buck niggah; he wuz de bigges niggah I ever seed, an' Burrus wuz near 'bout as big, an' dey 'spized Marse Jordan wus'n pizen.

I wuz sort of Mis' Sally, too. When Marse Jordan wusn' roun' she was sweet an' kind, but when he wuz roun', she wuz er "yes, suh, yes, suh," woman. Everythin' he tole her to do she done. He made her slap Mammy one time, 'kaze when she passes his coffee she spilled some in de saucer. Mis'Sally hit Mammy easy, but Marse jorad say, "Hit her, Sally. Hit de black bitch like she 'zerve to be hit. " Den Mis' Sally draw back her hand an' hit Mammy in de face, pow. Den she went back to her place at the table an' play like she eatin' her breakfas'. Den, when Marse Jordan leave, she come in de kitchen an' put her arms roun' Mammy an' cry, an' Mammy pat her on de back an' she cry, too. I loved Mis' Sally when Marse Jordan wuzn' roun'."

" Marse Jordan's two sons went to de War. Dey went ali dressed up in dey fightin' clothes. Young Marse Jordan wuz jus' like Mis' Sally, but Marse Gregory wuz like Marse Jordan, even to de bully way he walk. Young Marse Jordan never come back from de War, but 'twould take more den er bullet to kill Marse Gregory. He too mean to die anyhow, 'kaze de Debil didn' want him an' de Lawd wouldn' have him. One day Marse Gregory come home on er furlow. He think he look pretty wid his sword clankin' an' his boots shinin'. He wuz er colonel, lootenent, er somethin'. He wuz struttin' roun' de yard showin off, when Leonard Allen say under his breath, "Look at dat goddamn sojer. He fightin' to keep us niggahs from bein' free. " 'Bout dat time Marse Jordan come up. He look at Leonard an' say, "Wat yo' mumblin' 'bout?"

" Dat big Leonard wuzn' skeered. He say, "I say, 'Look at dat goddamn sojer. He fightin' to keep us niggahs from bein' free!' " Marse Jordan~ face begun to swell. It turned so red de blood near 'bout bust out. He turned to Pappy an' tole him to go an' bring him his shotgun. When Pappy come back Mis' Sally come wid him. De tears wuz streamin' down her face. She run up to Marse Jordan an' caught his arm. Ole Marse flung her off an' took de gun from Pappy. He leveled it on Leonard an' tole him to pull his shirt open. Leonard opened his shirt and stood dere big as er black giant, sneerin' at Ole Marse."

---

71 Georgia Baker, narrative in Mellon, *Bullwhip Days*, 3.

'Den Mis' Sally run up again an' stood 'tween dat gun an Leonard. Ole Marse yell to Pappy an' tole him to take dat woman out of de way, but nobody ain't moved to touch Mis' Sally an' she didn't move neither; she jus' stood dere facin' Ole Marse. Den Ole Marse let down de gun. He teached over an' slapped Mis' Sally down, den picked up de gun an' shot er hole in Leonard~ ches' big as yo' fis'. Den he took up Mis' Sally an' toted her in de house. But I wuz so skeered dat I run an' hid in de stable loft, an' even wid my eyes shut I could see Leonard layin' on de groun' wid dat bloody hole in his ches' an' dat sneer on his black mouf."

The Catholic Church defines loving someone as acting in their best interest even when it is in conflict with one's own interest. That kind of love generates the same in return.

"When de War ended Mis' Sally come to Mammy an' say, "Fanny, I's sho' glad yo's free. Yo' can go now an' yo' won' ever have to be er slave no more. "

But Mammy, she ain't had no notion of leavin' Mis' Sally. She put her arms roun' her an' call her "Baby, " an' tell her she goin' to stay wid her long as she live. An' she did stay wid her. Me an' Mammy bofe stayed wid Mis' Sally 'twell she died."[72]
Fanny Cannady

Master John Mixon:" de best old Master what ever was"

In the section titled "Liberated African American identity" of chapter 2, John Mixon's slave, Eliza, was whipped for saying *"I ain't no nigger, I's a Negro, and I'm Miss Liza Mixon. "* Like Alex Steven's, John Mixon was also a racist but treated his slaves well. Eliza believed the common myth that her African ancestors were wild in Africa and were enslaved by white people for their own good. Mixon's slaves however were well fed, treated humanely and Eliza's mother was taught to read and write. As a result, Liza enjoyed her life as a slave but at the same time she appreciated being called a Negro instead of *nigger* and having a last name. The Steal Away movement was not observed on Mixon's plantation and slave religion was practiced openly. Eliza's narrative includes a vivid description of plantation life that includes a detailed description of *patrollers*. as well as a description of the slave trade, although the accuracy is questionable.

"I sho' remember de days when I was a slave and belonged to de best old Master what ever was, Mr. John Mixon. We lived in Selma, Dallas Countu, Alabama.

My grandma was a refugee from Africa. You know dey was white men who went slipping 'round and would capture or entice black folks onto their boats and fetch them over here and sell 'em for slaves. Well, Grandma was a little girl 'bout eight or nine years old and her parents had sent her out to get wood. Dey was going to have a feast. Dey was going to roast a baby. Wasn't that awful! Well, they captured her and put a stick in her mouth, The stick held her mouth wide open so she wouldn't cry out. When she gor to de boat she was so tired out she didn't do nothing.

They was a lot of more colored folks on de boat. It took about four months to get across on de boat and Mr. John Mixon met the boat and bought her. I thin he gave five hundren dollars for her. She was named Gigi, but Master John told her he'd never sell none of her chillun. He kept dat promis and he never did sell any of her grandchillun either. He thought it was wrong to separate famblys. She was one hundred and three years old when she died. I guess her mind got kind of feeble 'cause she wandered off and fell into a mill race and was drowned.

---

72 Fanny Cannady, narrative in Mellon, *Bullwhip Days,* 78.

Master John Mixon had two big plantations. I believe he owned about four hundred slaves. Chillun and all. He allowed us to have church one time a month with de white folks and we had prayer meeting every Sunday. Sometimes when de men would do something like being sassy or lazy and dey knowed dey was gonna be whipped, dey's slip off and hide in de woods. When dey's slip back to get some food dey would all pary for 'em dat Master wouldn't have 'em whipped to hard, and for fear the patroller would hear 'em they'd put their faces down in a dinner pot. I's sit out and watch for the Patroller. He was a white man who was appointed to catch runaway niggers. We all knew him. His name was Howard Campbell. He had a big pack of dogs. The lead hound was named Venus. There was five or six in the pack, and they was vicious too.

My father was a carriage driver and he allus took the family to church. My mother went along to take care of the little chilluns. She'd take me too. They was Methodist and after they would take the sacrament we would allus go up and take it. The niggers could use the whitefolk's church in the afternoon.

De Big House was a grand place. It was a two-story house made out of logs dat had been peeled and smoothed off. There was five big rooms and a big open hall wid a wide front porch clean across de front. De porch had big posts and pretty banisters, I was painted white and had green shutters on de windows. De kitchen was back of de big House.

De slaves quarters was about a quarter of a mile from de Big House. Their houses was made of logs and the cracks was daubed with mud. They would have two rooms. Our bedsteads was made of poplar wood and we kept them scrubbed white with sand. We used ropes woven together for slats. Our mattresses were made of cotton, grass, or even shucks. My mother had a feather bed. The chairs was made from cedar with split white oak bottoms.

Each family kept their own home and cooked and served their own meals. We used wooden trays and wooden spoons. Once a week all the cullud chillun went to the Big House to eat dinner. The table was out in de yard. My nickname was "Speck." I didn't like to eat bread and milk when I went up there and I'd just sit there. Finally they'd let me go in de house and my mother would feed me. She was the house woman and my Anutie was cook. I don't know why they had us up there unless it was so they could laugh at us.

Non of the old Master's young niggers did much work. He say he want 'em to grow up strong. He gave us lots to eat. He had a store of bacon, milk, bread, beans and molasses. In summer we had vegetables. My mother could make awful good corn pone. She would take meal and put slat in it and pour boiling water over it and make into pones. She'd wrap these pones in wet cabbge or collard leaves and roll dem into hot ashes and bake dem. They sho' was good. We'd have possum and coon and fish too.

The boys never wore no pritches in de summer time. Boys fifteen years old would wear long shirts with no sleeves and they went barefooted. De girls dressed In shimmys. They was a sort of dress with two seams in it and no sleeves.

Old Master had his slaves to get up about five o'clock. Dey did an ordinary day's work. He never whipped them unless they was lazy or sassy or had a fight. Sometimes his slaves would run away but they allus come back. We didn't have no truck with railroaders (underground) 'cause we like our home.

A woman cussed my mother and it made her mad and they had a fight. Old Master had them both whipped. My mother got ten licks and de other woman got twenty-five. Old Mistress sho' was mad 'cause mother got whipped. Said he wouldn't have done it if she had known it. Old Mistress taught mother how to read and write and mother taught my father. I went to school jest one day do I can't read and write now.

Weddings was big days. We'd have big dinners and dances once in a while and when somebody died they'd hold a wake. They'd sit up all night and sing and pry and talk. At midnight they'd serve sandwiches and coffee. Sometimes we'd all get together and play ring plays and dance.

Once the Yankee soldiers come. I was big enough to tote pails and piggins them. These soldiers made us chillun tote water to till their canteens and water their horses. We totted the water on our heads. Another time we heard the Yankees was coming and Old Master had about fifteen hundred pounds of meat. They was hauling it off to bury it and hide it when the Yankees caught them. The soldiers ate and wasted every bit of that good meat. We didn't like them a bit…

I'se getting old now and can't work no more. I jest sits here and thinks about old times. They was good times. We didn't want to be freed, We hated the Yankee soldiers. Abe Lincoln was a good man, though, wasn't he? I tries to be a good Christian 'cause I wants to go to Heaven when I die."[73]

Grandpappy Jake Crawford

Few slave masters were loved more than Grandpappy Jake Crawford. He thought of slaves as people and not just assets. Martin Jackson recalled that Grandpappy said "I ain't a man that cares for wealth. Everything I got you niggers made it out'n you' sweat. And I want you to take time to set and enjoy it. I got more things that I want to do than to set and count money." A slave named Henry was sold to a man in Denver Colorado and walked back from Denver to Mississippi to be back with Grandpappy. Grandpappy paid for the slave and promised to never sell another slave against his will.

Grandpappy loved the slave children as well. He saw them as people that deserved to be loved instead of property.

"He was always one with a foundering for the little babies. He goes out to the nursing house every day and looks at the little niggers and pokes them in they bellies and fusses if they are not fat and full. He heists them up in the air and says, "This is a fine youn-un." Sometimes he shout out, :Change they swaddling's, plenty hippins. Ain't no good for white or black to lay in muck."[74]
Martin Jackson

Not even Grandpappy however, allowed his slaves to pray because they prayed for freedom. Henry's wife would pray for freedom late at night into a bucket of water, so no one would hear. Praying was not allowed by slaves on most plantations but they prayed anyway.

---

73 OK Gen Web Oklahoma Genealogy & History, *The Slave Narrative Collection, Eliza Evens,* http://www.okgenweb.org/collection/narrative/evans_eliza.htm

74 Martin Jackson, *Bullwhip Days, The Slaves Remember,* page 305

CHAPTER 9

The Abolitionist Movement: Blessed Are Those Who Hunger and Thirst for Righteousness

"You may do your best to keep us in wretchedness and misery, to enrich you and your children; but God will deliver us from under you"

David Walker

MANY ANTISLAVERY WHITES were motivated by their religion. They saw slavery as inhumane and not representing Christian behavior. Fighting slavery was considered righteous and serving God makes them slaves of God as well. Antislavery whites and abolitionists often placed the interest of the persecuted above their own. Modern examples of this Christian or "slave of God" activism are included in the latter part of the chapter. The abolitionists worked within the establishment to sway public opinion against slavery. There were many abolitionists who made important contributions. I will mention here several abolitionists who published material to fight slavery.

David Walker was a free black proprietor of a secondhand clothing store in Boston. In 1829 he published his *Appeal*, an incendiary pamphlet that called upon the slaves to rise against their masters. Walker died under suspicious circumstances.

> "I speak, Americans, for your good. We must and shall be free, I say, in spite of you. You may do your best to keep us in wretchedness and misery, to enrich you and your children; but God will deliver us from under you. And woe, woe, will be to you if we have to obtain our freedom by fighting."[75]
> David Walker

William Lloyd Garrison

William Lloyd Garrison began publishing a militant antislavery newspaper, *The Liberator*, in that same city as Walker:

> "The Southern planter's career," he said, "is one of unbridled lust, of filthy amalgamation, of swaggering braggadocio, of haughty domination, of cowardly ruffianism, of boundless dissipation, of matchless insolence, of infinite self-conceit, of unequalled oppression, of more than savage cruelty."[76]

---

75 David Walker, *Appeal* (Boston, 1829).

76 Geoffrey C. Ward, *The Civil War: An Illustrated History* (New York: Knopf, 1992), 14.

Frederick Douglass

Fredrick Douglass assisted Lloyd Garrison in his fight against slavery. Douglass's manner, however, made some skeptical that he had ever been a slave. To convince the public that he was once a slave, he published his autobiography, *The Life and Times of Frederick Douglass*. His book convinced the public that he was a former slave, but it also exposed him to slave catchers. This forced him to flee to England for asylum. He used this as an opportunity to continue his fight against slavery.

Frederick Douglass had the enormous task of convincing the world of the evils of American slavery. But first he had to convince the world that all men are equal and basically the same. Slavery dehumanized the slave, and Douglass had to remind the world that slaves were people. He chose to use a common trait among the races, which is the need to love and be loved. The following is taken from a speech that he delivered to the British people on May 2, 1846, while he was exiled to England.

"The woman was placed on the auctioneer's block; her limbs, as is customary, were brutally exposed to the purchasers, who examined her with all the freedom with which they would examine a horse. There stood the husband, powerless; no right to his wife; the master's right preeminent. She was sold. He was next brought to the auctioneer's block. His eyes followed his wife in the distance; and he looked beseechingly, imploringly, to the man that had bought his wife to buy him also. But he was at length bid off to another person. He was about to be separated forever from her whom he loved. No word of his, no word of his, could save him from this separation. He asked permission of his new master to go and take the hand of his wife at parting. It was denied him. In the agony of his soul he rushed from the man who had just bought him, that he might take a farewell of his wife; but his way was obstructed, he was struck over the head with a loaded whip, and was held for a moment; but his agony was great. When he was let go, he fell a corpse at the feet of his master. His heart was broken. Such scenes are the every-day fruits of American slavery."[77]
Frederick Douglass

Toni Braxton's hit "Breathe Again"[78] was released shortly before I discovered this Fredrick Douglass speech. Every time that I thought of this man losing his wife, I couldn't stop thinking of this song.

Harriet Tubman

Harriet Tubman is a well-known conductor of the Underground Railroad. The PBS website, Judgment Day series[79], has an excellent summary of her work conducting the Underground Railroad.

Harriet Tubman's original name was Araminta Ross. She was born a slave in Dorchester County, Maryland around 1820. She performed   house servant duties as a child and worked in the fields when she became a teenager. She supported abused slaves during her teenage years. On one occasion she tried to protect a slave from an angry slave overseer and received a permanent head injury. Harriet married John Tubman in 1844.

Tubman escaped to Philadelphia in 1849. Most runaway slaves were from Border States such as Maryland. The distance between Border States and Free States was short requiring a minimal amount of support for runaway slaves. She returned the next year to help her sister and her sisters two kids escape to freedom. The next year she rescued her brother and two other men. She returned the following year to rescue her husband but he had remarried. She found other slaves ready to escape and she led them to freedom.

---

77 Frederick Douglass, *Life and Writings of Frederick Douglass, Early Years, 1817–1849, Appeal to the British People*, 158–59.

78 Youtube, *Toni Braxton - Breathe Again*, https://www.youtube.com/watch?v=pRFEz2MjZgg.

79 PBS, Judgment Day, Part 4: 1831–1865, People and Events, Harriet Tubman, c.1820–1913; http://www.pbs.org/wgbh/aia/part4/4p1535.html

Tubman carried a gun with her on her trips to liberate slaves and threatened to use it if tired or scared slaves wanted to turn back, saying "you'll be free or die." As Harriet continued to make trips south to free slaves, risk of her capture significantly increased. By 1856 a reward of $40,000 was posted for her capture. Tubman however returned to the south nineteen times by 1960 freeing slaves and eluding capture. Frederick Douglass referred to Tubman as "Mosses," and John Brown called her "General Tubman." John Brown recognized Tubman's leadership skills and courage.

Mr. Tabb's Underground Railroad

Harriet Tubman is well known for leading slaves to freedom on the Underground Railroad. However, less well known is the role that Arnold Gragson played in helping slaves obtain freedom. Mr. Tabb of Mason County Kentucky (near Cincinnati, Ohio) was a liberal slave master who went as far as arguing against slavery. He gave his slaves a lot of freedom to come and go, as well as teaching them to read and do math. Arnold Gragson used his freedom to help hundreds of people escape from slavery across the Ohio River, and did not escape himself until his operation was revealed. Arnold Gragson's heroism is buried in the slave narratives.

"MOST of the slaves didn't know when they was born, but I did. You see, I was born on a Christmas mornin'- it was in 1840. I was a full-grown man when I finally got my freedom. Before I got it, though, I helped a lot of others get theirs--Lawd only knows how many; might have been as much as two, three hundred. It was way more than a hundred, I know."

" It took me a long time to get over my scared Feelin', but I finally did, and I soon found myself goin' back across the river with two or three people, and sometimes a whole boatload. I got so I used to make three and four trips a month. What did my passengers look like? I can't tell you any more about it than you can, and you wasn't there. After that first girl--I never did see her again -I never saw my passengers. It would have to be the "black nights" of the moon when I would carry them, and I would meet them out in the open or in a house without a single light. The only way I knew who they were was to ask them, "What you say?" And they would answer, "Menare." I don't know what that word meant--it came from the Bible. I only know that that was the password I used, and all of them that I took over told it to me before I took them."[80]
Arnold Gragson

---

80 Arnold Gragson, narrative in Mellon, *Bullwhip Days*, 263.

CHAPTER 10

John Brown: Mine Eyes Have Seen the Glory of the Coming of The Lord

"I can recover all the lost capital occasioned by that disaster; by only hanging a few moments by the neck"

John Brown Arms the Negroes

JOHN BROWN WAS an abolitionist, but unlike most abolitionists, he felt that violence would be required to end slavery. John Brown felt that fighting to end slavery was his way of serving God; it was his calling. Fighting mental slavery is my calling as well, and I feel an attachment to John Brown by name. John Brown was an old white man determined to end slavery. I, on the other hand, am an old brown man named John White who is struggling to end mental slavery. This coincidence in name similarity often inspires me to persevere when I feel like giving up; I see it as God's plan.

Brown was not alone; he had six secret supporters who shared his vision of ending slavery. Brown met with Frederick Douglass to get his support. Douglass wrote:

"Captain Brown did most of the talking on the other side of the question. He did not at all object to rousing the nation; it seemed to him that something startling was just what the nation needed. He had completely renounced his old plan, and thought that the capture of Harper's Ferry would serve as notice to the slaves that their friends had come, and as a trumpet to rally them to his standard. He described the place as to its means of defense, and how impossible it would be to dislodge him if once in possession... Our talk was long and earnest; we spent the most of Saturday and a part of Sunday in this debate-Brown for Harper's Ferry, and I against it; he for striking a blow which should instantly rouse the country, and I for the policy of gradually and unaccountably drawing off the slaves to the mountains, as at first suggested and proposed by him.

When I found that he had fully made up his mind and could not be dissuaded, I turned to Shields Green and told him he heard what Captain Brown had said; his old plan was changed, and that I should return home, and if he wished to go with me he could do so. Captain Brown urged us both to go with him, but I could not do so, and could but feel that he was about to rivet the fetters more firmly than ever on the limbs of the enslaved.

In parting he put his arms around me in a manner more than friendly, and said: "Come with me, Douglass; I will defend you with my life. I want you for a special purpose. When I strike, the bees will begin to swarm, and I shall want you to help hive them." But my discretion or my cowardice made me proof against the dear old man's eloquence-perhaps it was something of both which determined my course. When about to leave I

asked Green what he had decided to do, and was surprised by his coolly saying, in his broken way, "I b'leve I'll go wid de ole man."[81]
Frederick Douglass

Thinking that Brown's plan was suicide, Douglass refused to join John Brown at Harpers Ferry. Brown also shared his plan with Harriet Tubman. Tubman did not accompany John Brown on his raid, but she assisted John Brown with recruiting former slaves.[82]

On October 16, 1859 John Brown executed his plan of arming the Negroes. He entered the village of Harper's Ferry with five black men and thirteen white men including his sons. He brought a wagon load of arms, which included two hundred rifles, two hundred pistol and a thousand pikes. He was defeated however, by a man in charge who would become synonymous with the southern cause named "Robert E. Lee." Brown wrote to his wife, "I have been whipped, as the saying is, but I am sure I can recover all the lost capital occasioned by that disaster; by only hanging a few moments by the neck; and I feel quite determined to make the utmost possible out of a defeat."[83]

John Browns was found guilty of treason at his trial, and he was asked if he wanted to make a statement. He appeared to refer to the New Testament, Matthew 25:40, as his motive: "The King will reply, 'Truly I tell you, whatever you did for one of the least of these brothers and sisters of mine, you did for me.'"

"I have, may it please the court, a few words to say… I went into Missouri and there took slaves without the snapping of a gun on either side, moved them through the country, and finally left them in Canada. I designed to have done the same thing again on a larger scale. That was all I intended. I never did intend murder, or treason, or the destruction of property, or to excite or incite slaves to rebellion, or to make insurrection… I see a book kissed here which I suppose to be the Bible, or at least the New Testament. That teaches me that all things whatsoever I would that men should do to me, I should do even so to them. It teaches me, further, to "remember them that are in bonds, as bound with them." I endeavored to act up to that instruction… I believe that to have interfered as I have done as I have always freely admitted I have done--in behalf of His despised poor was not wrong, but right. Now, if it is deemed necessary that I should forfeit my life for the furtherance of the ends of justice, and mingle my blood further with the blood of my children and with the blood of millions in this slave country whose rights are disregarded by wicked, cruel, and unjust enactments--I submit; so let it be done!"[84]
John Brown

It is believed by many that the hanging of John Brown started the Civil War. John Brown inspired antislavery activists and abolitionists. Herman Melville called him "the meteor of the war." Henry Wadsworth Longfellow likewise predicted that "this day will be a great day in our history—the date of a new Revolution—quite as much needed as the old one." Henry David Thoreau saw similarities between Brown's hanging and the crucifixion of

---

81 Frederick Douglass, *Life and Writings of Frederick Douglass, Early Years, 1817–1849*, 350–354.

82 Wikipedia, *Harriet Tubman*, https://en.wikipedia.org/?title=Harriet_Tubman.

83 Geoffrey C. Ward, *The Civil War: An Illustrated History* (New York: Knopf, 1992) 2–5.

84 "John Brown Sentenced to Death," *The New York Times*, Thursday, November 3, 1859.

Christ. William Lloyd Garrison said, "In firing his gun, John Brown has merely told what time of day it is. It is high noon, thank God."[85]

John Copeland was one of five black men who were with John Brown at Harpers Ferry, Virginia. He was hung with Brown, and the following is part of a letter he wrote to his brother.

"To this freedom they were entitled by every known principle of justice and humanity; and, for the enjoyment of it, God created them. And now, dear brother; could I die in a more noble cause? Could I, brother, die in a manner and for a cause which would induce true and honest men more to honor me, and the angels more readily to receive me to their happy home of everlasting Joy above? I imagine that I hear you, and all of you, mother, father, sister and brothers, say, (, No, there is not a cause for which we, with less sorrow, could see you die! "
" Your affectionate Brother,
"JOHN A. COPELAND."[86]

The effect that John Brown's death had on the abolitionist movement was eloquently expressed by Frederick Douglass many years later, when he addressed Storer College in 1881:

"John Brown's zeal in the cause of freedom was infinitely superior to mine. Mine was as the taper light; his was as the burning sun. I could live for the slave; John Brown could die for him. The American people and the Government at Washington may refuse to recognize it for a time but the inexorable logic of events will force it upon them in the end; that the war now being waged in this land is a war for and against slavery."[87]
Frederick Douglass

On the second floor rotunda of the Kansas State capitol building is a mural of John Brown. The mural was painted by John Stuart Curry to represent important historical events of Kansas. The mural places John Brown at the center of the Civil War and suggests that his influence started it. Brown frequently referred to the Bible during his trial. Note that he is depicted in the mural as having a musket in one hand and a Bible in the other. This theme is repeated in a prayer of a soldier belonging to the South Carolina Colored Volunteers. The prayer was recorded by Colonel T. W. Higginson, who was a secret supporter of John Brown and also a minister. The soldier said, "Let me lib wid de musket in one hand, an' de Bible in de oder dat if I die at de muzzle of de musket, die in de water, die on de land, I may know I hab de bressed Jesus in my hand, an' hab no fear."

It was alleged that on the way to the gallows, John Brown stopped to kiss a colored child. The legend angered slavery supporters, who felt the slaves were not deserving of respect or love. John Brown haters are quick to disclaim the legend, and it has not been proven that it is true. However, as we examine John Brown's passion to end slavery, it is clear that John Brown would have kissed the colored child had he been given the opportunity. William Wells Brown wrote the following about John Brown's execution.

---

85 Ward, *The Civil War*, 2–5.
86 W. W. Brown, *The Negro in the American Rebellion*, 47.
87 Frederick Douglass, "His Soul Goes Marching On, The Life and Legacy of John Brown," Address at the Fourteenth Anniversary of Storer College, Harpers Ferry, West Virginia, May 30, 1881 (Dover, NH: Morning Star Job Printing House, 1881).

"When John Brown was led out of the Charlestown jail, on his way to execution, he paused a moment, it will be remembered, in the passage-way, and, taking a little colored child in his arms, kissed and blessed it. The dying blessing of the martyr will descend from generation to generation; and a whole race will cherish for ages the memory of that simple caress, which, degrading as it seemed to the slaveholders around him, was as sublime and as touching a lesson, and as sure to do its work in the world's history, as that of Him who said, " Suffer little children to come unto me.'"[88]
W. W. Brown pg201

Apparently, the legend of John Brown kissing the Negro child actually originated from his comments to a special *New York Daily Tribune* correspondent. Although his comments are more complex than a simple kiss, they are a lot more powerful. He didn't want slavery-supporting ministers to come between God and himself and would rather have been escorted to the gallows by a slave mother and her children. He felt that liberating the slaves would get him a lot closer to God than clergy who accepted slavery.

Three weeks after John Brown's execution (December 22, 1859), John Greenleaf Whittier published a poem in the *New York Independent* called "Brown of Ossawatomie" that refers to Brown kissing a colored child at the gallows.[89]

John Brown of Osawatomie spoke on his dying day:
"I will not have to shrive my soul a priest in Slavery's pay;
But let some poor slave-mother whom I have striven to free,
With her children, from the gallows-stair put up a prayer for me!"

John Brown of Ossawatomie, they led him out to die;
And lo! a poor slave-mother with her little child pressed nigh:
Then the bold, blue eye grew tender, and the old harsh face grew mild,
As he stooped between the jeering ranks and kissed the negro's child!

The shadows of his stormy life that moment fell apart,
And they who blamed the bloody hand forgave the loving heart;
That kiss from all its guilty means redeemed the good intent,
And round the grisly fighter's hair the martyr's aureole bent!

Perish with him the folly that seeks through evil good!
Long live the generous purpose unstained with human blood!
Not the raid of midnight terror, but the thought which underlies;
Not the borderer's pride of daring, but the Christian's sacrifice.

Nevermore may yon Blue Ridges the Northern rifle hear,
Nor see the light of blazing homes flash on the negro's spear;

---

88 W. W. Brown, *The Negro in the American Rebellion*, 201.
89 The Lost Museum Archive, *John Brown of Ossawatomie*, http://chnm.gmu.edu/lostmuseum/lm/144/.

But let the free-winged angel Truth their guarded passes scale,
To teach that right is more than might, and justice more than mail!

So vainly shall Virginia set her battle in array;
In vain her trampling squadrons knead the winter snow with clay!
She may strike the pouncing eagle, but she dares not harm the dove;
And every gate she bars to Hate shall open wide to Love!

John Brown, although at times willing to argue with the local clergy upon religious matters, has absolutely rejected all appearance of spiritual comfort at their hands, even maintaining that those who were capable of countenancing Slavery, were not fit to come between him and his God. The other day, he said, that instead of any clergyman of Charlestown, if they would suffer him to be followed to the place of execution by a family of little negro children, headed by a pious slave mother, it would be all he would ask. The

Fig. 14. Top: *The Last Moments of John Brown,* by Thomas Hovenden, 1884 (Library of Congress) and *New York Daily Tribune,* December 5, 1859
Bottom: *The Tragic Prelude, John Brown,* by John Steuart Curry (Courtesy Kansas State Historical Society)

Battle Hymn of the Republic; Link between the Steal Away and the Abolitionist Movements

Slaves were banned from reading, but the cat was out the bag. Praying for freedom at night became an unlawful practice, the "invisible institution." One spiritual that was sung was called "Say, brothers, will you meet me at Canaan's happy shore?" The land of Canaan was the Promised Land. This song made it north to Boston, where it was published. The tune had been one of John Brown's favorite. Union soldiers converted the melody and rhythm to a marching song called "John Brown's Body."

"John Brown's Body"

There was a "secret six" of abolitionists who supported John Brown's raid; they were Thomas Wentworth Higginson, Samuel Gridley Howe, Theodore Parker, Franklin Benjamin Sanborn, Gerrit Smith, and George Luther Stearns. Both Smith and Sterns were wealthy, while Higginson and Parker were Unitarian ministers. Colonel T. W. Higginson, later led the First South Carolina Volunteers, the first ex-slave regiment organized during the Civil War.

Samuel Howe was a secret supporter of John Brown and a doctor. Howe was married to Julia Ward Howe. The couple visited Abraham Lincoln at the White House in November of 1861. Julia and friends watched Union troops marching to the tune of a popular Union marching song, "John Brown's Body." Julia had wanted to rewrite the song to captured John Brown's new movement, but the words had not come to her. That night the words came to her while sleeping; she awoke and wrote the words down. Julia Howe rewrote "John Brown's Body" to become "The Battle Hymn of the Republic," which served as the American national anthem until 1931. She said that the words came to her in a dream.[90] If Julia Howe saw "the glory of the coming of the Lord," it would have been God's answer to the countless prayers of slaves.

Mine eyes have seen the glory of the coming of the Lord.
He is trampling out the vintage where the grapes of wrath are stored;
He hath loosed the fateful lightning of his terrible swift sword:
His truth is marching on

Chorus:
Glory Hally, Hallelujah!
Glory Hally, Hallelujah!
Glory Hally, Hallelujah!
His truth is marching on

In his final speech in Memphis, Tennessee, Dr. Martin Luther King Jr. repeated a line from this song when he said, "Mine eyes have seen the glory of the coming of the Lord."

---

90 Ward, *The Civil War,* 104.

INDIANA

JOHN BROWN SONG.

John Brown's body lies a mouldering in the grave,
John Brown's body lies a mouldering in the grave,
John Brown's body lies a mouldering in the grave,
   His soul's marching on!

         Chorus.

Glory Hally, Hallelujah! Glory Hally, Hallelujah! Glory
   Hally, Hallelujah!
   His soul's marching on!

He's gone to be a soldier in the army of our Lord,
He's gone to be a soldier in the army of our Lord,
He's gone to be a soldier in the army of our Lord,
   His soul's marching on!

Chorus: Glory Hally, Hallelujah! Glory Hally, Hallelujah!
   Glory Hally, Hallelujah!
   His soul's marching on!

John Brown's knapsack is strapped upon his back,
John Brown's knapsack is strapped upon his back,
John Brown's knapsack is strapped upon his back,
   His soul's marching on!

Chorus: Glory Hally, Hallelujah! Glory Hallelujah!
   Glory Hally, Hallelujah!
   His soul's marching on!

His pet lamps will meet him on the way, —
His pet lamps will meet him on the way, —
His pet lamps will meet him on the way. —
   They go marching on!

Chorus: Glory Hally, Hallelujah! Glory Hally Hallelujah!
   Glory Hally, Hallelujah!
   They go marching on!

They will han Jeff Davis to a tree!
They will hang Jeff Davis to a tree!
They will hang Jeff Davis to a tree!
   As they march along!

Chorus: Glory Hally, Hallelujah! Glory Hally, Hallelujah
   Glory Hally, Hallelujah!
   As they march along!

Now, three rousing cheers for the Union!
Now, three rousing cheers for the Union!
Now, three rousing cheers for the Union!
   As we are marching on!

Chorus: Glory Hally, Hallelujah! Glory Hally, Hallelujah!
   Glory Hally, Hallelujah!
   Hip, hip, hip, hip, Hurrah!

675

Fig. 15. John Brown's Original Marching Song, Duke University Libraries, Digital Collection's

CHAPTER 11

Soldiers of the Cross

"Religious sentiment-call it fanaticism, such as like that which made the soldiers of Cromwell invincible"

Do You Think I'll Make a Soldier?

AT THE BEGINNING of the Civil War, Union generals were indifferent to the plight of Negroes. General Benjamin Butler would become a staunch supporter of black troops, however. At the Charleston Convention in 1860, he supported Jefferson Davis, who became the president of the Confederacy. As president of the Confederacy, Davis was conservative and unyielding. Although Butler did not want to use black troops, he saw the value of their labor to the South. On May 24, 1861, Butler declared slaves "contraband of war." Runaway slaves would not be returned to the South, and all slaves acquired by war were under the control of the United States.

Like most Union Generals, Butler was a Democrat, which was the conservative party of that time period. Butler wrote:

"A large majority of the officers of the army were of Democratic inclination, or, to speak more accurately, were in favor of the Union as it was; that is to say, believed in states rights, including the restoration of the negroes to slavery. Certain it was that the almost universal feeling of ' the army was against the employing of negroes as soldiers, and that volunteering had so far stopped unless we were able to conquer the Rebellion with what troops we had it would be very difficult to get many more. I doubted whether the people would be willing to sustain the emancipation proclamation unless the negroes could be so far employed as to show that they were willing to fight for their freedom, a thing which no considerable portion had yet been permitted to do."[91]
Benjamin F. Butler

Most Union generals felt that blacks would not fight and would just endanger the lives of white Union troops. General William Tecumseh Sherman was one of those that felt blacks would not make good soldiers; he argued:

"I have had the question put to me often, 'Is not a negro as good as a white man to stop a bullet?' Yes: and a sand-bag is better; but can a negro do our skirmishing and picket duty? Can they improvise bridges, sorties, flank movements, etc., like the white man? I say no."[92]

---

91 Benjamin F. Butler, *Butler's Book* (Boston: A. M. Thayer & Co., 1892), 581.
92 Ward, *The Civil War*, 246.

General Hunter

General David Hunter was an abolitionist from the state of Illinois, like President Lincoln. Hunter corresponded with Lincoln about the ills of slavery and was invited by Lincoln to come to Washington shortly after the war started. He joined the army and served as a colonel during the Battle of Bull Run. He was severely injured in the neck. Following his recovery, he was appointed commander of the Department of the South in the spring of 1862. In the spring of 1862, he became the first man to use his authority in the Union army to end slavery. He imposed martial law over the states of Georgia, Florida, and South Carolina and outlawed slavery there.

At Hilton Head, South Carolina, in May of 1862, Hunter became the first person to organize black soldiers into regiments when he formed the First South Carolina Colored Volunteers. These men were taken from local plantations around Beaufort, South Carolina, which angered plantation owners. They claimed that many slaves were taken by the point of a bayonet and forced into the army. This objection was ironic, since they were slaves who had been forced into plantation labor. One must be very careful when reviewing historical information, since much of it is proslavery.

When Lincoln got word of Hunter's actions, he was furious. At that time, white Northerners were against arming Negroes, and plantation owners were complaining of hardship due to lost slave labor. Under Lincoln's orders, the regiment was disbanded in August 1862.

Butler and the Louisiana Native Guard

General Butler initially resisted the enlistment of black troops into the Union army. In early August of 1862, Brigadier General John W. Phelps requested permission from Butler to start a black regiment. Butler refused, stating that only Lincoln had the authority to start black regiments under the Second Confiscation Act of July 17, 1862. Phelps was ordered to use the Negroes as laborers instead of soldiers. Phelps was angered by the order and resigned.

What changed Butler's mind about using blacks as soldiers was, perhaps, a case of brutality that he had to rule on in New Orleans. On May 1, 1862, General Benjamin Butler was put in charge of New Orleans. Similar to Hunter, he was stationed in the South to maintain order. A young lady was brought to his attention at his headquarters in New Orleans. The girl was beautiful and may have reminded him of one of his own children. Her back was scarred and disfigured by the repeated tear of the bullwhip. The perpetrator was her father and her master. Reports of the incident suggested that Butler was deeply shaken, stunned, and never the same again. Butler witnessed in New Orleans how the dehumanization of slaves dehumanized the slaver and infuriated tenderhearted observers.

"

"One Sunday morning, while General Butler was seated at the breakfast table, Major Strong, a gentleman who was not given to undue emotion, rushed into the room, pale with rage and horror.

"General," he exclaimed, "there is the most list damnable thing out here!"... The woman who was the object of so much attention, was nearly white, aged about twenty-seven..."Look here, General," said Major Strong, as he opened the dress of this poor creature.

Her back was cut to pieces with the infernal cowhide. It was all black and red-red where and the infernal instrument of torture had broken the skin, black where it had not. To convey an idea of its appearance, General Strong used to yon say that it resembled a very rare beefsteak, with Ire the black marks of the gridiron across it.

No one ever saw General Butler so profoundly for moved as he was while gazing upon this pitiable ten spectacle. Who did this?" he asked the girl.

"Master," she replied.

"Who is your master?"

"Mr. Landry"

Landry was a respectable merchant living in near by quarters, not unknown to the members of the staff.

"What did he do it for?" asked the general.

"I went out after the clothes from the wash," said she, "and I stayed out late. When I then came home, master licked me and said he would teach me to run away."…At this moment Major Strong whispered in the general's ear a piece of information which I caused him to compare the faces of the master and the slave. The resemblance between them was striking.

"Is this woman your daughter?" asked the met general.

"There are reports to that effect," said Landry. … The general, for once, seemed deprived of his power to judge with promptness. He remained for some time," says an eye-witness, "apparently lost in abstraction. I shall never forget the singular expression on his face.

"I bad been accustomed to see him in a storm of passion at any instance of oppression or flagrant injustice; but on this occasion he was too deeply affected to obtain relief in the usual way.

"His whole air was one of dejection, almost listlessness; his indignation too intense, and his anger too stern, to find expression even in his countenance… …I close this chapter of horrors. Each of these anecdotes illustrates one phase of the accursed thing, and all of them tend to show what has been already remarked, that the worst consequences of slavery fall upon the white race. It is better to be murdered than to be a murderer. It is better to be the victim of cruelty than to be capable of inflicting it. Mrs. Kemble judges rightly, when she says, in her recent noble and well-timed work, that it were far preferable to be a slave upon a Georgian rice plantation than to be the lord of one, with all that weight of crime upon the soul which slavery necessitates, and to become so completely depraved as to be able to contemplate so much suffering and iniquity with stolid indifference…But a woman's bleeding back, the master's brutal insensibility, the absolute destruction in the character of slave-owners of all that redeems human nature, such as sense of truth, pity the helpless, regard for the sanctities of domestic life; the flighty inferiority of their minds, their stupid improvidence, their incurable wrong-headedness and wrong-heartedness, their childish vanity and shameful ignorance, their boastful at emptiness and contempt for all people and nations more enlightened than themselves; these things appealed to him, these things he marked and inwardly digested. Impatient as he had previously been at the slow progress of the war, he now became more reconciled to it, because he saw that every month of its continuance made the doom of slavery more certain and more speedy. He was now perfectly aware that the United States could never realize General of Washington's modest aspiration, that it might become "a respectable nation," much less a great and glorious one, nor even a nation homogeneous enough to be truly powerful, until slavery had ceased to exist in every part of it.

Those who lived on intimate relations with the general, remarked his growing abhorrence of It slavery. During the first weeks of the occupation of the city, he was occasionally capable, in the hurry of indorsing a peck of letters, of spelling negro with two g's. Not so in the later months. Not so when he had seen the torn and bleeding and blackened backs of fair and delicate in women. Not so when he had reviewed his noble colored regiments. Not so when he had learned that the negroes of the South were among the heaven-destined means of restoring the integrity, the power, and the splendor of his in country. Not so when he had learned how the oppression of the negroes bad extinguished in the white race almost every trait of character se which redeems and sanctifies human nature.

"God Almighty himself is doing it," he would say, when talking on this subject. "No man's hand can stay it. It is no other than the omnipotent God who has taken this mode of destroying slavery. We are but *the instruments in his hands. We could not prevent it if we would. And let us strive as we might, the judicial blindness of the rebels would do the work of God without our aid, and in spite of all our endeavors against it. "AMEN!"*[93]

General Benjamin Butler was to become as fanatical a supporter of Negro rights as John Brown and Frederick Douglass. He now believed he would be serving God by destroying slavery. One thing made him different from other abolitionists, however. Butler had the ear of the president. Although Butler was a Democrat and President Lincoln was a Republican, Lincoln reached across the aisle and confided in Butler. Butler was a high-ranking general and was so well thought-of by Lincoln that he would be asked to be Lincoln's running mate in the 1864 presidential election.

A year before Butler assumed control of New Orleans, on May 2, 1861, the Confederacy had organized a regiment of free black soldiers in New Orleans called "Native Guard, Colored." At that time, New Orleans had a population of 150,000, including 18,000 slaves and 10,000 free blacks.[94] Free blacks had previously been enrolled by Andrew Jackson in the War of 1812 and represented 10 percent of his army at the Battle of New Orleans.[95] Although the Louisiana Native Guard was initially composed of black Confederates, it was the first black Civil War regiment to be formed and had the distinction of being the only black regiment to be commanded by black officers. Some of the soldiers were slave owners, and some were mulattos, but they were primarily free blacks.

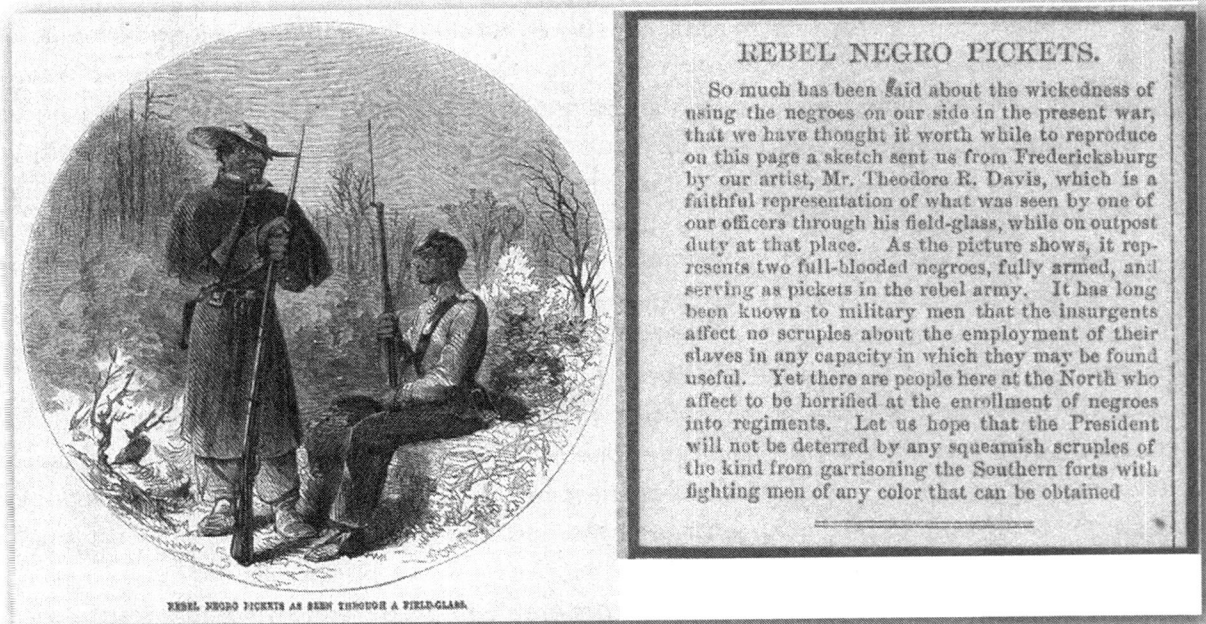

REBEL NEGRO PICKETS.

So much has been said about the wickedness of using the negroes on our side in the present war, that we have thought it worth while to reproduce on this page a sketch sent us from Fredericksburg by our artist, Mr. Theodore R. Davis, which is a faithful representation of what was seen by one of our officers through his field-glass, while on outpost duty at that place. As the picture shows, it represents two full-blooded negroes, fully armed, and serving as pickets in the rebel army. It has long been known to military men that the insurgents affect no scruples about the employment of their slaves in any capacity in which they may be found useful. Yet there are people here at the North who affect to be horrified at the enrollment of negroes into regiments. Let us hope that the President will not be deterred by any squeamish scruples of the kind from garrisoning the Southern forts with fighting men of any color that can be obtained

REBEL NEGRO PICKETS AS SEEN THROUGH A FIELD-GLASS.

Fig. 16. Louisiana Native Guard (Author's Collection)

Following the defeat of the Confederacy at New Orleans in May of 1861, the Louisiana Native Guard remained in the city. By May of 1862, General Hunter had formed the First South Carolina Colored Volunteers, and Governor James H Lane had started the First Kansas Colored Volunteers, but these regiments were not authorized by President Lincoln. Butler, however, had a great deal of power in New Orleans, but he was short of men. Butler wondered if the

---

93 *Atlanta Monthly*, July 1863, 143–145. Also, *General Butler in New Orleans*, 145, and Brown, *The Negro in the American Rebellion*.
94 James Parton, *General Butler in New Orleans* (New York: Mason Brothers, 1864), 130.
95 Ibid., 134.

Native Guard would switch sides and fight for the freedom of all blacks. Butler had the following conversation with a group of them:

"But," I said, "I want you to answer me one question. My officers, most of them, believe that negroes won't fight."
"Oh, but we will, "came from the whole of them.
"You seem to be an intelligent man, "said I, to their spokesman;
" answer me this question: I have found out that you know just as well what this war is about as I do, and if the United States succeed in it, it will put an end to slavery." They all looked assent.
"Then tell me why some negroes have not in this war struck a good blow somewhere for their freedom?
"General, will you permit a question?"
"Yes."
"If we colored men had risen to make war on our masters, would not it have been our duty to ourselves, they being our enemies, to kill the enemy wherever we could find them? and all the white men would have been our enemies to be killed?"
"I don't know but what you are right," said I. "I think that would be a logical necessity of insurrection."
"If the colored men had begun such a war as that, General, which general of the United States army should we have called on to help us fight our battles?"
That was unanswerable.
"Well," I said, "why do you think that your men will fight?"
"General we come from a fighting race. Our fathers were brought here slaves because they were captured in war, and in hand to hand fights, too. We are willing to fight. Pardon me, General, but the only cowardly blood we have got in our veins is the white blood."[96]
Benjamin F. Butler

The First Regiment of Louisiana Native Guard was mustered into the US Army on August 22, 1862. By December of 1862, there were three Native Guard regiments: the First, Second, and Third Louisiana Native Guard.

When Butler first came to New Orleans, he occasionally used the word "nigger" to describe blacks. His biographer, James Parton, said, "Not so in the later months. Not so when he had seen the torn and bleeding and blackened backs of fair and delicate women." While in New Orleans, Butler became a strong supporter for the use of black soldiers and felt they could be the key to a Union victory. Butler believed in John Brown's plan of "arming the Negroes." Butler was impressed by the ease it took to drill and train them, he wrote:

"Better soldiers never shouldered a musket. They were intelligent, obedient, highly appreciative of their position, and fully maintained its dignity. They easily learned the school of soldier. I observed a, very remarkable trait about them. They learned to handle arms and to march more readily than the most intelligent white men. My drillmaster could teach a regiment of negroes that much of the art of war sooner than he could have taught the same number of students from Harvard or Yale...

Again, their ear for time as well as tune was exceedingly apt; and it was wonderful with what accuracy and steadiness a company of negroes would march after a few days' instruction...

96 Butler, *Butler's Book*, 492.

Again, white men, in case of sudden danger, seek safety by going apart each for himself. The negroes always cling together for mutual protection."[97]
Benjamin F. Butler
*

After mustering black soldiers into service, Butler had to address the prejudices that his officers had for black troops. An example of this prejudice was that of General Godfry Weitzel who was second in command to Butler in New Orleans and helped him organize the Louisiana Native Guard. Butler had promoted Weitzel from lieutenant of engineers to brigadier-general of volunteers. Butler organized an expedition to control rich Louisiana farm land that was to be commanded by Weitzel. The expedition was to include the Louisiana Native Guard which angered Weitzel. Weitzel wrote:

"I cannot command those negro regiments…I beg you therefore to keep the negro brigade directly under your own command or pace someone over both mine and it,"[98]

Like Butler, Weitzel would change his opinion of black troops. Weitzel would eventually command the largest black army in the history of the United States the XXV Corps.

Shortly after Hunter started organizing black units in South Carolina, in the summer of 1862, Senator/General James H. Lane started recruiting black soldiers in Kansas. They were similarly called the First Kansas Volunteer Infantry. Again, Lincoln did not authorize the enlistment of black soldiers.

Colonel Higginson and the Gospel Army

Following Butler's enlistment of the Louisiana Native Guard, the First South Carolina Volunteers were allowed to reorganize. On November 10, 1862, Colonel Thomas Wentworth Higginson assumed command of the First South Carolina Volunteers. Colonel Higginson was another abolitionist who had been one of John Brown's "secret six" supporters The black men called themselves "The Gospel Army."

"It used to seem to me that never since Cromwell's time, had there been soldiers in whom the religious element held such a place. " A religious army," ' a gospel army," were their frequent phrases. In their prayer meetings there was always a mingling, often quaint enough, of the warlike and the pious. " If each one of us was a paying man" said Corporal Thomas Long in a sermon, " it appears to me that we could fight as well with prayers as with bullets, for the Lord has said that, if you have faith' even as a grain of mustard seed cut into four parts, you can say to the sycamore-tree, Arise, and it will come up." And though Corporal Long may have got a little perplexed in his botany, his faith proved itself by works, for he volunteered and went many miles on a solitary scouting expedition into the enemy' country in Florida, and got back safe, after I had given him up for lost."
* Col. T. W. Higginson,
First South Carolina Volunteers[99]

Slaves believed that they would be reunited with lost loved ones in heaven. Most black Civil War soldiers were ex-slaves, and many had families who were still slaves in the land of bondage. The following prayer was made

---

97 Butler, *Butler's Book*, 491.
98 Butler, *Butler's Book*, 497.
99 T. W. Higginson, *Army Life in a Black Regiment*, (Boston: Fields, Osgood & Co., 1870) 55.

by a member of the Gospel Army and recorded by Colonel Higginson. This soldier looked forward to seeing his family in heaven.

"

' Let me so lib dat when I die I shall hab manners ; dat I shall know what to say when I see my heabenly Lord.

" 'Let me lib wid de musket in one hand, an' de Bible in de oder dat if I die at de muzzle of de musket, die in de water, die on de land, I may know I hab bressed Jesus in my hand, an' hab no fear.

"'I hab lef my wife in de land o' bondage ; my little ones dey say eb'ry night, " Whar is my fader?" But when I die, when de breseed mornin' rises, when I shall stan' in de glory, mid one foot on de water an' one foot on do land, den, O Lord ! I shall see my wife an' my little chil'en once more."'

Col. T. W. Higginson,

First South Carolina Volunteers[100]

W. W. Brown

Note that the soldier refers to having a musket in one hand and a Bible in the other. John Brown is portrayed in chapter 10 with a musket in one hand and a Bible in the other as well.

During the Civil War a questionnaire was given to contraband camp superintendents to better understand the ex-slaves that the Union Army had captured. One of the questions on the survey examined religious practices. Results were published in the book Free At Last: A Documentary History of Slavery, Freedom, and the Civil War[101], edited by Ira Berlin.

INTERROGATORY 18   What of their religious notions and practice?

ANSWERS.

Corinth. Very religious- always orthodox- mostly Methodists, Baptists & Presbyterians. Not withstanding their peculiar notions, when any one dies, they often pray & sing all night.

Cairo Naturally religiously inclined. During my six months' connection with them, I have not heard over ten colored men swear. their religious meetineis are both solemn and interesting.

Grand Junction. During the cold months, no house for church. Their religious notions & practices have failed of any marked manifestation. Show a strong religious inclination.

Holly Springs and Memphis. Great majority religious--Baptists or Methodists. Their notions of the leading doctrines of the Bible are remarkably correct. Justification, repentance, faith, holiness, heaven, hell are not troubled, like educated white men, with unbelief.

Bolivar. Exceeding those of the whites in the army.

Slave Athleticism

Slavery gave blacks little experience with muskets; however, a slavery-system priority was to create strong, athletic bodies. The statue below is named *Free* and was created by Emma Cadwallader-Guild of Zanesville, Ohio, in the 1880s. Guild tried to capture the athletic slave body described by Colonel Higginson.

---

100 W. W. Brown, *The Negro in the American Rebellion*, 132.

101 Ira Berlin, *Free At Last: A Documentary History of Slavery, Freedom, and the Civil War*, page 197

Fig. 17. *"Free"*, Statue by Emma Cadwallader-Guild, 1880s, Courtesy Crystal Bridges Museum

Hard work in slavery blessed the ex-slaves with athletic bodies. Their physical condition is seldom mentioned in history, nor is slave breeding mentioned, but it was a common practice. Again, dehumanization of slaves dehumanizes both slave and slaver; in this case both are ashamed.

" In speaking of the military qualities of the blacks, I should add, that the only point where I am disappointed is one I have never seen raised by the most incredulous newspaper critics, - namely, their physical condition. To be sure they often look magnificently to my gymnasium-trained eye; and I always like to observe them when bathing, - such splendid muscular development, set off by that smooth coating of adipose tissue which makes them, like the South-Sea Islanders, appear even more muscular than they are"[102]
Col. T. W. Higginson,
First South Carolina Volunteers

102 Higginson, *Army Life in a Black Regiment*, 55.

South Carolina Volunteer Service; The Gospel Army

The Gospel Army was the first black regiments to go into battle.

"The first actual fighting by organized colored troops of which there is official record took place on St. Helena Island, South Carolina, October 26, 1862, when the pickets of company A, 1st. south Carolina Volunteers, under Captain Trowbridge, fired upon and drove back two boat-loads of Confederates who had attempted a landing."[103]
Thomas Wentworth Higginson

Below is the unit history of the First South Carolina Volunteer Infantry (US) taken from Dyer's Compendium.

"Before muster, 3 companies on Expedition along the coast of Georgia and Florida on during November 3-10, 1862. Spalding's, on Sapello River, GA, November 7 (Company "A"). Doboy River Island until March 1863. Expedition from Beaufort up the St. Mary's River in Georgia and Florida during January 23 - February 1. Skirmish at Township on January 26. Expedition from Beaufort to Jacksonville, FL, on March 23-31. Skirmish near Jacksonville on March 29. At Beaufort, SC, until January 1864. Expedition up South Edisto River during July 9-11, 1863. Action at Williston Bluff, Pon Pon River on July 10. Expedition to Pocotaligo, SC, during November 23-25 (Companies "E" & "K").

Skirmish near Cunningham's Bluff on November 24. (Companies "C" and "K" at Hilton Head, SC, until September, 1863, returning to Beaufort, SC; Companies "A" & "F" moved to Hilton Head, SC, during January, 1864. Expedition to Jacksonville, FL, during February 6-8. Designation of Regiment changed to 33rd Infantry Regiment, USCT on February 8, 1864"[104]

---

103 Thomas Wentworth Higginson, *"Colored Troops Under Fire"*, The Century Illustrated Monthly Magazine, Volume 32; Volume 54, Scribner & Company; The Century Company, 1897 - American literature, 194.
104 Frederick Henry Dyer, *A compendium of the War of the Rebellion* (Des Moines, Iowa: The Dyer Publishing Company, 1908), 1636.

Fig. 18. Top: First South Carolina Colored Volunteers, from a sketch by Colonel Brewerton (Author's Collection)
Bottom: Captioned "The War in South Carolina—a Negro regiment attacked by rebels and bloodhounds—
from a sketch by our special artist, W. T. Crane," (*Frank Leslie's Illustrated*, March 5, 1864)

Harriet Tubman was popular among the Massachusetts abolitionists. Governor John Andrew of Massachusetts asked Tubman to assist General Hunter in South Carolina with the thousands of newly freed slaves. Tubman recruited and led scouts into Confederate territory to report troop movement and strength. Tubman also recruited troops for the Second South Carolina volunteers with Colonel Montgomery. Hunter asked Tubman to "go with several gunboats up the Combahee River, the object of the expedition being to take up the torpedoes placed by the rebels in the river, to destroy railroads and bridges, and to cut off supplies from the rebel troops." Tubman agreed and asked for the appointment of Colonel Montgomery; he was given command of the Second South Carolina Volunteers (Colored). The expedition made Tubman the first woman in American history to lead an army into battle. The following article was published in the *Boston Commonwealth*, a Boston newspaper, on July 10, 1863.

"Col. Montgomery and his gallant band of 300 black soldiers, under the guidance of a black woman, dashed into the enemy's country, struck a bold and effective blow, destroying millions of dollars worth of commissary stores, cotton and lordly dwellings, and striking terror into the: heart of rebellion, brought off near 800 slaves and thousands of dollars worth of property, without losing a man or receiving a scratch. It' was a glorious consummation."[105]

Big Bob, Preacher and Leader

It was difficult for Southerners to admit that they needed Negroes to win the Civil War. Putting blacks in gray uniforms was a plan doomed to fail from the beginning. Southerners controlled blacks with chains and bullwhips. Controlling blacks who were holding bayonets and muskets was a more difficult task. As with the present day, black preachers played an important leadership role in the African American and slave community. A century later, Dr. Martin Luther King Jr. articulated their belief in "church activism," when he said that "the pastor has the responsibility of teaching the word of god as well as leading his flock to do 'God's Will.'"

The preacher Big Bob was a classic black leader, hero, minister, and martyr. Big Bob's history is preserved by William Wells Brown.

"The siege of Washington, N.C., March 30-April 20, 1863, had carried consternation among the planters of the surrounding country, and contrabands were flocking in by hundreds. when, just at day-break one morning, a band of seventeen came to the shore, and hailed the nearest gunboat. The blacks were soon taken on board, when it was ascertained that they had travelled fifty miles the previous night, guided by their leader, a negro whom they called "Big Bob." This man was without a drop of Anglo Saxon blood in his veins, if color was a true index. It was also soon known that he was a preacher, or had been, among his fellow-slaves. These men all expressed a desire to be put to work, and, if allowed, to fight for " de ole flag." " Big Bob " sported a suit of rebel gray, which his fellow-slaves could not ; and the way in which he obtained it was rather amusing. In the region from which they escaped, the blacks were being enrolled in the rebel army ; and Bob and his companions were taken, and put under guard, preparatory to their being removed to the nearest military post. Bob, however, resolved that he would not fight for the rebel cause, and induced his comrades to join in the plan of seizing the guard, and bringing him away with them ; which they ' did, Bob claiming the rebel soldier's clothes, when that individual was dismissed, after a march of thirty miles from their home. Bob made an amusing appearance, heing above six feet in height, and dressed in a suit, the legs of the pants of which were five or six inches too short, and the arms of the coat proportionally short.

A few days after the arrival of the contrabands, their services were needed in an important expedition in the interior."[106]

The preacher Big Bob led his band of "home boys" or congregation on a number of raids behind enemy lines, generating the terror that Butler would describe to President Lincoln.

---

105 Lerone Bennett Jr., *Before the Mayflower* (Penguin Books, New York, New York) 207.
106 Brown, *The Negro in the American Rebellion*, 215.

"*The blacks numbered less than forty ; while the whites were more than one hundred. The negroes were called upon to surrender; but Bob answered, " No, I never surrenders." and then he cried out, " Come on, boys! ef we's captud, we's got to hang; and dat's a fack. And nobly did they fight, whipping their assailants, and reaching the gunboats with but the loss of' three men killed and ten wounded. Bob and his companions were greatly praised when once more on the fleet.*"

"*But Bob's days were numbered; for the next day a flat full of soldiers, with four blacks, including Bob, attempted to land at Rodman's Point, but were repulsed by a terrible fire of rebel bullets, all tumbling into the boat, and lying fiat to escape being shot. Meanwhile the boat stuck fast on the sand-bar, while the balls were still whizzing over and around the flat. Seeing that something must be done at once, or all would be lost, Big Bob exclaimed, "Somebody's got to die to get us out of this, and it may as well be me ! " He then deliberately got out, and pushed the boat of, and fell into it, pierced by five bullets.*"[107]

President Lincoln and General Butler resurrects John Brown's Plan

On September 22, 1862, exactly one month after the First Regiment of Louisiana Native Guard was mustered into the US Army, President Lincoln unveiled the Emancipation Proclamation. The Emancipation Proclamation simply freed slaves in Confederate controlled states. Historians argue that the announcement of the Emancipation Proclamation purposely followed a Union victory which occurred five days earlier at the Battle of Antietam. When the Emancipation Proclamation took effect on January 1, 1863, it was accompanied by the Union Army's authorization to recruit black troops and muster them into the Union Army. The idea of arming the Negroes appears to have result from President Lincoln's consultation with General Butler. General Butler did not belong to Lincoln's political party but was an aide to the president. General Butler met with President Lincoln to discuss "the Negro problem" and implementing John Browns plan of arming the Negro. I am not curtain of the date of the meeting, but the meetings content suggest that it had to have occurred before the Emancipation Proclamation took effect in January 1863. The plan called for first freeing slaves then arming them. Mustering the Louisiana Native Guard into the US Army would have been a first step to implementing John Brown's plan. Butler describes his meeting with President Lincoln as follows:

"*We then talked of a favorite project he had of getting rid of the negroes by colonization, and he asked me what I thought of it. I told him that it was simply impossible; that the negroes would not go anyway, for they loved their homes as much as the rest of us, and all efforts at colonization would not make a substantial impression upon the number of negroes in the country.*"

"*Reverting to the subject of arming the negroes, I said to him that I thought it might be possible to start with a sufficient army of white troops, and, avoiding a march which might deplete their ranks by death and sickness, to take them in ships and land them somewhere on the Southern coast. These troops could then come up through the Confederacy, gathering up negroes, who could be armed at first with arms that they could handle, so as to defend themselves and aid the rest of the army in case of rebel charges upon it. In this way we could establish ourselves down there with an army that would be a terror to the whole South.*"

"*He asked me what I would arm them with. I told him John Brown had intended, if he got loose in the mountains of Virginia, to arm his negroes with spears and revolvers; and there was a great deal in that. *"

"*That is a new idea, General," said he.*

---

107 Ibid.

"No, Mr. President," I answered, "it is a very old one. Fathers of these negroes, and some of the negroes themselves, fought their battles in Africa with no other weapon, save a club. Although we have substituted the bayonet for the spear, yet as long as the soldier can shoot he is not inclined to use the bayonet."[108]
General Benjamin F. Butler

General Hunter's Letter

In a letter to then-Governor Andrews of Massachusetts, General Hunter encouraged the establishment of black regiments and described the Gospel Army.

HEADQUARTERS DEPARTMENT OF THE SOUTH
Hilton Head, Port Royal, SC, May 4, 1863

To His Excellency the Governor of Massachusetts, Boston, Mass.

"I am happy to be able to announce to you my complete and eminent satisfaction with the results of the organization of negro regiments in this department. In the field so far as tried, they have proved brave, active, enduring, and energetic, frequently outrunning, by their zeal, and familiarity with the Southern country, the restrictions deemed prudent by certain of their officers. They have never disgraced their uniform by pillage or cruelty, but have so conducted themselves, upon the whole, that even our enemies, though more anxious to find fault with these than with any other portion of our troops, have not yet been able to allege against them a single violation of any of the rules of civilized warfare."

"These regiments are hardy, generous, temperate, patient, strictly obedient, possessing great natural aptitude for arms and deeply imbued with that religious sentiment-call it fanaticism, such as like that which made the soldiers of Cromwell invincible. They believe that now is the time appointed by God for their deliverance; and, under the heroic incitement of this faith, I believe them capable of showing a courage, and persistency of purpose, which must, in the end, extort both victory and admiration."

D. HUNTER
Major General Commanding[109]
W. W. Brown

---

108 Butler, *Butler's Book*, 578.
109 Brown, *Negro in American Rebellion*, 131.

CHAPTER 12

United States Colored Troops

"Shall we leave this inheritance of shame to our children? No!"

Every Round Goes Higher, Higher

ON MARCH 25, 1863, General Lorenzo Thomas was authorized by Secretary of War Edwin Stanton to enlist Negro troops into the Union army. On May 22, 1863, the war department established the Bureau of Colored Troops (USCT) and launched an aggressive campaign to recruit black soldiers. By the end of the war, there were over 130,000 black soldiers in the field at once. Wikipedia list the USCT regiments as follows:

- *6 Regiments of Cavalry [1st-6th USC Cavalry]*
- *1 Regiment of Light Artillery [2nd USC (Light) Artillery]*
- *1 Independent USC (Heavy) Artillery Battery*
- *13 Heavy Artillery Regiments [1st and 3rd-14th USC (Heavy) Artillery]*
- *1 unassigned Company of Infantry [Company A, US Colored Infantry]*
- *1 Independent USC Company of Infantry [Southard's Independent Company, Pennsylvania (Colored) Infantry]*
- *1 Independent USC Regiment of Infantry [Powell's Regiment, US Colored Infantry]*
- *135 Regiments of Infantry [1st-138th USC Infantry] (The 94th, 105th, and 126th USC Infantry regiments were never fully formed)*

(Wikipedia, *United States Colored Troops*, http://en.wikipedia.org/wiki/United_States_Colored_Troops)

The USCT was composed of 175 regiments representing 178,895 black men by the end of the war. Forty-four percent of the men were recruited from Northern states, and 56 percent were recruited from Southern states.

Men of Color to Arms

Men like Frederick Douglass believed that black Americans must earn their own freedom, or else black youth would inherit a history of shame. These men used words similar to the following to recruit free blacks into the Union army. This is a copy of a 8 foot tall sign that appeared on a Philadelphia building in 1863:

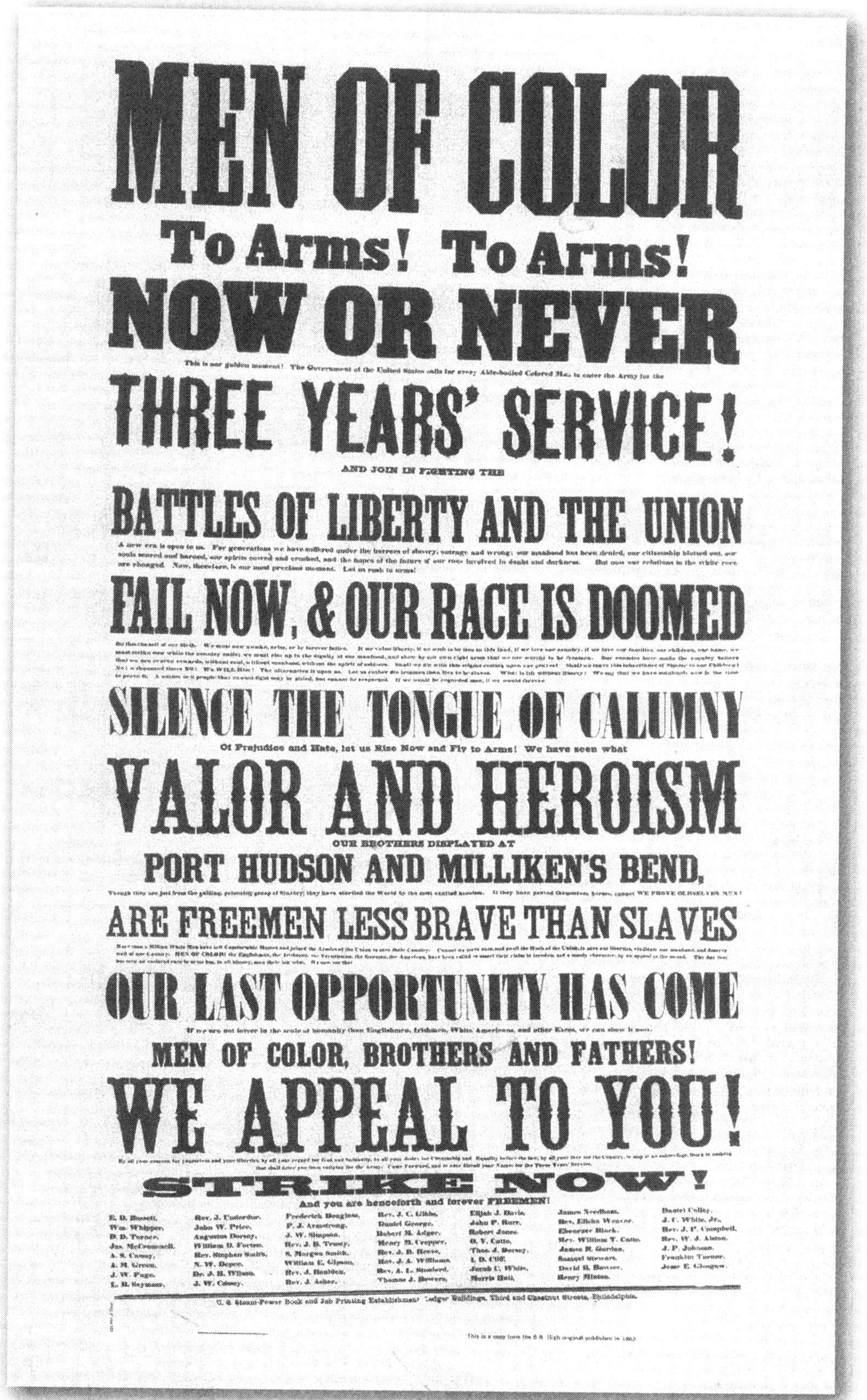

Fig. 19. Men of Color! To Arms! To Arms! (Philadelphia 1863), Library of Congress

"'Men of color. To arms! To arms! Now or never...For generations we have suffered under the horrors of slavery, outrage and wrong; our manhood has been denied, our citizenship blotted out, our souls scared and burned, our spirits cowed and crushed, and the hopes of the future of our race involved in doubts and darkness. But now the whole aspect of our of our relations to the white race is changed. Now therefore is our most precious moment. Let us, Rush to Arms! Fail Now and Our Race is Doomed on this the soil of our birth. We must now awake, arise, or be forever fallen. If we value liberty, if we wish to be free in this land if we love our country, if we love our families, our children, our homes, we must strike NOW while the Country calls : must rise up in the dignity of our manhood, and show by our own right arms that we are worthy to be freemen. Our enemies have made the country believe that we are craven cowards, without soul, without manhood, without the spirit of soldiers. Shall we die with this stigma resting on our graves? Shall we leave this inheritance of shame to our children? No! A thousand times No ! We WILL Rise!"[110]

White Officers

A great deal of care was taken by the Union army to assure that arming the Negroes was a success. Significant prejudice and resistance toward black troops existed, and it was believed that a lack of intelligence played a major role in promoting racism. Poorly educated people rely more on traditions and less on good judgment than well-educated people. The white officers in the USCT had high morals and were the most intelligent men in the army. It was required that officers pass an intelligence test as well as be committed to lifting the black race. This was not a requirement in other branches of the military. Due to the enormous prejudice against black men, a great deal of effort was made in selecting officers who had faith in both the ability and potential of black troops. After joining the USCT, the white men endured heavy fatigue duty and humiliation from their families. They were criticized for joining the USCT by their colleagues as well.

Strong relationships grew between black soldiers and their white officers. J. T. Glatthaar reviewed personal letters written by white officers who served in the USCT. Glatthaar's work is published in a book called *Forged in Battle*. Glatthaar said that officers in black units were "a better class of men, more moral, more religious, better educated and understand their business better than those in white reg'ts."

White officers who fought with black men were subject to be called niggers as the establishment defines it. *For example, led by their white officer, the 2ⁿᵈ USCT marched through Philadelphia to catch a train and were confronted by an angry racist mob. Their white officer was called a 'white nigger'*[111] by a civilian and a black soldier knocked him down.
The moral convictions of the white officers were often revealed by their courage. Many Confederate soldiers believed that black soldiers fought them because they were led and forced to fight by their white officers. They hoped that if they shot the white officers, the black men would turn and retreat. This was not the case; in fact, it made the black men more tenacious. However, the white skin among black faces and blue uniforms made them a distinguishable target.

---

110 W. A. Gladstone, *Men of Color* (Gettysburg, PA: Thomas, 1993) 110.

111 Glatthaar, *Forged in Battle*, 244.

First Kansas Colored Volunteers Follow John Brown into Battle

Fig. 20. "A Negro Regiment in Action," *Harper's Weekly*, March 14, 1863

On October 28, 1862, the First Kansas Colored Volunteers repulsed and drove off a superior force of rebels at Island Mound, Missouri. The First Kansas Colored Volunteers marched into battle singing this song:

"Old John Brown's body lies a moldering in the grave,
While weep the sons of bondage, whom he ventured to save;
But though he lost his life in struggling for the slave,
His soul is marching on.
    Glory, glory, Hallelujah !
    Glory, glory, Hallelujsh !
    Glory, glory, Hallelujah 1
    His soul is marching on !

Jobn Brown was a hero, undaunted, true, and bave,
And Kansas knew his valor, when he fought her rights to save ;
And now thongh the grass grows green above his grave,
    His soul Is marching on.

He captured Harper's Ferry with his nineteen men so few,
And he frightened ' Old Virginny ' till she trembled through and through :
They hang him for a traitor, themselves a traitor crew,
    For his soul is marching on, &c.

John Brown was John the Baptist, of the Christ we are to see, -
Christ, who of the bondman shall the Liberator be ;
And soon throughout the sunny South the slaves shall all be free,
    For his soul is marching on, &c.

The conflict that he haralded, he looks from heaven to view,
On the army of the Union, with its flag, red, white, and blue ;
And heaven shall ring with anthems o'er the dead they mean to do,
    For his soul is marching on, &c.

Ye soldiers of freedom then strike, while strike ye may,
The death. blow of oppression in a better time and way ;
For the dawn of old John Brown has brightened into day,

    And his soul is marching on.
    Glory, glory, Hallelujah !
    Glory, glory, Hallelujsh !
    Glory, glory, Hallelujah !
    And his soul is marching on."[112]

On April 18, 1864 First Kansas Colored Volunteers fought a superior force at Poison Springs, Arkansas. They smashed through confederate lines but sustained heavy casualties.

"On the 29th, we skirmished in the forenoon. In the afternooa, the venturing-out of a detachment beyond the distance ordered brought on a severe though short general engagement. At least one hundred and twenty of the rebel cavalry made a charge upon this detachment of twenty-four men. Before we could brirg up re-enforcements, these fearfully disproportioned parties were engaged in a desperate hand-to-hand encounter.

I was on the field, doing, with the other officers, the best we could to bring up re-enforcerments. There was no flinching, no hesitation, or trembling limbs among the men; but fierce determination flashing in their eyes, and exhibiting an eager, passionate haste to aid their comrades, and vindicate the manhood of their race. The air was rent with their yells, as they rushed on, and the difficulty manifested was in holding them well in rather than in fa.tering. Among the detachment cut off; of whom only six escaped unhurt, nothing I have ever seen, read, or

---

112 Browr., *Negro in the American Rebellion*, 212.

heard in the annals of war, surpasses the desperate personal valor exhibited by each and every man. Bayonets came in bloody, as did the stocks of gun ; and the last charge was found gone from cartridge-boxes." [113]

W. W. Brown

Battle of Port Hudson

On May 27, 1863, the first large battle that included a black regiment occurred at Port Hudson, Louisiana. Butler had mustered the regiment into Union service, making it the first black regiment to serve the Union and the only black regiment to have black officers. The men in Butler's First Regiment of Louisiana Native Guard lived up to their promise to Butler that they would fight with courage and honor. They attacked a heavily defended Confederate fort over five times, until their force of nine hundred men was cut down to fewer than three hundred. A review of Fox's Regimental Losses[114], reveal that these are the greatest casualties absorbed by a Union regiment in a single battle during the Civil War. William Wells Brown published several newspaper articles that described the battle. The battle drew national attention. The following articles appeared in the *New York Herald* and *New York Tribune*.[115]

"The New-York Herald, June 6—

"The First Regiment "The First Regiment Louisiana Native Guard, Col. Nelson, were in this charge. They went on the advance, and, when they came out, six hundred out of nine hundred men could not be accounted for. It is said on every side that they fought with the desperation of tigers. One negro was observed with a rebel soldiers in his face with his teeth?? (John are there some words missing here? This line doesn't make sense), other weapons having failed him. There are other incidents connected with the conduct of this regiment that have raised them very much in my opinion as soldiers. After firing one volley, they did not deign to load again, but went in with bayonets; and, wherever they hail a chance, it was all up with the rebels."

"The New-York Tribune, June 8, 1863-"Nobly done, First Regiment of Louisiana Native Guard! Though you failed to carry the rebel works against overwhelming numbers, you did not charge and fight and fall in vain. That heap of six hundred corpses, lying there dark and grim and silent before and within the rebel works, is a better proclamation of freedom than even President Lincoln's. A race ready to die thus was never yet retained in bondage, and never can be. Even the Wood copperheads, who will not fight themselves, and try to keep others out of the Union ranks, will not dare to mob negro regiments if this is their style of fighting. " [116]

113 Brown, *Negro in the American Rebellion*, 233

114 Fox's Regimental Losses, *"Chapter II"*, http://www.civilwarhome.com/foxschapter2.html

115 Brown, *Negro in the American Rebellion*, 175.

116 Brown, *William Wells, The Negro in the American Rebellion*, 175.

Fig. 21. Top: Battle of Port Hudson (Library of Congress)
Bottom: Funeral of Capt. Andre Cailloux in New Orleans, July 29, 1863,
from the August 29, 1863, edition of *Harper's Weekly*

As mentioned above, the Louisiana Native Guard was the only black regiment that fought in the Civil War with black officers. One of the officers who died in the Battle of Port Hudson was a local free black named Capt. Andre Cailloux. His funeral gained national attention in the North; however, his accomplishment was not a part of New Orleans black history. I discovered this black Civil War history was hidden when I visited New Orleans the summer before Hurricane Katrina. I toured the area with a very knowledgeable black tour guide. He was aware of all New Orleans history except black Civil War history. He said that he had never heard of the Louisiana Native Guard or the Battle of Port Hudson. This history is common knowledge because it was published in the North, but it remains unknown to blacks in New Orleans.

"The death of Capt. Andre Cailloux created a profound sensational throughout Louisiana, and especially in New Orleans, where the deceased had lived from childhood. This feeling of sorrow found vent at the funeral, which took place on the 11th of July, 1863. We give the following, written at the time by a correspondent of a New.York Journal :-

—"NEW ORLEANS, Saturday, Aug. 1, 1863.
"The most extraordinary local event that has ever been seen within our borders, and, I think, one of the most extraordinary exhibitions brought forth by this Rebellion, was the funeral of Capt. Andre Callioux, Company E, First Louisiana National Guards. Here, in this Southern emporium, was performed a funeral ceremony that for numbers and impressiveness never had its Superior in this city; and it was originated and carried through in honor of a gallant soldier of the despised race, to enslave which, it is said, will soothe this State back into the Union."[117]

Sergeant Spencer

During the siege of Port Hudson, a new schoolhouse was erected for the black soldiers who had been enlisted in that vicinity. When the school opened, the following speech was made by a colored soldier called Sergeant Spencer. Spencer gave the following speech at the school's dedication:

" I has been a-thinkin' I was old man; for, on de plantation, I was put down wid de old hands, and I quinsicontly felt myself dat I was a old man. But since I has come here to de Yankees, and been made a soldier for de Unite States, an' got dese beautiful clothes on. I feels like one young man ; and I doesn't call myself a old man nebber no more. An' I feels dis ebenin' dat, if de rebs came down here to dis old Fort Hudson, dat I could jus fight um as brave as any man what is in the Sebenth Regiment. Sometimes I has mighty feelins in dis ole heart of mine, when I considers how dese ere ossifers come all de way from de North to fight in de cause what we is fighten fur. How many ossifers has died, and how many white soldiers has died, in dis great and glorious war what we is in ! And now I feels dat, fore I would turn coward away from dese ossifers, I feels dat I could drink my own blood, and be pierced through wid five thousand bullets. I feels sometimes as doe I ought to tank Massa Linkern for dis blessin' what we has ; but again I comes to de solemn conclusion dat I ought to tank de Lord, Massa Linkern, and all dese ossifers. 'Fore I would be a slave 'gain, I would fight till de last drop of blood was gone. I has 'cluded to fight for my liberty, and for dis eddication what we is now to receive in dis beautiful new

---

117 Brown, *Negro in the American Rebellion*, 186.

house what we has. Also I hasn't got any eddication nor no book-learnin', I has rose up dis blessed ebenin' to do my best afore dis congregation. Dat's all what I has to say now ; but, at some future occasion, T may say more dan I has to say now, and edify you all when I has more preparation. Dat's all what I has to say. Amen."[118]

Milliken's Bend

Fig. 22. Battle of Milliken's Bend (Frank Leslie's 'The Negro in The War')

White Southerners believed that their slaves would not fight them. Brown wrote, "The planters had boasted, that, should they meet their former slaves, a single look from them would cause the negroes to throw down their weapons, and run." Milliken's Bend would test their belief.

Similar to white planters, most white officers and Union troops also initially did not welcome black troops onto the battle field. The belief that black troops would not fight was deeply rooted. On June 7, 1863, the first regular battle was fought between the blacks and whites in the valley of the Mississippi. At Milliken's Bend, Illinois cavalrymen encountered colored troops and some of them sneered, "A man ud be a dam fool to try to make soldiers out ah niggers…Any one ought to know a nigger won't fight: they'r running now before they seen a reb…We will show them how it is done if we find any of them. "[119] A few minutes later, the Illinois cavalrymen encountered a group of Confederate cavalrymen. Without firing a shot the Illinois group retreated and raced past the black troops. The black troops formed a firing line and fired a volley into the charging Confederates, halting their charge.

W. W. Brown described the battle from an account of an eyewitness:

118 Ibid., 281.
119 Glatthaar, *Forged in Battle*, 131–35.

"My information states that a force of about five hundred negroes, and two hundred men of the Twenty=third Iowa, belonging to the second brigade, Carr's division (twenty-third Iowa had been up the river with prisoners, and was on its way back to this place), was surprised in camp by a rebel force of about two thousand men. ...the rebels drove our force towards the gunboats, taking colored men prisoners and murdering them. This so in raged them that they rallied, and charged the enemy more heroically and desperately than has been recorded during the war. It was a genuine bayonet charge, a hand-to-hand fight, that has never occurred to any extent during this prolonged conflict. Upon both sides men were killed with the butts of muskets. White and black men were lying side by side, pierced by bayonets, and in some instances transfixed to the earth....If facts prove to be what they are now represented, this engagement of Sunday morning will be recorded as the most desperate of this war.

This battle satisfied the slave-masters of the South that their charm was gone; and that the negro, as a slave, was lost forever." [120]

Brigadier General Edward A. Wild

Brigadier General Edward Wild was an abolitionist and friend of Harriet Beecher Stowe, the author of Uncle Tom's Cabin. General Wild recruited blacks for the USCT as well as white officers. Wild recruited Stowe's half-brother James C. Beecher as an officer in the USCT. General Wild commanded a brigade of Black troops known as *Wild's African Brigade.* Wild's brigade was composed of the 54th Massachusetts Infantry as well as the 2nd and 3rd North Carolina Colored Volunteers. In the latter months of 1863 Wild led his black troops on an expedition into North Carolina to liberate slaves. The following article appeared in Harper's Weekly on January 23, 1864.

Fig. 23. "Colored troops under General Wild, Liberating slaves in North Carolina."

120 Brown, *Negro in the American Rebellion*, 137–9.

GENERAL WILD'S late raid into the interior of North Carolina abounded in incidents of peculiar interest, from which we have selected a single one...the liberation by the negro battalion of the slaves on Mr. Terrebee's plantation. As the reader may imagine, the scene was both novel and original in all its features. General Wild having scoured the peninsula between Pasquotank and Little Rivers to Elizabeth City, proceeded from the latter place toward Indiantown in Camden County. Having encamped overnight, the column moved on into a rich country which was covered with wealthy plantations. The scene in our sketch represents the colored troops on one of these plantations freeing the slaves. The morning light is shining upon their bristling bayonets in the back-ground, and upon a scene in front as ludicrous as it is interesting. The personal effects of the slaves are being gathered together from the outhouses on the plantation and piled, regardless of order, in an old cart, the party meanwhile availing themselves in a promiscuous manner of the Confiscation Act by plundering hens and chickens and larger fowl; and after all of these preliminary arrangements the women and children are (in a double sense) placed on an eminence above their chattels and carted off in triumph, leaving "Ole Massa" to glory in solitude and secession.

The Army of the James

In March 1864, General Ulysses S. Grant was put in charge of the Union army. General Grant organized a coordinated invasion of the South. General William T. Sherman's army invaded Georgia and marched toward Atlanta. General Franz Sigel invaded the Shenandoah Valley. Meanwhile, General Crook's and General Averill's mission was to destroy railroad supply lines in West Virginia, and General Banks was sent to capture Mobile, Alabama. General Grant and General George C. Meade attacked General Robert E. Lee's Army of Northern Virginia. Butler's mission was to capture the Confederate capital of Richmond, Virginia, with his Army of the James.

General Butler was given command of the Army of the James in April 1864. It was composed of thirty-three thousand troops, thirteen thousand, or 40 percent, of whom were black. On May 5, 1864, Butler traveled down the James River by means of the US Navy and established his headquarters at a small village called Bermuda Hundred, Virginia. This was the same day that General Grant engaged Confederate General Robert E. Lee at the Battle of the Wilderness.

Before attacking Richmond, Butler first had to attack Petersburg to destroy an important railway supply to Richmond. Butler, however, had to contend with the Confederate army, led by Confederate General PGT Beauregard. His subordinate was General George Pickett, who had led Pickett's Charge at the Battle of Gettysburg and guarded Petersburg.

By this stage of the war, Butler had fully implemented John Brown's plan of arming the Negro. Although Brown was dead, it was believed that his soul was marching on in the army of the Lord. Butler's goal was to go to Richmond; find the president of the Confederacy, Jeff Davis; and hang him "on a sour apple-tree." A favorite marching song of the Army of the James's colored troops was "John Brown's Body." A verse was added that refers to hanging Jeff Davis.[121]

John Brown's body lies a moulding in the grave,
John Brown's body lies a moulding in the grave,
John Brown's body lies a moulding in the grave,
His soul is marching on.

---

121 Williams, *Negro Troops in the Rebellion 1861–1865* (Franklin Square, NY: Harper & Bros., 1887) 300.

Chorrus:
Glory Hally, Hallelujah! Glory Hally, Hallelujah!
Glory Hally, Hallelujah!
His soul's marching on.

We'll hang Jeff Davis on an sour apple-tree
We'll hang Jeff Davis on an sour apple-tree
We'll hang Jeff Davis on an sour apple-tree
His soul is marching on.

Chorrus:
Glory Hally, Hallelujah! Glory Hally, Hallelujah!
Glory Hally, Hallelujah!
His soul's marching on.

Butler told President Lincoln that a black army would be "an army that would be a terror to the whole South." His prediction came true. When Pickett heard of a movement of the Army of the James, the Southern Gettysburg hero expressed his concerns to Adjutant General Cooper[122]:

"Butler's plan, evidently, is to let loose his swarm of blacks upon our ladies and defenseless families, plunder and devastate the country. Against such a warfare there is but one resource to hang at once every one captured belonging to the expedition, and afterwards every one caught who belongs to Butler's department. Let us come to a definite understanding with these heathen at once. Butler cannot be allowed to rule here as he did in New Orleans. His course must be stopped"

Fort Pillow Massacre and the KKK

Confederate General Nathan Bedford Forest also had a zero tolerance for slave disobedience, his inhumane treatment of blacks eventually led to him and his followers creating inhumane acts. On April 12, 1864, General Forest and fifteen hundred men captured Fort Pillow, in Tennessee. The fort was manned by 550 federal troops, half of whom were black. It was alleged that Forest murdered most of the prisoners, including black women and children. Black men were burned and buried alive. Forest went on to found the Ku Klux Klan following the war.

"All the negroes found in blue uniform or with any outward marks of a Union soldier upon him was killed—I saw some taken into the woods and hung…confined until the following morning when the remainder of the black soldiers were killed."[123]

---

122 R. S.H George W. olzman, *Stormy Ben Butler*, 137.
123 McPherson, *Battle Cry of Freedom*, 793.

Fig. 24. *The Fort Pillow Massacre,* Louis Kurz and Alexander Allison, Chicago, Illinois

The Fort Pillow Massacre significantly affected prisoner exchange between the North and South. Grant ordered General Benjamin F. Butler to demand that black prisoners be treated identically to whites and state that a refusal to do so would result in the end of prisoner exchange. Confederates refused Grant's demand, which resulted in an end to prisoner exchange. This decision led to the death of many white Union soldiers held in Confederate prisons. Confederate prisons were kept in very poor condition.

The hatred of black soldiers was a focal point for the KKK. A film was released in 1915 called *The Birth of a Nation*. It was shown on Cspan3 in recognition of the films one-hundredth anniversary. The film was the first blockbuster feature film; however, it was extremely racist. Black leaders tried to censor the film in 1915, but they were unsuccessful, and the film went on to inspire the KKK. The KKK membership ignited from a small number of radicals to six million members in the 1920s. Black Cspan3 viewers called again for censorship, but the curator of the African American Museum, Hari Jones, supported viewing and having a dialogue on the film. I agree with Jones; we can learn a lot about the fears of racists when we analyze the film.

The greatest fear that white southerners had was the arming of the Negro. Why? They believed in their racial superiority. If blacks were armed and had power over them, they could not expect blacks to treat them better than they had treated blacks for the past three hundred years. It was a tradition in the South for slave owners to have sex with their slaves and for slaves to wet-nurse their white babies as well.

I only saw the last hour of the three-hour film, but the last hour included black Civil War soldiers, which I have studied extensively. The film portrayed what would happen if the South was under black control. Following the Civil War, carpetbaggers invade the South with a massive black Civil War army. Blacks are portrayed by whites with black faces. The black army allows all blacks to vote, and they end up with an all-black government and legislature. This black legislature "cuts up." They eat chicken, take their shoes off, and drink alcohol during legislative proceedings. The first law that they pass allows them to marry white women. The black army also demands respect. Whites must salute their captain, and the black army also ties white men to trees and whips them. Things reach a climax when white women feel threatened with being molested by black soldiers, and one woman chooses death first. This sparks the KKK, who comes to the rescue and defeats the black army.

As well as inspiring the KKK, the film may also have led to hiding black Civil War history, since the history is not popular at all. Note that the "Battle Hymn of the Republic" was replaced as the national anthem in 1931, close to the peak period of political power for the KKK.

Never Avenge Yourselves

Jesus said, "Never avenge yourselves" (Rom. 13:19). Instead, feed your enemy if he is hungry. If he is thirsty give him something to drink, and you will be "heaping coals of fire on his head." In other words, he will feel ashamed of himself for what he has done to you. Don't let evil get the upper hand but conquer by doing good (Rom. 13:19–21).

Despite what Jesus said, the law of the land was "an eye for an eye and a tooth for a tooth." Men have retaliated after being attacked for thousands of years. Retaliation is justified by those unwilling to become a "doormats" of the hard-hearted. If the Negroes were capable of fighting, then all that could be expected was savagery, since the race had been raped for two hundred years. Southerners thought they would want revenge, as Nat Turner did on his revenge ride. Nat killed anyone in his path who was white.

Blacks saw white southerners as individuals rather than a single race. This is largely because blacks were a minority. It is much more common for blacks to associate with whites than the other way around. Whites with no contact with blacks require public opinion to judge them. Blacks recognized that there were some slave masters who loved their slaves and treated them with respect and kindness. In return, their slaves treated them with respect when they were not forced.

"Uncle Henry, the young fellow who figured in the whipping by Old Major, came back to the farm once at the head of a dozen soldiers. He had become a recruiting officer--now, I think they call it "drafting." Old Major was sitting in his favorite chair on the porch when he saw Henry coming with those soldiers, and he almost fell, he was that scairt. You see, so many times the slaves had returned to kill their masters, and poor Old Major thought Henry remembered that whipping."

" But Henry drew the men up in front of Old Major and he said, "This is my master, Major Holden. Honor him, men." And the men took off their caps and cheered Old Major. And he nearly fell again such a great big burden was off his shoulders, then. When Henry commanded his men to stack arms, they all stacked their guns together in front of Old Major, except one soldier who was the lookout. The others then went into the house to see Mis' Nancy; and Mis' Nancy sent out to have some chickens killed, and in no time at all those men were all seated around the dining room table having a regular feast--that is, all but the one who had to watch the guns, and he was fed later. "[124]
Rachel Cruze

---

124 Mellon, *Bullwhip Days*, 210–211.

Black men were not interested in molesting white women, but were interested in protecting black women. Chaplain Henry M. Turner said, "The fact is, when colored Soldiers are about they [whites] are afraid to kick colored women and abuse colored people on the Streets, as they usually do."[125]

Butler Is Lincoln's Pick for Vice President

Simon Cameron was an aide and friend to President Lincoln. He met with Butler to inform him of Lincoln's desire to have Butler as his running mate in the 1864 presidential election. Apparently President Lincoln was trying to reach across the aisle for a moderate Democratic vice president. Butler, however, was pleased with his assignment of capturing Richmond with the Army of the James, so he chose to stay on the battlefield. Butler described his conversation with Cameron:

> *"The President as you know," intends to be a candidate for re-election, and as his friends indicate that Mr. Hamptin should no longer be a candidate for Vice-President, and he is from New England, the President thinks his place should be filled by someone from that section. Besides reasons of personal friendship which would make it pleasant to have you with him, he believes that as you were the first prominent Democrat who volunteered for the war, your candidature would add strength to the ticket, especially with the War Democrats, and he hopes that you in that you will allow your friends to co-operate with his to place you in that position."*
>
> *"Please say to Mr. Lincoln," I replied, "that while I appreciate with the fullest sensibilities his act of friendship and the high compliment he pays me, yet I must decline. Tell him that I said laughingly that with the prospects of a campaign before me I would not quit the field to be Vice-President even with himself as Vice President, unless he would give me bound in sureties in the full sum of his four years' salary that within three months after his inauguration he will die unresigned. "*[126]
>
> *Benjamin F. Butler*

Battle of Petersburg

On May 4, 1864, Ulysses S. Grant attacked Robert E. Lee's Army of North Virginia. Grant moved south toward Richmond, engaging in a number of major battles. General Butler with the Army of the James attacked from the south. By 1864 the Confederacy was low on men, and they had adopted a defensive strategy of holding territory with defensive works and hoping for a resolution to the war that maintained slavery. Confederate defenses were primarily composed of forts, breastworks, earthworks, rifle entrenchments, and abatis. In order to dislodge the Confederacy, frontal attacks were required, which were very costly for Union lives. Recall that the Emancipation Proclamation only set slaves free in territory taken from the Confederacy.

---

125 Glatthaar, Forged in Battle, 13
126 Butler, *Butler's Book*, 634.

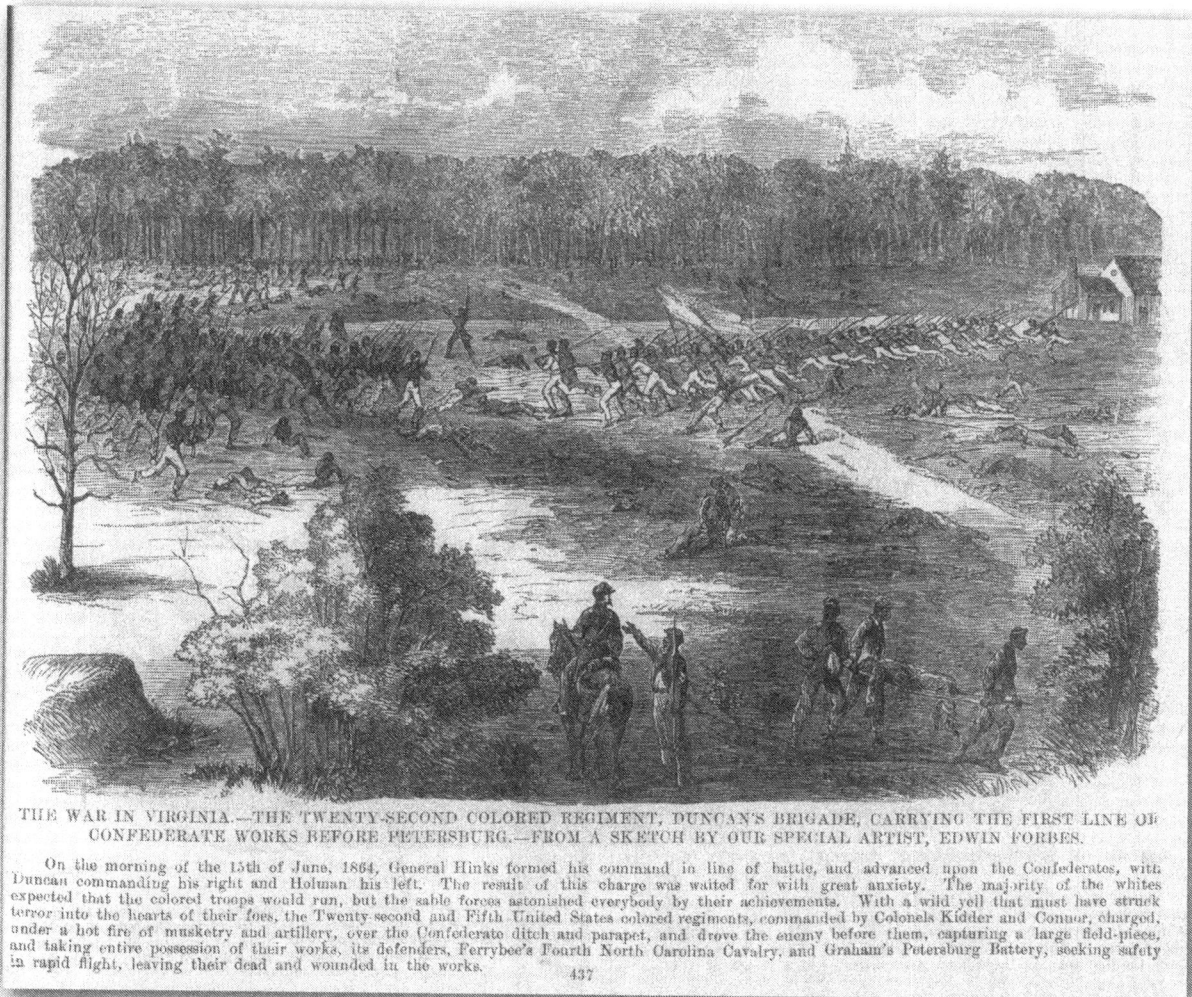

THE WAR IN VIRGINIA.—THE TWENTY-SECOND COLORED REGIMENT, DUNCAN'S BRIGADE, CARRYING THE FIRST LINE OF CONFEDERATE WORKS BEFORE PETERSBURG.—FROM A SKETCH BY OUR SPECIAL ARTIST, EDWIN FORBES.

On the morning of the 15th of June, 1864, General Hinks formed his command in line of battle, and advanced upon the Confederates, with Duncan commanding his right and Holman his left. The result of this charge was waited for with great anxiety. The majority of the whites expected that the colored troops would run, but the sable forces astonished everybody by their achievements. With a wild yell that must have struck terror into the hearts of their foes, the Twenty-second and Fifth United States colored regiments, commanded by Colonels Kidder and Conner, charged, under a hot fire of musketry and artillery, over the Confederate ditch and parapet, and drove the enemy before them, capturing a large field-piece, and taking entire possession of their works, its defenders, Ferrybee's Fourth North Carolina Cavalry, and Graham's Petersburg Battery, seeking safety in rapid flight, leaving their dead and wounded in the works. 437

Fig. 25. The war in Virginia - the 22nd Colored Regiment, Duncan's brigade, carrying the first line of Rebel works before Petersburg (Library of congress, Illus. in: Frank Leslie's illustrated newspaper, 1864 July 9, p. 244.)

Black troops attacked Petersburg with success but were ordered to stop before taking the city. A ten-month siege of Petersburg followed.

Black troops performed well at charging Petersburg's Confederate defenses. They mounted their bayonets and rush the Confederate works with screams. Black soldiers wrote letters to black and abolitionary newspapers describing their Civil War battle experiences. Congressional Medal of Honor recipient Milton Holland wrote a letter that described his charge of a Confederate works at Petersburg. Holland wrote:

" One thing that I must mention which attracted the attention of the whole division. It was that brave and daring but strange personage that rides the white charger. We could see him plainly riding up and down the rebel lines, could hear him shouting from the top of his voice to stand, that they had only niggers to contend with. This peculiar personage seems possessed with supernatural talent. He would sometimes ride his horse at lightning speed, up and down his lines amid the most terrific fire of shot and shell. But when the command was given to us, "Charge bayonets! Forward double quick!" the black column rushed forward raising the battle yell, and in a few moments more we mounted the rebel parapets. And to our great surprise, we found that the boasted Southern chivalry had fled. They could not see the nigger part as the man on the white horse presented it. We captured here one gun and caisson. "[127]

Milton M. Holland,
Orderly Sergeant
Co. C, 5th USCI
Petersburg Virginia, July 24, 1864

The Battle of the Crater

At the siege of Petersburg on July 30, 1964, General Ambrose E. Burnside developed an elaborate plan to tunnel under the Confederate defenses. The tunnel was to be filled with explosives that would damage the Confederate defenses. Black troops would then rush in to seize the town. Black troops had gained a reputation for fighting with significant determination and tenacity when charging Confederate works, and they trained for the attack. General Grant, however, was not comfortable with Burnside's reason for using black troops and substituted them with a more experienced but untrained white division. The switch resulted in a disaster. The black troops had been trained to go around the crater created by the explosion. The white troops, however, went into the crater instead of going around it and suffered heavy casualties. General Grant then sent the black troops into the crater to save the white troops, but the element of surprise had been lost. Black troops pushed the rebel line back but suffered heavy losses when the rebels were reinforced.

Congress called General Grant to come to Washington and explain.

"Earlier in his testimony, Grant had said: 'General Burnside wanted to put his colored division in front, and I believe, if he had done so, it would have been a success."[128]

General Grant took the blame for the failure of the attack due to his decision to switch black troops for white troops. The Joint Committee agreed with General Grant and suggested that black troops should be used at any hazard if dictated by the situation.

"Your Committee desire to say that, in the statement of facts and conclusions which they present in their report, they wish to be distinctly understood as in no degree censuring the conduct of the troops engaged in this assault. While they confidently believe that the selection of the division of colored troops by General Burnside to lead the assault was, under the circumstances, the best that could have been made, they do not intend thereby to have it inferred that the white troops of the Ninth Corps are behind any troops in the service in those qualities which have placed our volunteer troops before the world as equal, if not superior to any known to modern warfare."[129]

General Grant also testified that he switched the use of black troops for white troops in the battle to avoid excessive losses of black troops. A more plausible reason is that General Grant's white troops suffered over forty thousand casualties (The Battle of the Wilderness) on the way to Petersburg just two month earlier. Letting black troops carry the ball into the end zone because they might be better could have been too humiliating to accept.

---

127 Edwin S. Redkey, ed, *A Grand Army of Black Men: Letters from African-American Soldiers in the Union Army, 1861–1865*, Cambridge Studies in American Literature and Culture 63 (New York: Cambridge University Press, 1993), p106.

128 Henry Pleasants, and George H. Straley, *Inferno at Petersburg*, Chilton Book Company, 1961, 163.

129 Henry Pleasants, *Inferno at Petersburg*, 163–164.

Fig. 26. Top: Abatis at Petersburg in 1865. (Library of Congress)
Bottom: "The Colored Infantry Bringing in the Captured Guns, amid the Cheers of the Ohio Troops," *Frank Leslie's Illustrated*, July 9, 1864

LOSION OF THE MINE BEFORE PETERSBURG.—Beauregard had made the place almost impregnable, and after various attacks Grant, becoming convinced that capture by assault was impossible, began the erection of intrenchments to lay siege to the place. General Burnside, with a regiment of Schuylkill miners, constructed a mine extending from his rifle pits, 170 yards, to a point within the Confederate lines, with lateral galleries extending 37 feet right and left. Upon the exploding of the mine the Ninth Corps Artillery (in the fore ground, to silence the enemy's batteries not affected by the explosion, made a charge. The fort was found to have been converted into a yawning crater, burying guns and men, and stunning Elliott's brigade, which was panic-stricken. The Federals swarmed in and beyond the crater, subjected all the while to the concentrated fire of all the batteries, while Beauregard rallied his men and, after one of the bloodiest hand to hand conflicts of the war, finally drove the Federal forces back. The loss on both sides was frightful, and the affair was characterized as most discreditable to the National Armies.—Sketched by Andrew McCallum.

Fig. 27. Battle of the Crater (Author's Collection)

CHAPTER 13

The Battle of New Market Heights

"After that in the Army of the James a negro regiment was looked upon as the safest flanking regiment that could be put in line."

Lincoln's Reelection

ON SEPTEMBER 19, 1864, General Butler developed a plan to capture Richmond using black troops. General Butler believed, as did John Brown and Frederick Douglass, that black men must earn their own freedom or forever be second-class citizens whom white men had to rescue. Butler was looking for a good blow against slavery to prove once and for all that all men are created equal.

Another important benefit of a big Negro victory was that it might bolster Lincoln's chances of being reelected. At this stage, Lincoln's reelection in November 1864 was in jeopardy. Lincoln had asked Butler to be his running mate in the election, but Butler had refused, saying that he would rather remain on the battlefield. Lincoln was behind his anti-war opponent, George McClellan, who did not support the Emancipation Proclamation. Lincoln's defeat in November would have meant a compromise over the slavery issue. President Lincoln wrote a letter to his cabinet and asked them to sign and support preserving the Union.

"On August 23, 1864 Lincoln wrote "It seems probable that this administration will not be re-elected. Then it will be my duty to so co-operate with the President elect, as to save the Union between the election and the inauguration; as he will have secured his election on such ground that he cannot possibly save it afterwards."[130]

Butler's Plan

Until that point, black troops had fought in a number of battles but had not gained the public's attention or respect. The "affair at the mine" would have given them that sought-after eminence had not General Grant switched the black soldiers' role in the Battle of the Crater. Publicly, blame for the defeat was put on the black troops. Butler had become the most hated man in the Civil War due to his relentless support of Negro troops. His leadership was constantly criticized during the Civil War, and he is not well thought-of by modern historians either. In a magazine, General William F. Smith described Butler as a "child, incapable of giving an order in the field." Butler wanted his Negro troops and himself as well to have one major victory that would significantly change the Civil War and make them the heroes of the day.

---

130 The Civil War Trust, *"Lincoln's Blind Mimo"*, http://www.civilwar.org/education/history/primarysources/blind-memo.html.

In September 1864, the Union army was south of Richmond and unable to control the territory north of the James River. Butler's headquarters was located at Deep Bottom, on the south shore of the James River. Butler developed a plan in which black troops would attack New Market Heights, which was a heavily fortified redoubt on the left flank of the Confederate line protecting Richmond. The plan called for white troops to simultaneously attack the middle of the Confederate line at Fort Harris.

Richmond was protected by three thousand entrenched Confederate troops, and most of these were positioned close to New Market Heights and in front of Butler at Deep Bottom. New Market Heights was heavily fortified. White troops had twice failed to take the target in prior attempts. In fact, cadets from a nearby military school had successfully defeated a Union attack there earlier that year.

If the black troops succeeded, it would prove their value once and for all. Butler told his black men to "take New Market Heights at any cost."

Most Civil War generals used Napoleonic battle tactics. First, skirmishers would be sent out to draw enemy fire and assess battlefield-terrain obstacles such as ravines, underbrush, and swamps. Generals could watch the skirmishers and determine the best attacking route. Assaults were made with columns of troops standing shoulder to shoulder. One column of soldiers would fire at the enemy while another column reloaded.

Musket reloading was a chore that required nine steps. Gun powder and ball had to be packed into the barrel with a ramrod. The hammer was set to half cock, and a percussion cap was placed on the hammer. The hammer was pulled back to full cock, and now the musket was ready to be fired. When the trigger was pulled, the hammer was released, and the force of the hammer ignited the percussion cap. A flame propagated to the powder in the barrel through a small channel. The barrel powder ignited and pushed the ball out the barrel.

The advantage of the Napoleonic tactic was that the columns could direct a large amount of firepower at the enemy. At any instance, a column was fully loaded, and if the enemy charged, the column would fire. The disadvantage, however, is that the column was an easy target for a concealed enemy behind barricades in breastworks. The concealed soldiers were protected by breastworks and were often allowed to "fire at will." An experienced soldier could get off as many as three shots per minute.

In contrast to these Napoleonic tactics, the regular "dash," as Butler called it, put emphasis on the charge. Skirmishers were not used, and the soldiers in the charging column did not stop to discharge their weapons. Black men did not possess the experience with muskets that white Union soldiers had. This tactic used the athleticism of the black men and represented the fighting style of their ancestors in Africa. Butler made certain of this by removing percussion caps from their muskets so that they could not fire. He told his black men to take New Market Heights at any cost and let "Remember Fort Pillow" be the battle cry.

General Butler discussed his attack on Richmond with General Grant, and he also described his dual objective:

"I further told him that I had another thing in view. The affair of the mine at Petersburg, which had been discussed between us, had convinced me that in the Army of the Potomac negro troops were thought of no value, and with the exception of an attack under Smith on the 15th of June, where they were prevented from entering Petersburg by the sloth, inaction, or I believe worse, of Smith, the negro troops had had no

chance to show their valor or staying qualities in action. I told him that I meant to take a large part of my negro force, and under my personal command make an attack upon Newmarket Heights, the redoubt to the extreme left of the enemy's line. If I could take that and turn it, then I was certain that I could gain the first line of the enemy's entrenchment's around Richmond. I said:" I want to convince myself whether, when under my own eye, the negro troops will fight; and if I can take with the negroes, a redoubt that turned Hancock's corps on a former occasion, that will settle the question." I proposed to try this in a manner that I had not before seen attempted, either in the Army of the Potomac or else where, - that is, by a regular "dash" such as I had read of in the history of the wars of Europe."[131]
General Benjamin F. Butler

Butler estimated that enemy defenses of 2,875 men held the eight-mile-long New Market line defense. All but Johnson's Brigade, Chaffin Farm Heavy Artillery, and militia reserves were positioned near New Market Heights.

CONFEDERATE UNIT	COMMANDER	SIZE
Bushrod Johnson's (Tennessee) Brigade	Hughs	450
Twenty-Fifth Virginia (City Brigade)	Elliot	200
Grigg's Texas brigade	Bass	400
Seventh South Carolina Cavalry	Gary	400
Twenty-Fourth Virginia Cavalry	Gary	400
Benning's (Georgia) Brigade	DuBose	400
Militia reserves (Second Virginia Reserve Battalion)	Guy	175
Chaffin Farm Heavy Artillery		100
Wade Hampton's Legion		400

Black troops had demonstrated in places like Fort Hudson, Milliken's Bend, and Fort Wagner that they were effective at charging Confederate works. Their charges were often described as determined and tenacious. Butler's plan called for them to not stop and fire their muskets during their charge but continue until they entered the Confederate works. This tactic would use their strength of charging works. The joint committees had warned General Grant after the "affair at the mine" to use black troops when the situation called for their talents. General Grant therefore approved Butler's plan.

"At half past four o'clock I found the colored division, rising three thousand men, occupying a plain which shelved towards the river, so that they mere not observed by the enemy at Newmarket Heights. They were formed in close column of division right in front. I rode through the division, addressed a few words of encouragement and confidence to the troops. I told them that this was an attack where I expected them to go over and take a work which would be before them after they got over the hill, and that they must take it at all hazards, and that when they went over the parapet into it their war cry should be, " remember Fort Pillow."

"The caps were taken from the nipples of their guns so that no shot should be fired by them, for when ever a charging column stops to fire, that charge may as well be considered ended. As their was to be no halt after they turned the brow of the hill, no skirmishers were to be deployed."[132]

---

131 Butler, *Butler's Book*, 731–733.
132 Ibid.

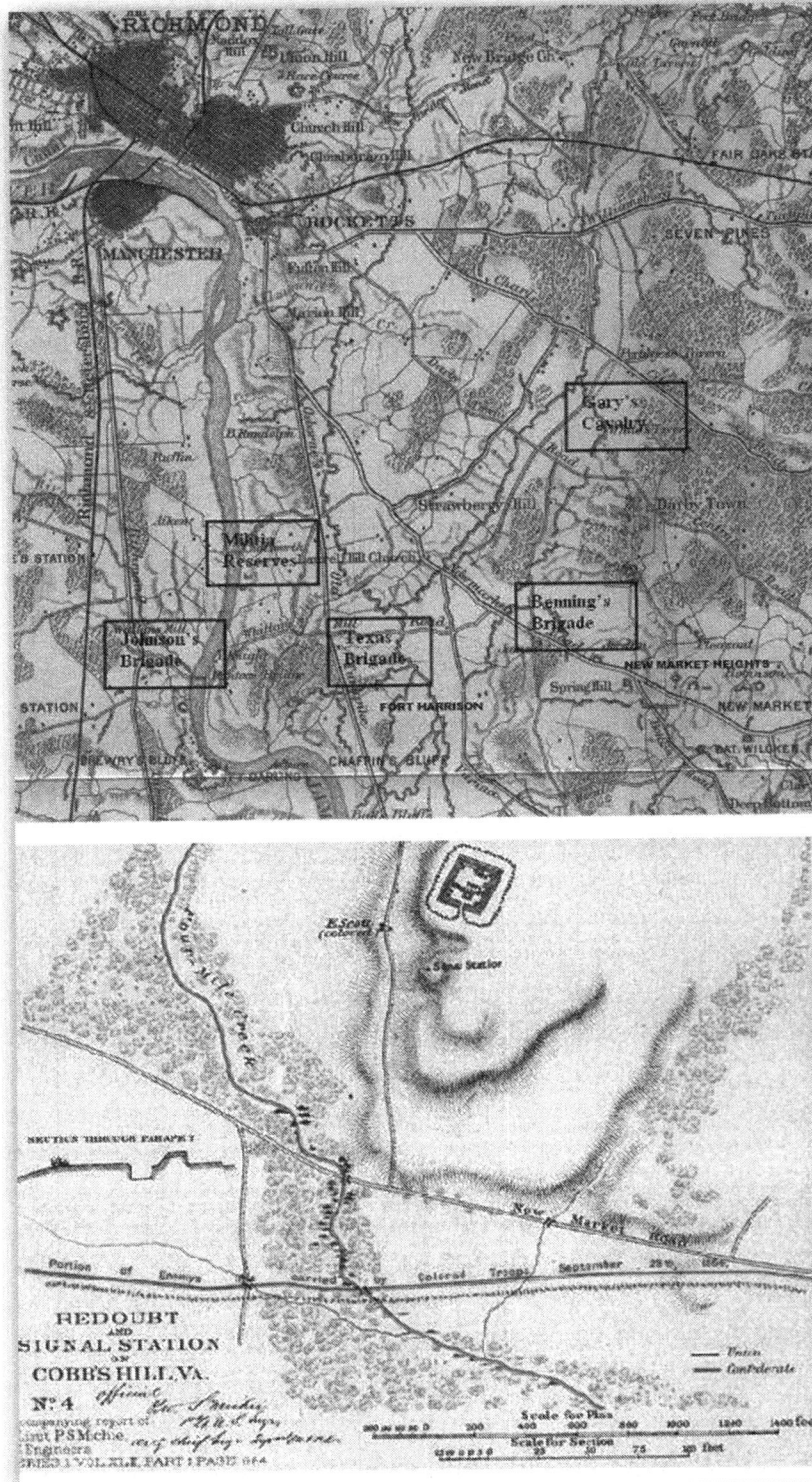

Fig. 28. Top: Polley's description of Confederate positions guarding Richmond Virginia at New Market Heights, September 29, 1864, Burk & McFetridge, environs of Richmond Bottom: *Redoubt and Signal Station on Cobb's Hill, Va.*

No official Confederate battle records of the Battle of New Market Heights exist. Joseph Benjamin Polley was a Confederate soldier and a member of the Texas Brigade. Polley fought with the Texas Brigade at New Market Heights. Polley wrote his account of the battle many years following the Civil War. Polley claimed that Benning's Brigade was stationed at New Market Heights and the Texas Brigade was a mile and a half from them.

Polley's troop strength at New Market Heights prior to the battle agrees with Butler's prebattle intelligence; it therefore assumed that his described distribution of Confederate troops at New Market Heights is reliable. Polley wrote:

"Along toward the last days of September General Grant believed the time ripe for renewed activity on the north side; wherefore, he started 40,000 men in that direction, under General Ord, with instructions to proceed without delay into Richmond."

"On the 27th these crossed the James River at Deep Bottom, got well into position on the 28th, and at daylight of the 29th, with negro troops in the van and covering their entire front, moved forward against the 3000 Confederates, all told, then between them and their goal. Of this 3000, Johnson's brigade was on the river above Drury's Bluff, Benning's, at New Market Heights, Gary's, guarding the Charles City Road-and the Texas, at the Phillips house, between Benning's and Johnson's, two miles to the right of the one and three to the left of the other. Half way between the Texas and Johnson's commands, was Fort Harrison, then occupied by a small force of Confederate artillery. On the inner line of intrenchments around the city, a mile and a half in rear of the Texas Brigade, and a like distance in rear of Fort Harrison, was Fort Gilmer, which was defended by a few heavy siege guns, under the management of a few trained artillerists and the City Battalion, composed of old men and boys, and such clerks in governmental departments as were able to bear arms. The line to be defended against the 40,000 Federal soldiers extended from Drury's Bluff down the river about eight miles."[133]

J. B. Polley

Colonel Duncan's Charge

Brevet Major General Alfred H. Terry lined a division of white troops on the New Market battle line, which included Abbott's Second Brigade, Pond's First Brigade, and Plaisted's Third Brigade. Brig. General Charles Paine's Third Division of Colored Troops would attack New Market Heights on the left flank of Terry's Second Brigade under Colonel Joseph C. Abbott. First he sent in the Third Brigade under Colonel Samuel A. Duncan, which consisted of the Fourth USCT, Sixth USCT, and the Second USCT Cavalry.

Apparently, Terry did not understand Butler's "dash" tactic. Terry deployed these regiments as skirmishers to reveal the strength of the Confederate line, and they were told to capture the heights if possible. Skirmishers typically fire at will. On the other hand, Butler ordered the black men to not act like skirmishers, remove their firing caps from their rifles, and not break the charge to fire them. Butler described the battle as follows:

---

133 J. B. Polley, *Hood's Texas Brigade*, 252.

Fig. 29. Company E, Fourth US Colored Infantry, Ft. Lincoln, defenses of Washington (Library of Congress)

"We waited a few minutes, and the day fairly shining, the order was given to go forward, and the troops marched up to the top of the hill as regularly and quietly as if on parade."

"Then the scene that lay before us was this: there dipped from the brow of the hill quite a declivity down through some meadow land. At its foot ran a brook of water only a few inches deep, a part of the bottom, as I knew, being gravely and firm. The brook drained a marsh which was quite deep and muddy, a little to the left of the direct line. The column of division unfortunately did not oblique to the right far enough to avoid that marsh wholly. Then rose steadily, at an angle of thirty to thirty five degrees, plain, hard ground to within hundred and fifty yards of the redoubt. At this point there was a very strong line of abatis."

At one hundred yards above that, the hill rising a little faster, was another line of abatis. Fifty yards beyond was a square redoubt mounting some guns en barbette, that is, on top of the embankment, and held by not exceeding one thousand of the enemy.

I rode with my staff to the top of the first hill, where everything was in sight, and watched the movement of the Negroes. "

Crossing the brook their lines broke in little disorder, the left of the divisions having plunged into the morass, but the men struggling, held their guns above their heads to keep them dry. The enemy directed its fire upon them; but, as in all cases of firing downward from a fort the fire was too high. The leading battalion broke, but its Colonel maintained his position at its head. Words of command was useless as in the melee

they could not be heard; but calling his bugler to him the rally rang out, and at its call his men formed around him. The division was at once reformed, and then at double quick they dashed up to the first line of abatis. The axe men laid to, vigorously chopping out the obstructions. Many of them went down. Others seized the axes. The enemy concentrated on the head of the column. It looked at one moment as if it might melt away. The colors of the first battalion went down but instantly they were up again but with new color bearers."[134]
General Benjamin F. Butler

In his book *Hood's Texas Brigade*, Polley described Duncan's attack as follows:

""With daylight came a dense, obscuring fog, and through it was heard a roar that sounded like the bellowing of ten thousand wild bulls; it was the shout of the negroes as they valorously charged the picket line in their front. A minute later it was learned that the first attack would be up a narrow creek valley across which ran the Confederate line, and thither the Texas Brigade hastened. In this little valley the fog was so thick as to render large objects, a hundred feet distant, indistinguishable. Forming in single line, six feet apart, the Texans and Arkansans awaited the onset of the enemy. They could distinctly hear the Federal officers, as in loud tones they gave such commands as were needed to keep their men moving in line, but until the line approached within a hundred feet, could see nothing; even then, only a wavering dark line was visible. As it became so, and as was usual in those days, without waiting for orders, the Confederates sprang to the top of the low breastworks, and commenced firing" shooting at shadows," one of them said.

About the same instant a Federal officer shouted in stentorian voice, "Charge, men-Charge!" But only by 'the negroes immediately in front of the First Texas was the order obeyed by a rush forward that carried a regiment of the poor wretches up to, and in one or more places, across the breast-works, and right in among the First Texans. The latter, since Spottsylvania Court House well-provided with bayonets, were experts in the use of them, defensively and offensively, and in less than three minutes one-half of the assailants were shot down or bayoneted, and the other half, prisoners. In front of the other regiments the darkey charge lasted but a second or two, and covered not more than five paces. It was, in fact, simply a spasmodic response to the order. Then the black line halted, and for a moment stood motionless, obviously deliberating whether the more danger was to be apprehended from the Southern men in front, or the Northern men in rear. Apparently, they decided on a compromise, for the half of those that survived the terrible fire poured into their ranks, threw down their guns, and wheeling, fled to the rear, and the other half dropped fiat on the ground, and lay there until they were led away as captives.

In effect, it was a massacre. Not a dozen shots in all were fired by the blacks, not a man in the Texas Brigade received a wound, and save in the First Texas, not a man was for a second in danger. The firing lasted not exceeding five minutes, but in that short space of time, if the New York Herald be good authority, a Confederate brigade numbering scant 800 men, killed 194 negroes and 23 of their white officers. Estimating the killed as one-fifth of the total loss, it will appear that about 1000 of the colored defenders of the Union were shot out of service in that five minutes. Of the many negroes who dropped to the ground unhurt, quite a number preferred to serve their individual captors as slaves, to confinement in Southern prisons, and did so serve them until the close of the war."[135]
J. B. Polley

---

134 Butler, *Butler's Book*, 731–733.
135 Polley, *Hood's Texas Brigade*, 254.

Colonel Duncan was wounded in the battle and did not report on his failed charge of the rebel works. However, black Civil War correspondent Thomas Chester covered Duncan's charge and reported the following from the field:

"In the onward to Richmond move of the 29th ult. the 4th United States Colored troops, raised in Maryland, and the sixth United States colored Troops, from Pennsylvania, gained for themselves undying laurels for their steady and unflinching courage displayed in attacking the Rebels at great disadvantage. These two regiments were deployed as skirmishers.

"It was just light enough to see as they pushed out of a skirt of woods from our breastworks at Deep Bottom ; and a soon as emerging from it they were fired upon by the rebel sharpshooters, who fell back before these advancing regiments. They pushed on across a ravine, where they were exposed to a severe enfilading fire by the enemy's sharpshooters, occupying a house in a skirt of wood on our left. It was under that fire the first men of these regiments were killed, among whom was Captain S. W. Vannuys. The sharpshooters were soon dislodged and our troops entered another woods, pushed beyond it and crossed the Three Mile Creek. On account of the marshy state of the ground, slush, timber, undergrowth and brush, this line became somewhat confused, but some advancing beyond these difficulties, they reached the enemy's abatis in front of his breastworks which they charged with cheering. Two lines of abatis had here to be overcome, which was handsomely accomplished. It was here that many of the colored troops fell while attempting to force a passage over the abatis. There was no flinching of these two regiments in this terrible position, but they manfully received and returned the fire until they were three times ordered to fall back which they did in good order. In the attempt of the fourth and the sixth regiments to pass over the abatis, the fourth lost it's entire color guard. Alfred B. Hilton, of the fourth carried the American flag, which was presented to it by the colored ladies of Baltimore, to the very edge of the breastworks, and, lying down, held aloft the national colors. When they were ordered to fall back, this brave man was shot down, but is not dangerously wounded and his exclamation was, " Save the Flag !" Sergeant Major Fleetwood successfully brought the colors back riddled with thirty rents, with no other loss to himself than a shot to his bootleg."[136]
Thomas Morris Chester
Black Civil War Correspondent

Their courage in saving the flag was recognized by Congress. Fleetwood, Veal, and Hilton of the Fourth Regiment, as well as Sergeant Alexander Kelly and Sergeant Thomas R. Hawkins of the Sixth Regiment, received Congressional Medals of Honor. Hilton died of his wounds a month later.

Casualties were heavy, between four hundred and five hundred men. Colonel Duncan was badly wounded. In forty minutes of fighting, Company D of the Sixth USCT lost 87 percent of its men, which was the highest reported loss of a Union company during a single charge in the Civil War. Company D of the Sixth Regiment lost twenty-seven of thirty enlisted men.

Out of twelve flag bearers, all were killed or wounded but one. One of the flag bearers was Alfred Hilton, who carried two flags, one belonging to a dead flag bearer and the other belonging to himself. As men were being shot, he struggled to keep the flags from touching the ground until he was shot in the leg. He said, "Boys, save the colors."

---

136 R. J. M. Blackett, *Thomas Morris Chester Black Civil War Correspondent His Dispatches from the Virginia Front*, Plenum Publishing Corporation, New York, New York, 1989, 139–141.

Private Charles Veal grabbed the regimental flag, and Sergeant Christian Fleetwood grabbed the American flag. They continued their charge. Outnumbered, with many dead and wounded, they retreated back to their skirmish line, which was still entangled in the abatis. Fleetwood rallied the survivors around his flag for another attack. Some men made it to the top, and, as Butler requested, they said, "Remember Fort Pillow!" Completely outnumbered, however, they were killed or captured and then murdered.

At the same time General Terry deployed Duncan's Brigade, he also deployed Abbott's Second Brigade of white troops on Duncan's right flank. They were composed of Third New Hampshire Regiment, which were three hundred men, and the Seventh Connecticut Volunteers as skirmishers. Abbott wrote:

"Having thrown out the Seventh Connecticut, Capt. S.S. Atwell commanding, as skirmishers I advanced, following the skirmishers at about 250 yards toward the enemy's works on the New Market road. Between my first position and those works there was a difficult ravine and swamp, and my line was enfiladed by a sharp artillery fire from the enemy's battery-on my right. Captain Atwell having reported that the enemy's works were well manned, and the skirmishing being sharp, I strengthened the skirmish line by sending forward the Third New Hampshire, Maj. J. F. Randlett commanding, with orders to press forward strongly, while I followed with the main line as before."[137]
J. C. Abbot

Major James F. Randlett advanced the Third New Hampshire within five hundred yards of the works and halted. He wrote:

"Colonel Abbott instructed me to advance my line as rapidly as possible, reporting success to him, exercising my own discretion. When in full view of enemy and his works, 500 yards across the opening, I advanced a light line and drew from the enemy the disposition of his forces."[138]
J. F. Randlett

It appears that the Confederates followed Duncan's retreat and pushed the line of battle back to the area of Four Mile Creek. Confederates were massing at the point of Duncan's attack; after Duncan's dash stalled, Major Randlett, having a small force of three hundred men, asked Abbott for reinforcements. He wrote:

"Finding my line flanked on the left by works similar to those in my front, and discovering that he was re-enforcing the flank, I ordered my men to lie down, the advantage of the rolling ground being such as to entirely protect them from his infantry while his artillery played over us into the ravine. I then dispatched a messenger to Colonel Abbott, informing him of disposition of my command, respectfully suggesting that a force be sent to relieve my left flank. Was informed that General Terry had sent a detachment of colored troops to that duty."[139]
J. F. Randlett

---

137 J.C. Abbot, O.R. 86:702-703.
138 J. F. Randlett, O.R. 86:702-703.
139 J. F. Randlett, O.R. 86:702-703.

Colonel Draper's Charge

Butler's "dash" tactic may have worked better on good terrain. New Market Heights, however, contained ravines and swampy ground, which broke portions of the column's charge. But now Paine understood where the good footing was and conducted a second charge.

Apparently, Draper was sent in to support the retreating Duncan's Brigade and protect Abbott's left flank. Paine deployed his Second Brigade of colored troops consisting of the Thirty-Sixth, the Thirty-Eighth, and the Fifth USCT under Col. Draper, a total of thirteen hundred men. The First Brigade, the Twenty-Second USCT under Col. Holman, was acting as skirmishers in front of Draper. Draper moved to the right so the Twenty-Second were in front and to the left of Draper. The Twenty-Second followed Duncan's trail, but they did not continue to the works. Like Duncan, the Twenty-Second got hung up in the underbrush. In his battle report, Albert James said, "The line moved forward through a dense tangle of underbrush and felled trees."[140] This slowed the charge down. On the other hand, Draper had moved to the right of Duncan's trail, missing the tangled underbrush. He only encountered three hundred yards of young pines, so he continued to Four Mile Creek ahead of the Twenty-Second. Draper charged across the open plain until they reached Four Mile Creek, where the charge was halted.

Like Duncan, Draper's men took heavy losses at Four Mile Creek as well. Their "dash" was broken to a crawl as they crossed Four Mile Creek about thirty yards in front of the Confederate abatis. Some of the men started to discharge their weapons, which added to the confusion and halted the progress of the dash.

Draper's skirmish line was pinned down between Four Mile Creek and the first abatis. It was reinforced and picked up new momentum from the support of the Twenty-Second USCT. Once out of the "dense tangle of underbrush and felled trees," the Twenty-Second charged across the open plain where Draper's charge had stalled. Part of the Twenty-Second approached Draper's skirmish line on the right and entered the works with them. In his battle report, Captain Albert Janes of the Twenty-Second wrote, "As the charging column came up to the support of the skirmish line a part of the regiment assembled on the right and moved forward into the works, driving the enemy in confusion from them."

In his battle report, Draper took credit for the rally when he said:

> *"After half an hour of terrible suspense, by starting the yell among a few, we succeeded in getting them in motion. The entire brigade took up the shout and went over the rebel works...When the brigade were making their final charge, a rebel officer leaped upon the parapet, waved his sword and shouted, "Hurrah, my brave men." Private James Gardiner,(+) Company I, Thirty-sixth U.S. Colored Troops, rushed in advance of the brigade, shot him, and then ran the bayonet through his body to the muzzle."[141]*
> *Col. Alonzo G. Draper, Thirty-Sixth US Colored Troops, commanding Second Brigade, September 29.*

Once the Confederates evacuated the works in front of Draper, the whole Confederate line evacuated. The small brigade of white troops charged the works with little resistance. Abbott wrote:

---

140 Albert James, *The War of the Rebellion XLII Part 1, Report. No 331.*
141 *Draper, O.R.—SERIES I—VOLUME XLII/1 [S# 87] AUGUST 1–DECEMBER 31, 1864.—The Richmond (Virginia) Campaign., No. 333.* US War Dept., *The War of the Rebellion: a Compilation of the Official Records of the Union and Confederate Armies, Govt. Print. Off., Washington,* (1880–1901).

"Major Randlett having reported that the enemy were advancing on my left and massing in front, I went forward to the skirmish line to make an examination. I ordered him again to press forward and at once advanced the main line. Just at that time Paine's division commenced a vigorous attack upon the enemy upon my left, which was successful, and as my line advanced into the open ground, the enemy evacuated their works in my front, having a few minutes previous taken off their artillery from the height on my extreme right. I advanced into the works, the Third New Hampshire occupying the deserted battery on the right."[142]
J. C. Abbot

Polley wrote very little about the second charge, only that his Texas Brigade was redeployed.

"The firing had hardly ceased when word came that Gary's cavalry and Benning's brigade had been driven from their positions, and were in rapid retreat to the inner line of intrenchments on which stood Fort Gilmer, and that if the Texas Brigade did not "get a move on," and a fast one at that, it would be cut off from Richmond and its comrade commands on the north side. Immediately following that information, came a courier from General Gregg with the more alarming intelligence that Fort Harrison had been captured by the enemy, and with an order that the Texas Brigade report as quickly as possible to Gregg at that point. The capture of the fort, as every man knew, placed the brigade in a critical position, and within a minute it was double-quicking up the outer line of intrenchments it had so long guarded-the broad, level ditch affording not only the shortest route, but as well, the best footing for rapid travel. It had not gone a mile, though, before it was a long, straggling line of panting, perspiring and almost exhausted men."[143]
J. B. Polley

From Butler's viewpoint he watched the men charging over the abatis. He wrote:

"Wonderfully they managed to brush aside the abatis, and then at double quick the reformed column charged the second line of abatis."Fortunately they were able to remove that in a few minutes, but it seemed a long time to the lookers on. Then, with a cheer and a yell that I can almost hear now, they dashed upon the fort. But before they reached even the ditch, which was not a formidable thing, the enemy ran away and did not stop until they had run four miles, I believe. They were only fired at as they ran away and did not lose a man."[144]
General Benjamin F. Butler

During the second charge, most of the white officers were killed or wounded, and black sergeants took command. Sergeants given Congressional Medals of Honor for rallying their troops were First Sergeant Powhatan, First Sergeant James Bronson, and Sergeant Robert Pinn of the Ohio Fifth Regiment. Medals of Honor were also given to First Sergeant Edward Ratcliff, Sergeant James H. Harris, and Private William H. Barnes of the Thirty-Eighth Regiment. Corporal James Miles and Private James Gardiner of the Thirty-Sixth Regiment were among the first men to enter the rebel works. Casualties among black troops exceeded one thousand, while those for white troops were minimal.

After the Confederates evacuated New Market Heights, Butler rode his horse across the battlefield. Butler said:

---

142 Abbot, O.R. 86:702-703.
143 Polley, *Hood's Texas Brigade*, 254.
144 Butler, *Butler's Book*, 731–733.

" As I rode across the brook and up towards the fort along this line of charge, some eighty feet wide and three or four hundred yards long, there lay in my path five hundred and forty-three dead and wounded of my colored comrades. And, as I guided my horse this way and that way that his hoof might not profane their dead bodies, I swore to myself an oath, which I hope and believe I have kept sacredly, that they and their race should be cared for and protected by me to the extent of my power so long as I lived.

When I reached the scene of their exploit their ranks broke, but it was to gather around their general. They almost dragged my horse up alongside the cannon they had 'captured, and I felt in my inmost heart that the capacity of the negro race for soldiers had then and there been fully settled forever." [145]
General Benjamin F. Butler

Fort Harrison

Fort Harrison was actually the prize of the day. It was the strongest point on the Confederate line and protected the capital of the Confederacy, Richmond, Virginia. As a result, once it fell, the outer defenses around Richmond collapsed. By 7:00 a.m. Butler's men occupied Fort Harrison. The next day, General Robert E. Lee ordered that the fort be taken back. However, the Twenty-Second USCT had arrived at Fort Harrison and helped to defend the fort.

"On the morning On the morning of the 30th the regiment moved to the right of the fort refaced and repaired to earth-works adjacent to the fort. At 1 o'clock the enemy was seen making preparation for an attack. At 2 o'clock our pickets were driven in and five distinct lines of the enemy charged our line. The attack was general. The charging column was repulsed. A second time charged and second time repulsed. A counter-charge was then made by the Twenty-second, which added impetus to the already flying rebels. In this counter-charge the regiment encountered a strong [force] which was stationed under the lee of an isolated fort, and from which we received a volley of musketry which killed several men and wounded two officers (Maj. J. B. Cook and Capt. Jacob F. Force), but they, too, were put [to] flight, and, as no other advantage could be gained, the regiment again took its position in line behind the breast-works, in all the maneuvering the most unflinching bravery was displayed by both officers and men.
Very respectfully, your obedient servant,
ALBERT JANES,
Captain, commanding Regiment." [146]

Battle Aftermath

Confederate losses at New Market Heights were very light. They evacuated the trenches before the black troops fired their muskets. After the Confederates were defeated at New Market Heights and Fort Harrison, they evacuated the outer defenses around Richmond and retreated to works close to the city. Polley describes the aftermath of the battle:

" Their capture on the 29th of September, of Fort Harrison, was a distinct gain to the Federals. Holding it, General Lee had been able to confine the enemy on the north side to the valley of the James, below Drury's Bluff: losing it, he was compelled to withdraw his forces from the heights north of the James, and place

---

145 Ibid.
146 Albert James, O.R. 87:817, *The War of the Rebellion XLII Part 1 Report. No 331.*

them within a line of entrenchments encircling Richmond, and, at various points, not over three mile from the city. This gave the Federals outlet into the country north of Richmond." [147]
J. B. Polley

Fort Harrison was the prize, not New Market Heights. The black troops did, however, draw most of the Confederates to New Market Heights from Fort Harrison so that Fort Harrison could be easily taken. Butler made it clear that the Battle of New Market Heights was more than a battle; it was an important statement. For black troops to fight effectively alongside white troops, they would have to earn the respect of the white troops. Slavery had produced enormous disrespect of blacks. Free blacks would need respect to remain free. Black troops took heavy losses but destroyed the outer defenses of Richmond without firing a dozen shots. Earning respect cost lives, and Butler evaluated that cost.

"But in the attack on Newmarket Heights I did deliberately expose my men to the loss of greater numbers than I really believed the capture of the redoubt was worth; for if the enemy's lines at Fort Harrison were captured, as they were, then Newmarket Heights would have been evacuated without loss, for I do not know that they were ever reoccupied by either side afterwards during the war. Now comes the inquiry in the minds of reflecting men: "Why make the attack?" Because it was to be done with my negro troops. "Are we to understand that you would sacrifice your negro troops where you would not your white troops?" No; except for a great purpose in behalf of their race and in behalf of the Union. If I have tried to make anything apparent up to this time in what I have written, it is that from prejudice and ignorance of their good qualities it was not really believed in and out of the army by military men, with a very few exceptions, that the negroes would fight. My white regiments were always nervous when standing in line flanked by colored troops, lest the colored regiments should give way and they (the white) be flanked. This fear was a deep-seated one and spread far and wide, and the negro had had no sufficient opportunity to demonstrate his valor and his staying qualities as a soldier. And the further cry was that the negroes never struck a good blow for their own freedom. Therefore, I determined to put them in position, to demonstrate the fact of the value of the negro as a soldier, cotite qui coUte, and that the experiment should be one of which no man should doubt, if it attained success. Hence the attack by the negro column on Newmarket Heights.

After that in the Army of the James a negro regiment was looked upon as the safest flanking regiment that could be put in line." [148]
Benjamin F. Butler

Following the battle of New Market Heights, Colonel Alonzo Draper and Colonel Samuel A. Duncan were both promoted to general upon General Butler's recommendation to President Lincoln. When Richmond fell, Draper had seen that his Thirty-Sixth Colored Regiment was the first to enter the city.

In November 1864, Lincoln was reelected. Historians credit the capture of Atlanta and victories in Shenandoah Valley for the win. Atlanta fell September 2, 1864, a little over a week after Lincoln's expression of doubt of winning reelection. However, the Battle of New Market Heights may have been a bigger boost to the Union cause because it signaled the probable fall of the Confederate capital of Richmond, Virginia. Also, the battle demonstrated an answer to entrenched warfare, which was the use of black troops. By 1864 the Civil War was a war of slave liberation composed mostly of trench warfare. Cities such as Richmond, Petersburg, and Atlanta were under siege and protected by dwindling

147 Polley, *Hood's Texas Brigade*, 254.
148 Butler, *Butler's Book*, 741.

entrenched Confederate forces. Entrenched forces required frontal attacks to dislodge them, which resulted in heavy casualties of the attacking force—and the attacking force was usually white Union troops. The Battle of New Market Heights demonstrated that black troops could be used effectively to dislodge entrenched Confederate troops, reducing white Union troop casualties. This gave the Union an effective new weapon for which the Confederacy had no answer but to establish their own black army. The thought of relying on black men to save the confederacy was humiliating to proslavery racist. This new Union weapon was probably a bigger lift to the Union cause than the fall of Atlanta.

The media reported little on the achievement of the black men before the Confederate capital of Richmond, Virginia. General Grant was given the credit for destroying Richmond's outer defenses. The English media, however, gave a complete description of the battle.

The Butler Medal

At his expense, Butler had a large silver medal struck by Tiffany & Co. for his black troops that fought at New Market Heights. These medals remain the only medal made for black troops. Butler personally gave two hundred of the medals to black soldiers. He wrote:

"I had the fullest reports made to me of the acts of individual bravery of colored men on that occasion, and I had done for the negro soldiers, by my own order, what the government has never done for its white soldiers — I had a medal struck of like size, weight, quality, fabrication and intrinsic value with those which Queen Victoria gave with her own hand to her distinguished private soldiers of the Crimea....The obverse of the medal shows a bastion fort charged by Negro soldiers, and bears the inscription "Ferro iis libertas perveniet." (Freedom was won by them with the sword) The reverse bears the words, "Campaign before Richmond," encircling the words, "Distinguished for Courage."[149]
Benjamin F. Butler

Fig. 30. *Butler Medal*, engraving in *Butler's Book* and Medal from Authors Collection, Fleetwood's Medal of Honor, Smithsonian Institution

149 Butler, *Butler's Book*, 743.

Butler Medals are very rare, and only a few exist in museums such as the Smithsonian. I believe that they were not very popular and were melted down for their silver. I was able to obtain a Tiffany Butler Medal made of silver. It appears, however, to match Butler's engraving more than the Smithsonian medals that were given to soldiers. I had a jeweler cast a reproduction of silver for myself, and I wore it on chain. I felt that General Colin Powell deserved the medal more than me, so I mailed to him. Why? Because General Powell reached great success but never forgot where he came from. He is a staunch supporter of black military history and justice. He also has a tender heart. He started an organization called America's Promise to support young people. I also gave General Powell copies of *Butler's Book* and William Wells Brown's book, *The Negro in the American Rebellion*. General Butler would have been proud to know him and meet him, as I was.

Congressional Medals of Honor

Congress showed its gratitude by awarding the first Congressional Medals of Honor given to nonwhite soldiers in America's history to the black soldiers at the Battle of New Market Heights. The fourteen Congressional Medals of Honor awarded for the battle remains today the highest honor given to African Americans by Congress.

Fourteen of the fifteen Medals of Honor listed here were awarded for valor at New Market Heights. Note that some are recorded as having been earned at Chaffin's Farm, which is incorrect. The only medal not earned at New Market Heights is the one awarded to Decatur Dorsey at Petersburg. The Battle of New Market Heights is sometimes included in the Battle of Chaffin's Farm, which was a series of battles.

Following the war, two more Congressional Medals of Honor were belatedly awarded to Civil War colored troops. Sergeant William H. Carney was awarded a Congressional Medal of Honor for bravery at Fort Wagner in 1863. Carney is often identified as the first black soldier to earn a Congressional Medal of Honor, which is not accurate. Carney was not awarded the medal until May 23, 1900, which was over thirty years later. The first Congressional Medals of Honor awarded were for bravery at New Market Heights, Virginia, on September 29, 1864, and were awarded on April 6, 1865. The nation made an important statement when these medals were awarded: "All men are created equal," and it was proven at New Market Heights. This act was a terrible blow against proslavery racists and put them on the wrong side of history.

In January 2001 President Clinton posthumously awarded a Congressional Medal of Honor to Corporal Andrew Jackson Smith for gallantry during the Battle of Honey Hill, November 30, 1864.

Name.	Rank and organization	Date.	Awarded for--
O.R.—SERIES I—VOLUME XLII/1 [S# 87] *AUGUST 1–DECEMBER 31, 1864.—The Richmond (Virginia) Campaign.* *No. 350.—Medals of Honor awarded for distinguished services under Resolution of Congress,*			
Eronson, James H	First Sergeant, Company D, 5th U.S. Colored Troops	Sept. 29	Do
Beaty, Powhatan	First Sergeant, Company G, 5th U.S. Colored Troops	Sept. 29	Do
Barnes, William H	Private, Company C, 38th U.S. Colored Troops	Sept. 29	Among the first to enter the rebel works, although wounded, at Chaffin's Farm, near Richmond, Va.
Fleetwood, Christian A.	Sergeant-major, 4th U.S. Colored Troops	Sept. 29	Do.
Gardiner, James	Private, Company I, 36th U.S. Colored Troops	Sept. 29	Gallantry in action at Chaffin's Farm, near Richmond, Va.
Holland, Milton	Sergeant-major, 5th U.S. Colored Troops	Sept, 20	Gallantry in action at Chaffin's Farm, near Richmond, Va.
Hilton, Alfred B.	Sergeant, Company H, 4th U.S. Colored Troops	Sept. 29	Gallantry in action as color bearer at Chaffin's Farm, near Richmond, Va.
Harris, James H.	Sergeant, Company B, 38th U.S. Colored Troops	Sept, 29	Gallantry in action at New Market Heights, Va.
James, Miles	Corporal, Company B, 36th U.S Colored Troops	Sept. 30	Gallantry in action at Chaffin's Farm, near Richmond, Va.
Kelly, Alexander	First Sergeant, Company F, 6th U.S. Colored Troops	Sept, 29	Gallantry in action at Chaffin's Farm, near Richmond, Va.
Pinn, Robert	First Sergeant, Company I, 5th U.S. Colored Troops	Sept. 29	Gallantry in action at Chaffin's Farm, near Richmond, Va.
Ratclift, Edward	First Sergeant, Company C, 38th U.S. Colored Troops	Sept. 29	Gallantry in action at Chaffin's Farm, near Richmond. Va.
Veal, Charles	Private, Company D, 4th U.S. Colored Troops	Sept. 29	Do.

O.R.—SERIES I—VOLUME XL/1 [S# 80]
JUNE 13–JULY 31, 1864.—The Richmond (Virginia) Campaign.

Dorsey, Decatur	Sergeant, Company B, Thirty-Ninth US Colored Troops.	July 30, 1864	Bravery while acting as color sergeant of his regiment at Petersburg.
Hawkins, Thomas	Sergeant-major, Sixth US Colored Troops	July 30, 1864	Rescue of regimental flag at Deep Bottom, Virginia.

(US War Dept., *The War of the Rebellion: a Compilation of the Official Records of the Union and Confederate Armies*, Govt. Print. Off., Washington, (1880–1901))

Twenty-Fifth Corps

On December 3, 1864, 13,650 black troops were assigned to the XXV (Twenty-Fifth) Corps, making it the largest black army in the history of the United States. The remaining nineteen thousand white troops were reassigned to the Twenty-Fourth Corps.

The Twenty-Fifth Corps was commanded by General Godfrey Weitzel. Weitzel was in charge of the Louisiana Native Guard after they were mustered into service by General Butler (see chapter 11: Butler and the Louisiana Native Guard). General Butler procured Weitzel in April 1864 and he was promoted to major-general in Butler's Army of the James in December 1864.

Fort Fisher

Fort Fisher protected North Carolina's port of Wilmington, which by December of 1865 was the last remaining supply route for the Confederate army. Northern merchants were expressing concerns to President Lincoln that European trade was still being conducted by the Confederate states through Wilmington. General Grant ordered General Weitzel of the Army of the James to capture the fort. Since General Weitzel reported to General Butler, Fort Fisher became Butler's responsibility. Butler took a similar approach to General Burnside's when he tried to blow up the Confederate defenses at Petersburg. Butler worked with the navy to load a ship with explosives that was to approach the wall of the fort and detonate. It was planned that the explosion would destroy the wall of the fort, but the plan failed. The explosives detonated prematurely, and the fort walls were not harmed. Butler's plan had depended on the floating bomb destroying the fort, and he had not massed enough troops for a successful frontal attack. When President Lincoln inquired about the progress of capturing the fort, Grant described it as a failure and recommended Butler's removal. Recall that General Grant admitted that his interference with the affair at the mine at Petersburg caused that plan to fail. Nevertheless, Butler was removed as commander of the Army of the James. Fort Fisher fell a month later.

Butler demonstrated at New Market Heights that black troops could be used effectively at frontal attacks, but perhaps he was not as ready to perform frontal attacks as Grant desired. Butler had showed a fondness for his black troops. Perhaps it was like having a prize pit bull as a pet and not having the stomach to put it in a dog fight.

CHAPTER 14

Rise, Shine, Give God the Glory

"they all admit it was the hardest stroke that there cause has received—the arming of the negrow. Not a few of them told me that they would rather fight two Regiments of white Soldiers than one of Niggers"

The Battle of Nashville

Fig. 31. *Battle of Nashville*, by Louis Kurz and Alexander Allison, 1893

ON DECEMBER 15, 1864, black troops played a decisive role in running General John Bell Hood out of Tennessee. By the end of the Civil War, Union officers were using black troops effectively. The tactic was to put them on the flank of the Union line and let them attack at the Confederate flank "double-quick." The Confederate reaction was to over commit to stopping the black flank advancement at the expense of its opposite flank and center defenses. White troops would then attack and at times rout the Confederate defense. This scenario was played out at the battle of Nashville. By the summer of 1864, there were close to 24,000 black men stationed in Tennessee. Under Lt. Gen. George H. Thomas Black USCT regiments played a decisive roll defeating General Hood at the Battle of Nashville. On the first day of the battle two black regiments were placed on the left flank of the Union line. The two black regiments threaten the confederate right flank causing them to draw reinforcements from the Confederate left flank. The large main force of white Union soldiers overwhelmed the Confederate left flank.

On the second day, black troops again attacked the Confederates right flank at Overton Hill. Confederates stopped the charge of the black troops by over committing to their right flank weakening their center and left flank. White USCT officers ordered them to "Close up those rank…as great gaps were made in them by howitzer and grape shot guns loaded to the muzzle." Again, the large main force of white Union soldiers routed the Confederate left flank. At the Battle of Nashville "Black units sustained 630 casualties out of 3,500 men in the victory."[150]

Following the Battle of New Market Heights, General Butler said *"in the Army of the James a negro regiment was looked upon as the safest flanking regiment that could be put in line,"* Butler's words were supported at the Battle of Nashville.

The following slave narrative was given by a former black Civil War soldier who fought at the battle of Nashville. Note that his name is "Anonymous." This is one of two anonymous slave narrative that I found in *Bullwhip Days*. The southern establishment would have found his narrative to be very disturbing, since Confederate Civil War soldiers were still idolized when the book was originally published in the 1930s. At the time of his narrative, blacks were subjected to racism in the South, so he may have had his name removed for fear of reprisal.

"When I went to the War, I was turning seventeen. I was in the Battle of Nashville, when we whipped old General Hood. I went to see my mistress on my furlough, and she was glad to see me. She said, 'You remember when you were sick and had to bring you to the house and nurse you?" And I told her, "Yes m, I remember. " And she said, "And now, you are fighting me?" I said, "No'm, I ain't fighting you. I'm fighting to get free."[151]
Anonymous

The Black Cavalry

There were six colored cavalry regiments formed in the Civil War called 1st to 6th USC. The 1st USC[152] was organized December 22, 1863 however; the 1st Mississippi Cavalry was featured by *Frank Leslie's Illustrated*, on December 19, 1863. The emancipation Proclamation freed slaves in union occupied territory, which freed slaves in Louisiana, Kentucky, Tennessee and Mississippi. Freed slaves were enlisted into the union Army. The cavalry unit illustrated was formed in Mississippi and was designated the First Mississippi Cavalry (African Descent)[153]. Once the USCT was

---

150 Glatthaar, *Forged in Battle*, 167.

151 Anonymous, *Bullwhip Days*, 339.

152 The Civil War Archive, Union Regimental Histories, *United States Colored Troops Cavalry*, http://www.civilwararchive.com/Unreghst/uncolcav. htm

153 Jubilo! The Emancipation Century, *On Their High Horses: Black Cavalry Soldiers in Mississippi*, https://jubiloemancipationcentury.wordpress. com/tag/1st-mississippi-negro-cavalry/

established the First Mississippi Cavalry was federalized and became the 3rd USC. General Butler "raised in Virginia three thousand negro cavalry"[154] which became the 1st and 2nd USC.

Fig. 32. "The First Mississippi Cavalry Bringing into Vicksburg Rebel Prisoners Captured at Haines Bluff," *Frank Leslie's Illustrated*, December 19, 1863

In late 1364 two companies (150 USCC) of the 3rd U.S. Colored Cavalry defeated a Confederate regiment twice their size (300 Confederates) at a railroad bridge across the Big Black River in Mississippi. A large Union force had failed to capture the bridge on several occasions. Maj. J. B. Cook and two companies of his colored cavalry *"tried their hands"* and "routed the Confederates fighting parts of the battle "hand to hand". It was declared "one of the most daring and heroic acts of the war."[155]

Battle of Saltville; Blessed Are the Peacemakers

Between December 10 and 29, 1864, black troops from Kentucky fought at Saltville, Virginia. The following is exceptional historical material because it describes the action of a black cavalry unit at the battle of Saltville. This article

154 Butler, *Butler's Book*, 494
155 J. T. G atthaar, *Forged in Battle*, p152

is closely related to the article in the following section about the beating of Patsy Leach, the widow of a black soldier. Patsy was beaten by her owner after he discovered that her husband had nobly died fighting at Saltville. Both documents appear separately in Ira Berlin's book *Free At Last*.

Clearly, black troops who fought in the Civil War had not only justification for retaliation against their enemies but also the opportunity. They chose instead at Saltville to show their enemies kindness. Many people feel that kindness displayed toward an enemy without retaliation is a sign of weakness, but it is a teaching of Jesus the protector. No one should ever characterize these men as weak.

The Battle of Salt Works Virginia was described by Colonel James S. Brisbiny:

Letter from Col. James S. Brisbiny to Brig. General Lorenzo Thomas

Lexington Ky Oct 20/64

General I have the honor to forward herewith a report of the operations of a detachment of the 5th U.S. Colored Cavalry during the late operations in Western Virginia against the Salt Works. After the main body of the forces had moved, Gen'l Burbridge Comdg. District was informed I had some mounted recruits belonging to the 5th U.S. Colored Cavalry, then organizing at Camp Nelson and he at once directed me to send them forward. They were mounted on horses that had been only partly recruited* and that had been drawn with the intention of using them only for the purpose of drilling. Six hundred of the best horses were picked out, mounted and Col Jas. F. Wade 6th. U.S.C. Cav'y was ordered to take command of the Detachment. The Detachment came up with the main body at Prestonburg Ky and was assigned to the Brigade Commanded by Colonel R. W. Ratliff 12th O[hio].V. Cav.

On the march the Colored Soldiers as well as their white Officers were made the subject of much ridicule and many insulting remarks by the white Troops and in some instances petty outrages such as the pulling off the Caps of Colored Soldiers, stealing their horses etc. was practiced by the white Soldiers. These insults as well as the jeers and taunts that they would not fight were borne by the Colored Soldiers patiently or punished with dignity by their Officers but in no instance did I hear Colored soldiers make any reply to insulting language used toward [them] by the white Troops.

On the 2nd of October the forces reached the vicinity of the Salt Works and finding the enemy in force preparations were made for the battle. Col Ratliffs Brigade was assigned to the left of the line and the Bridge dismounted was disposed as follows. 5th U.S.C. Cav. on the left. 12th O[hio]. V.C. in the center and 11th Mich. Cav. on the right. The point to be attacked was the side of a high mountain, the Rebels being posted about halfway up behind rifle pits made of logs and stones to the heights of three feet. All being in readiness the Brigade moved to the attack. The Rebels opened upon them a terrific fire but the line pressed steadily forward up the steep side of the mountain until they found themselves within fifty yards of the Enemy. Here Col. Wade ordered his force to charge and the Negroes rushed upon the works with a yell and after a desperate struggle carried the entire line killing and wounding a large number of the enemy and capturing some prisoners There were four hundred black soldiers engaged in the battle. one hundred having been left behind sick and with broken down horses on the march, and one hundred having been left in the Valley to hold horses. Out of the four hundred engaged, one hundred and fourteen men and four officers fell killed or wounded. Of this fight I can only say that men could not have behaved more bravely. I have seen white troops fight in twenty-seven battles and I never saw any fight better. At dusk the Colored

Troops were withdrawn from the enemies works, which they had held for over two hours, with scarcely a round of ammunition in their Cartridge boxes.

On the return of the forces those who had scoffed at the Colored Troops on the march out were silent.

Nearly all the wounded were brought off though we had not an Ambulance in the command. The Negro 'soldiers preferred present suffering to being murdered at the hands of a cruel enemy. I saw one man riding with his arm off another shot, through the lungs and another shot through both hips.

Such of the Colored Soldiers as fell into the hands of the Enemy during the battle were brutally murdered. The Negroes did not retaliate but treated the Rebel wounded with great kindness, carrying them water in their canteens and doing all they could to alleviate the sufferings of those whom the fortunes of war had placed in their hands. Col. Wade handled his command with skill bravery and good judgment, evincing his capacity to command a much larger force. I am General Very Respectfully Your Obedient. Servant

James S. Brisbiny

*i.e., disabled or diseased horses that had been only partly rehabilitated.[156]

Beating of a Black Soldiers Slave Widow

Many slave owners had a fear of their slaves being armed that evolved into hatred. They treated their slaves inhumanely to maintain their obedience. Once their slaves were armed, it would be impossible to control them, and their nobility would demand respect. Their belief system was based on white supremacy. Traditional black and white relationships were in jeopardy.

Kentucky was a border state that was not under the influence of the Emancipation Proclamation. Black men were allowed to join the Union army, but their families remained in slavery. Patsy Leach was one slave who remained in bondage while her husband was fighting for their freedom at Saltville, Virginia. She probably never knew how bravely her husband and his unit fought at the salt works at Saltville, Virginia. When Patsy's owner found out that her husband had died in the battle of Saltville, he threatened to kill her, so she escaped without her children. She later appealed to the Union army for the return of her children. A description of her husband's unit's performance is described in the previous section about "The Battle at Saltville, Virginia."

"I am a widow and belonged to Warren Wiley of Woodford County Ky. My husband Julius Leach was a member of Co. D. 5" U.S. C[colored].Cavalry and was killed at the Salt Works Va. about six months ago. When he enlisted sometime in the fall of 1864 he belonged to Sarah Martin Scott County Ky. He had only been about a month in the service when he was killed. I was living with aforesaid Wiley when he died.

About three weeks after my husband enlisted a Company of Colored soldiers passed our house and I was there in the garden and looked at them as they passed. My master had been watching me and when the soldiers had gone I went into the kitchen. My master followed me and Knocked me to the floor senseless saying as he did so, "You have been looking at them darned Nigger Soldiers"

When I recovered my senses he beat me with a cowhide. When my husband was Killed my master whipped me severely saying my husband had gone into the army to fight against white folks and he my master would let me know that I was foolish to let my husband go he would "take it out of my back," he

---

156 Ira Berlin, *Free at Last*, 489.

would "Kill me by piecemeal" and he hoped "that the last one of the nigger soldiers would be Killed" He whipped me twice after that using similar expressions

The last whipping he gave me he took me into the Kitchen tied my hands tore all my clothes off until I was entirely naked, bent me down, placed my head between his Knees, then whipped me most unmercifully until my back was lacerated all over, the blood oozing out in several places so that I could not wear my underclothes without their becoming saturated with blood.

The marks are still visible on my back. On this and other occasions my master whipped me for no other cause than my husband having enlisted. When he had whipped me he said "never mind God dam you when I am done with you tomorrow you never will live no more." I knew he would carry out his threats so that night about 10 o'clock I took my babe and traveled to Arnolds Depot where I took the Cars to Lexington

I have five children, I left them all with my master except the youngest and I want to get them but I dare not go near my master knowing he would whip me again. My master is a Rebel Sympathizer and often sends Boxes of Goods to Rebel prisoners. And further Deponent saith not.

Her mark
Signed Patsey Leach"[157]

Confederate Respect for Black Soldiers

The following article was published in the *Savannah Republic*, a rebel newspaper, following the battle of Honey Hill, South Carolina. The article suggests that black troops were observed fighting in the front or advance of the attacking army on a regular basis.

"The negroes, as usual, formed the advance, and had nearly reached the creek, when our batteries opened upon them down the road with a terrible volley of spherical case."
"The Savannah Republic"[158]

By the end of the war, black soldiers had earned the respect of their enemies, the Confederates. At one point in the battle of Milliken's Bend two companies of Iowans were stampeded from the battlefield. Confederate General McColloch said "The white or true Yankee portion ran like whipped curs almost as soon as the charge was ordered." while the blacks resisted with "considerable obstinacy," yet they could not hold the levee." [159]

Even the word "nigger" had a new meaning. In a letter to his mother, a Union officer wrote:

" I have talked with numbers of Paroled Prisoners in Vicksburg, and they all admit it was the hardest stroke that there cause has received—the arming of the negrow. Not a few of them told me that they would rather fight two Regiments of white Soldiers than one of Niggers. Rebel Citizens fear them more than they would fear Indians."[160]

157 Ira Berlin, *Free at Last*, 400.
158 Brown, *The Negro in the American Rebellion*, 261.
159 Glatthaar, *Forged in Battle*, 131-135
160 Glatthaar, *Forged in Battle*, 155.

Most Southerners believed in the racism that supported slavery, so when the Confederates debated arming slaves in 1865, it required that they denounce racism. At the heart of the Civil War conflict was the belief that blacks were better off as slaves, and invincible black soldiers proved to be a significant contradiction. Toward the end of the Civil War, one out of every ten Union soldiers was black. The Confederacy needed a black army to counter the Union's black army. However, it was almost impossible to put blacks on the battlefield without accepting the notion of equality. The debate is included in the book *Battle Cry for Freedom*, by J. M. McPherson[161].

Robert Toombs believed that blacks were inferior and their inscription into the Confederate army would reduce the pride that they had for their Confederate troops. He said "The day that the army of Virginia allows a negro regiment to enter their lines as soldiers they will be degraded, ruined, and disgrace." A Mississippi congressman agreed and said "Victory itself would be robbed of its glory if shared with slaves." But it was more than degradation of Confederate soldiers that they feared; it was the lifting of the black race that feared the South. White southern superiority was based on black inferiority. The Charleston Mercury expressed the fear that poor whites could be at the level of the slave, when they wrote "the poor man . . . reduced to the level of a nigger." This fear was echoed by Senator Louis Wigfall of Texas who said that he "wanted to live in no country in which the man who blacked his boots and curried his horse was his equal." The Richmond Examiner agreed and said it was a case of southern identity, culture and heritage. Lifting blacks to the level of the Confederate soldier would: "surrender the essential and distinctive principle of Southern civilization". These racist views were the foundation of the theory of slavery.

It was General Howell Cobb of Georgia however, who took the debate one step farther. He defined the southern cause as based on the theory of slavery and the theory of slavery was results of battlefield nobility. Therefore racial superiority was determined on the battlefield and measured in terms of courage, character and fighting performance. He said that "the moment you resort to negro soldiers your white soldier will be lost to you. . . . The day you make soldiers of them is the beginning of the end of the revolution. If slaves will make good soldiers our whole theory of slavery is wrong. And was not that the theory the South fought for? "

Many Southerners felt that blacks were meant to be slaves and were better off as slaves, but they had to respect their fight for freedom. One Virginian politician said:

"While slavery is the normal condition of the negro as indispensable to [his] prosperity and happiness . . . as is liberty to the whites never the less "if the public exigencies require that any number of our male slaves be enlisted in the military service in order to [maintain] our Government, we are willing to make concessions to their false and unenlightened notions of the blessings of liberty."

It was the Confederacy's most influential military general, General Robert E. Lee, who influenced the debate. Lee had observed the fighting ability of former slaves at the battles of Petersburg and Richmond.

"we should employ them without delay [even] at the risk which may be produced upon our social institutions...not only expedient but necessary," wrote Lee. "The negroes, under proper circumstances, will make efficient soldiers. I think we could at least do as well with them as the enemy. Those who are employed should be freed. It would be neither just nor wise . . . to require them to serve as slaves."[162]
General Robert E. Lee

---

161 J. M. McPherson, *Battle Cry of Freedom*, 836.
162 Ibid.

Under Lee's insistence, the Confederacy adopted the policy of arming slaves, but it was too late.

White Union troops had gained a great deal of respect for black troops as well. The 13th Kentucky Cavalry opposed the enlistment of blacks to the point that some of them almost murdered a USCT recruiting officer. A captain in the 13th Kentucky however changed his option of black troops after watching them fight. He said "never saw troops fight like they did. The rebels were firing on them with grape and canister and were mowing them down by the Score but others kept straight on."[163]

The Fall of Richmond: "let them up easy"

Fig. 33. The Federal Army Entering Richmond, Virginia, April 3, 1865,
Frank Leslie's 1895 Book, History of the Civil War

On April 2, 1865, black troops were among the first to enter Petersburg. They marched to the tune of "John Brown's Body" and included the lyrics "We'll hang Jeff Davis on a sour apple-tree."

Richmond fell the day after Petersburg, on April 3, 1865. Black regiments of Major General Weitzel's XXV Corps (see chapter 13: Twenty-Fifth Corps) led the Union army on the day Richmond was liberated and were the first to enter the city. Black correspondent Thomas Morris Chester reported that the 36th USCT was reported to be the first regiment to enter Richmond. Commanding the brigade marching into Richmond was Brevet Brigade General Alonzo Draper, former regimental major of the black regiment Thirty-Sixth USCT. Six months earlier, Draper and his black troops had driven Confederates guarding Richmond from their outer defenses (see chapter 13: *Colonel Draper's Charge*). The victory at New Market Heights had resulted in General Lee pulling his Confederate troops from Petersburg and retreating to the inner

---

163 Glatthaar, *Forged in Battle*, 165.

defenses of Richmond. The victory had helped to get Lincoln reelected, and fourteen black troops had been rewarded with Congressional Medals of Honor. Draper was promoted from the rank of major to brevet brigadier general. Earlier in the war Draper was an officer in *Wild's African Brigade* (see chapter 12: *Brigadier General Edward A. Wild*).

Thomas Morris Chester described the fall of Richmond to newspapers back in Philadelphia. Chester wrote:

"When General Draper's brigade entered the outskirts of the city it was halted, and a brigade of Devin's division, 24th Corps, passed in to constitute the provost guard. A scene was here witnessed which was not only grand, but sublime. Officers rushed into each other's arms, congratulating them upon the peaceful occupation of this citadel... The pious old negroes, male and female, indulged in such expressions: "You've come at last"; "We've been looking for you these many days"; "Jesus has opened the way"; "God bless you"; "I've not seen that old flag for four years"; "It does my eyes good"; "Have you come to stay?"; "Thank God", and similar expressions of exultation.

There General Draper's brigade, with the gallant 36th U.S.C.T.'s drum corps, played "Yankee Doodle" and "Shouting the Battle Cry of Freedom," amid the cheers of the boys and the white soldiers who filed by them... For marching or fighting Draper's 1st Brigade, 1st Division, 25th Corps, is not to be surpassed in the service, and the General honors it with a pride and a consciousness which inspire him to undertake cheerfully whatever may be committed to his execution. It was his brigade that nipped the flower of the Southern army, the Texas Brigade, under Gary, which never before last September knew defeat. There may be others who may claim the distinction of being the first to enter the city, but as I was ahead of every part of the force but the cavalry, which of necessity must lead the advance, I know whereof I affirm when I announce that General Draper's brigade was the first organization to enter the city limits. According to custom, it should constitute the provost guard of Richmond.

Kautz's division, consisting of Draper's and Wild's brigades, with troops of the 24th Corps, were placed in the trenches around the city, and Thomas' brigade was assigned to garrison Manchester. Proper dispositions have been made of the force to give security, and, soldier-like, placed the defenses of the city beyond the possibility of a surprise.

As we entered all the Government buildings were in flames, having been fired by order of the rebel General Ewell. The flames soon communicated themselves to the business part of the city; and continued to rage furiously throughout the day. All efforts to arrest this destructive element seemed for the best part of the day of no avail. The fire department of Richmond rendered every aid, and to them and the cooperate labors of our soldiers belongs the credit of having saved Richmond from the devastating flames. As it is, all that part of the city lying between Ninth and Fourteenth streets, between Main street and the river inclusive, is in ruins. Among the most prominent buildings destroyed are the rebel War Department, Quartermaster General's Department, all the buildings with commissary stores, Shockoe's and Dibbrel's warehouses, well stored with tobacco, Dispatch and Enquirer newspaper buildings, the court house, (Guy) House, Farmers' Bank, Bank of Virginia, Exchange Bank, Tracers' Bank, American and Columbia hotels, and the Mayo bridge which unites Richmond with Manchester. The buildings of the largest merchants are among those which have been reduced to ashes.

The flames, in spreading, soon communicated to poor and rich houses alike. All classes were soon rushing, into the streets with their goods, to save them."[164]

---

164 Chester, *Black Civil War Correspondent*, 290–291.

Thomas Morris Chester
Black Civil War Correspondent
His Dispatches from the Virginia Front

One of the black soldiers who led the Union army into Richmond on the day it fell was Chaplin Garland White. He marched into the capital of the Confederacy, Richmond, Virginia, at the front of his regiment, the Twenty-Eighth USCI. White wrote:

"I have just returned from the city of Richmond; my regiment was among the first that entered that city. I marched at the head of the column, and soon I found myself called upon by the officers and men of my regiment to make a speech, with which, of course, I readily complied. A vast multitude assembled on Broad Street, and I was aroused amid the shouts of ten thousand voices, and proclaimed for the first time in that city freedom to all mankind. After which the doors of all the slave pens were thrown open, and thousands came out shouting and praising God, and Father, of Master Abe, as they termed him. In this mighty consternation I became so overcome with tears that I could not stand up under the pressure of such fullness of joy in my own heart. I retired to gain strength, so I lost many important topics worthy of note.

Among the densely crowded concourse there were parents looking for children who had been sold south of this state in tribes, and husbands came for the same purpose; here and there one was singled out in the ranks, and an effort was made to approach the gallant and marching soldiers, who were too obedient to orders to break ranks.

We continued our march as far as Camp Lee, at the extreme end of Broad Street, running westwards. In camp the multitude followed, and everybody could participate in shaking the friendly but hard hands of the poor slaves. Among the many broken-hearted mothers looking for their children who had been sold to Georgia and elsewhere, was an aged woman, passing through the vast crowd of colored, inquiring for [one] by the name of Garland H. White, who had been sold from her when a small boy, and was bought by a lawyer named Robert Toombs, who lived in Georgia. Since the war has been going on she has seen Mr. Toombs in Richmond with troops from his state, and upon her asking him where his body-servant Garland was, he replied: "He ran off from me at Washington, and went to 'Canada. I have since learned that he is living somewhere in the State of Ohio." Some of the boys knowing that I lived in Ohio, soon found me and said, "Chaplain, here is a lady that wishes to see you." I quickly turned, following the soldier until coming to a group of colored ladies. I was questioned as follows:

"What is your name, sir?"
"My name is Garland H. White."
What was your mother's name?"
"Nancy."
"Where was you born?"
"In Hanover County, in this State." "Where was you sold from?"
"From this city."
"What was the name of the man who bought you?"
"Robert Toombs."
"Where did he live?"
"In the State of Georgia."
"Where did you leave him?"

"At Washington."

"Where did you go then?"

"To Canada."

"Where do you live now?"

"In Ohio."

"This is your mother, Garland, whom you are now talking to, who has spent twenty years of grief about her son."

I cannot express the joy I felt at this happy meeting of my mother and other friends. But suffice it to say that God is on the side of the righteous, and will in due time reward them. I have witnessed several such scenes among the other colored regiments.

Late in the afternoon, we were honored with his Excellency, the President of the United States, Lieutenant-General Grant, and other gentlemen of distinction. We made a grand parade through most of the principal streets of the city, beginning at Jeff Davis's mansion, and it appeared to me that all the colored people in the world had collected in that city for that purpose. I never saw so many colored people in all my life, women and children of all sizes running after Father, or Master Abraham, as they called him. To see the colored people, one would think they had all gone crazy…Some people do not seem to believe that the colored troops were the first that entered Richmond. Why, you need not feel at all timid in giving the truthfulness of my assertion to the four winds of the heavens, and let the angels re-echo it back to the earth, that the colored soldiers of the Army of the James were the first to enter the city of Richmond. I was with them, and am still with them, and am willing to stay with them until freedom is proclaimed throughout the world. Yes, we will follow this race of men in search of liberty through the whole Island of Cuba. All the boys are well, and send their love to all the kind ones at home.

Garland H. White, Chaplain,

28th USCI,

Richmond, Virginia, April 12, 1865"[165]

Weitzel set up his headquarters in the Whitehouse of the Confederate President, Jefferson Davis. They raised the American flag over Richmond, opened the slave pens, freeing thousands, who praised God and President Lincoln.

The Confederate perspective of the fall of Richmond is expressed in a very popular 1969 song written by Canadian Robbie Robertson called "The Night they Drove Old Dixie Down."[166] A verse in the song describes the plight of the people of Richmond:

"In the winter of '65, we were hungry, just barely alive

By May the tenth, Richmond had fell, it's a time I remember oh so well"

The next day, Weitzel met with President Lincoln and expressed his concern about the people of Richmond. Richmond was under siege since June 9, 1864 and supplies to the city were cut March 25, 1865. Much of the city was destroyed and the people of Richmond were suffering. President Lincoln replied *"If I were in your position, General, I think I would let them up easy, let them up easy."*[167] The XXV Corps dispensed supplies to the people of Richmond and protected the city from looters.

---

165 E. S. Redkey, *A Grand Army of Black Men*, 175.

166 Goggle Play, *The Night they Drove Old Dixie Down*, https://play.google.com/music/preview/Tf7jrcmdxfephhd3cvmtwotlbiq?lyrics=1&utm_source=google&utm_medium=search&utm_campaign=lyrics&pcampaignid=kp-lyrics

167 Fort Pocahontas, *Major General Godfrey Weitzel United States Army*, http://www.fortpocahontas.org/Weitzel.html

The Twenty-Fifth Corps pursued Robert E. Lee's army and participated in the closing battle at Clover Hill on April 9, 1865, the day of Lee's surrender. Black troops continued to follow General Lee to Appomattox, where he surrendered.

Charleston Liberated

Fig. 34. Black Troops Entering Charleston, *Harper's Weekly,* March 18, 1865

South Carolina was the first state to succeed from the Union and the Civil War started in south Carolina at Fort Sumter. The first black regiment was formed in South Carolina as well making the state an important part of Civil War history. On February 18, 1865, black troops fighting in the advance of the Union army were the first to enter Charleston. The Harper's weekly illustration reads, *"Marching on!"–The Fifty-fifth Massachusetts Colored Regiment singing John Brown's March in the streets of Charleston, February 21, 1865."*

A parade was organized by emancipated blacks of Charleston to celebrate their liberation on March 21, 1865. A report of the parade appeared in the New York Daily Tribune on April 4, 1865 called, *"A Jubilee of Freedom": Freed Slaves March in Charleston, South Carolina.*[168]

There was the greatest procession of loyalists in Charleston last Tuesday that the city has witnessed for many a long year. The present generation has never seen its like. For these loyalists were true to the Nation without any qualifications of State rights, reserved sovereignties, or other allegiances; they gloried in the

---

[168] History Matters *"A Jubilee of Freedom": Freed Slaves March in Charleston, South Carolina, March, 1865,* http://historymatters.gmu.edu/d/6381/

flag, they adored the Nation, they believed with the fullest faith in the ideas which our banner symbols and the country avows its own. It was a procession of colored men, women and children, a celebration of their deliverance from bondage and ostracism; a jubilee of freedom, a hosannah to their deliverers.

The celebration was projected and conducted by colored men. It met on the Citadel green at noon. Upward of ten thousand persons were present, colored men, women and children, and every window and balustrade overlooking the square was crowded with spectators. This immense gathering had been convened in 24 hours, for permission to form the procession was given only on Sunday night, and none of the preliminary arrangements were completed till Monday at noon.

Gen. Hatch, Admiral Dahlgren and Col. Woodruff gave their aid to the movement; and thereby the 21st Regiment of U.S.C.T., a hundred colored marines and a number of national flags gave dignity and added attractions to the procession.

The procession began to move at one o'clock under the charge of a committee and marshalls on horseback, who were decorated with red, white and blue sashes and rosettes.

First came the marshals and their aid[e]s, followed by a band of music; then the 21st Regiment in full form; then the clergymen of the different churches, carrying open Bibles; then an open car, drawn by four white horses, and tastefully adorned with National flags. In this car there were 15 colored ladies dressed in white, to represent the 15 recent Slave States. Each of them had a beautiful bouquet to present to Gen. Saxton after the speech which he was expected to deliver. A long procession of women followed the car. Then followed the children of the Public Schools, or part of them; and there were 1,800 in line, at least. They sang during the entire length of the march:

John Brown's body lies a moulding in the grave,
John Brown's body lies a moulding in the grave,
John Brown's body lies a moulding in the grave,
His soul is marching on!
Glory! Glory! Glory! Hallelujah!
Glory! Glory! Glory! Hallelujah!
We go marching on!

This verse, however, was not nearly so popular as one which it was intended should be omitted, but rapidly supplanted all the others, until at last all along the [?] or more of children, marching two abreast, no other sound could be heard than

We'll hang Jeff. Davis on a sour apple tree!
We'll hang Jeff. Davis on a sour apple tree!
We'll hang Jeff. Davis on a sour apple tree!
As we go marching on!

A similar parade occurred again in Charleston a month later. A Confederate prison for Union soldiers was located in Charleston at the site of the elite *Washington Race Course and Jockey Club.* The site contained a mass grave of Union soldiers. Because of the *"no-quarter"* Confederate policy for captured black soldiers, prisoner exchange was halted and many Union soldiers died in unsupplied confederate prisons. Many of the Union soldier remains were exhumed and given a proper cemetery burial at the site. A parade of 10,000 people was organized to dedicate the Union cemetery, which was the first *Memorial Day* Celebration.[169] *The procession started at 9 am on May 1, 1865. At the head of the procession was three thousand black schoolchildren carrying roses and singing "John Browns Body." They were followed by several hundred*

---

169 David W. Blight, *The First Decoration Day, https://zinnedproject.org/materials/the-first-decoration-day/*

black women carrying flowers and wreaths. The men marched next followed by Union soldiers. At the cemetery the children sang ""We'll Rally around the Flag," the "Star-Spangled Banner," and several spirituals". Black ministers read from scripture: "for it is the jubilee; it shall be holy unto you… in the year of this jubilee he shall return every man unto his own possession."

USCT's at Appomattox Court House: "Surrender of Lee and his army"

I had planned to say nothing about the Appomattox Court House because I had little to add to the existing history. However, discovery of a family member that was at the court house when Lee surrendered led me to research the event and now I question the existing history.

I was attending my brother n-law, Vernon Douglas's funeral when I became aware that Vernon and my wife Nancy's great grandfather Wallace Douglas was a private in the 114th USCT, Company K, XXV Corps. Vernon's cousin Pat Spalding informed me that his regiment served at Appomattox Court House. The National Park Service acknowledges that the 114th was at Appomattox Court House[170] but they are not included in the Park Service's history of Lee's surrender.

The National Park Service published the official history of colored troops in the Appomattox Campaign in a webpage named "Black Soldiers on the Appomattox Campaign."[171] The article states ," There were seven black units (approximately 2,000 men, or 3% of the Federal force) which made the journey all the way to Appomattox Court House … the 29th and 31st U.S.C.T., along with the 116th U.S.C.T., assigned to them from another brigade. Colonel Ulysses Doubleday's brigade, 8th, 41st, 45th, and 127th U.S.C.T., were also present."

Bennie J. McRae, Jr. compiled USCT records and published them on the web in three sections, which are Border States,[172] Northern States and Southern States. I found the 114th in the Border States section and their official regiment record states "Pursuit of Lee April 3-9. Appomattox Court House April 9. Surrender of Lee and his army." The Park Service states that the 116th was the only black regiment from Border States at Appomattox Court House. I searched through the USCT regiment records of the other Border States USCT regiments and found five additional regiments that state that they were at "Surrender of Lee and his army," which are the 109th, 114th, 117th, 7th and 19th. The Park Service states that the Northern State USCT regiments 8th, 29th 31th, 41st, 45th, and 127th were at Appomattox Court House. A search of the Northern States USCT regiment records support the presents of five of these regiments at Lee's surrender however the 43rd was present at Appomattox Court House as well. The record of the 36th and 29th states that they were in the Appomattox Campaign but they did not mention being present at Appomattox Court House. Review of the Southern State USCT records revealed that the 23rd was present at Lee's surrender as well.

The Park Service states that there were seven USCT regiments at Appomattox Court House, however review of USCT records indicate that there were fourteen USCT regiments at Lee's surrender, if we include the 29th.

The Park Service may have also under counted the USCT's at Appomattox. The Park Service states that there were about 2000 USCT's at Appomattox Court House which breaks down to less than 300 men per regiment. Newly formed regiments are required to have 970 men.[173] The 114th would be newly formed since it was organized only ten months before Lee's surrender. I would estimate that the number of USCT soldiers

170 National Park Service, *114th Regiment, United States Colored Infantry* http://www.nps.gov/civilwar/search-battle-units-detail.htm?battleUnitCode=UUS0114RI00C

171 National Park Service, *Black Soldiers on the Appomattox Campaign*, http://www.nps.gov/apco/black-soldiers.htm

172 Bennie J. McRae, Jr., *Organization of the United States Colored Troops in the Border States*, http://www.lwfaam.net/cw/bord_states

173 National Park Service, *From Regiment to President: The Structure and Command of Civil War Armies*, http://www.nps.gov/resources/story.htm?id=299

at Lee's surrender could exceed 10,000 men or 15% of the Federal force. The Park Service needs to correct the history "Black Soldiers on the Appomattox Campaign."

My Families Journey from Slavery to the Promised Land

Biblical identity was deeply entrenched into slave and African American culture but certainly not the American establishment. As blacks assimilated into American culture, the Children of Israel identity was discarded because blacks viewed their enslavement with shame and themselves as victims. The Israelites view their enslavement as part of their sacred past, and they hold it as a testimony of the power of their God. This difference in the view of slavery makes blacks entrenched in being a victim, and it gives purpose to Israelis to be victors.

The tradition of relating to the Bible for identity was maintained in my family. My dad's mother lived to be close to one hundred years old, and I was often very curious about her past. Her name was Leona White, and her maiden name was Bunn. I often asked her to talk about the old days. Her mother was Jane Richards Bunn, and her grandmother was former slave Matildia Richards. She was not well acquainted with her Grand Mother Matildia, and only knew her as "Mammy." Frequently, she would say, "You need to find my mama's Bible." I searched for the Bible and found it stored by a cousin in Arkansas. When I received the Bible, I was disappointed to find in it only a record of the deaths and births of ancestors. My great-grandmother could not read or write, so a literate cousin had made death and birth recordings. The Bible contained her history and thus her identity.

African American genealogy is different from other groups because of slavery. Before liberation slaves had no last names and were property. I was fortunate to work with a wonderful African American genealogist named *Sandra Craighead*. Most of what I know of my ancestors is a result of Sandra's hard work.

The paper "The Genetic Ancestry of African Americans, Latinos, and European Americans across the United States, The American Journal of Human Genetics" states that African Americans are three-fourths African and one-fourth European. My great-grandma Jane was a mulatto as well as her sister Aunt Lou. My great-grandmother, Jane Richards Bunn, had a white father, which was not uncommon for that time period. For years, we were not curtain of who Jane's father was. Tradition said that he was from a family named Buchanan. The Buchanans treated Jane and her family as if she was a family member of theirs. One of the Buchanan doctors saved my aunt Mae Wilma White Wyatt's life when she was a very ill little girl. After my grandfather died, Dr. Buchanan offered to care for my grandmother in his home. However, with online genealogy and DNA services, we were able to discover that her father was not a Buchanan but a Harrington. Mr. Harrington was just a poor white farmer with a family of his own. Black women belonged to slave owners and were protected by them during slavery times. Once black women were freed, they were vulnerable to sexual abuse by men that were not their owners. Her uncle was a nineteen-year-old Confederate soldier, named Henry A. Harrington. He was a member of the Second Regiment, Arkansas Mounted Rifles, Company E from Clark County. He died on May 5, 1862, in a Mississippi hospital. Her father was too old to serve in the army during the Civil War.

Aunt Lou (Jane's sister) was a mulatto as well. Since Harrington did not live near Jane's mother, it is unlikely that he fathered both children. Jane's mother, Matilda, had a twin sister named Nancy. Nancy had a mulatto child born during the same period as Jane.

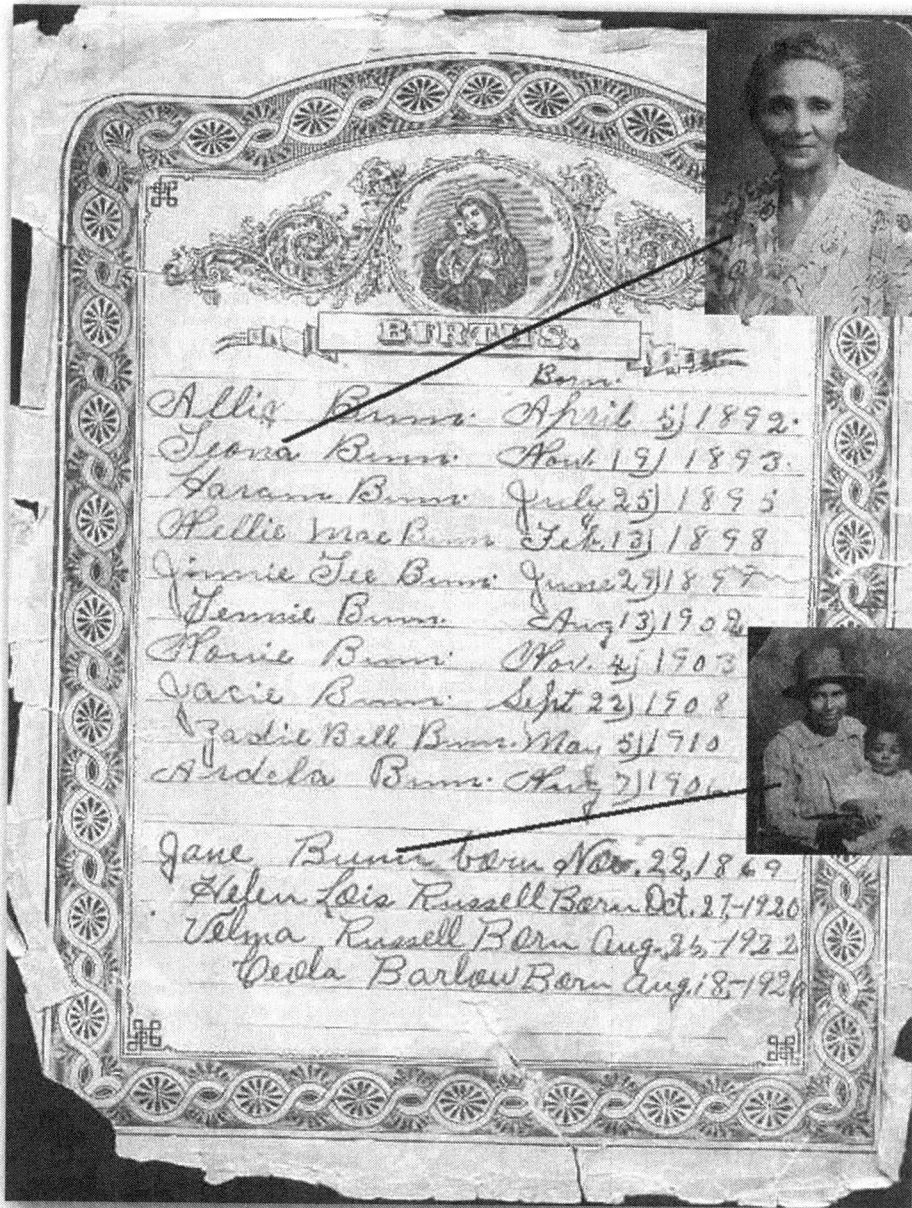

Fig. 35. Jane Richards Bunn's Bible

Matilda Richards was a slave and received the surname Richards from her mother's owner following the Civil War. The Richard family owned Matilda, her sister Nancy and their mother Maria. All three ancestors were from Tennessee and move to Arkansas with the Richard's in the 1850's. My great-grandmother was born several years after slavery ended.

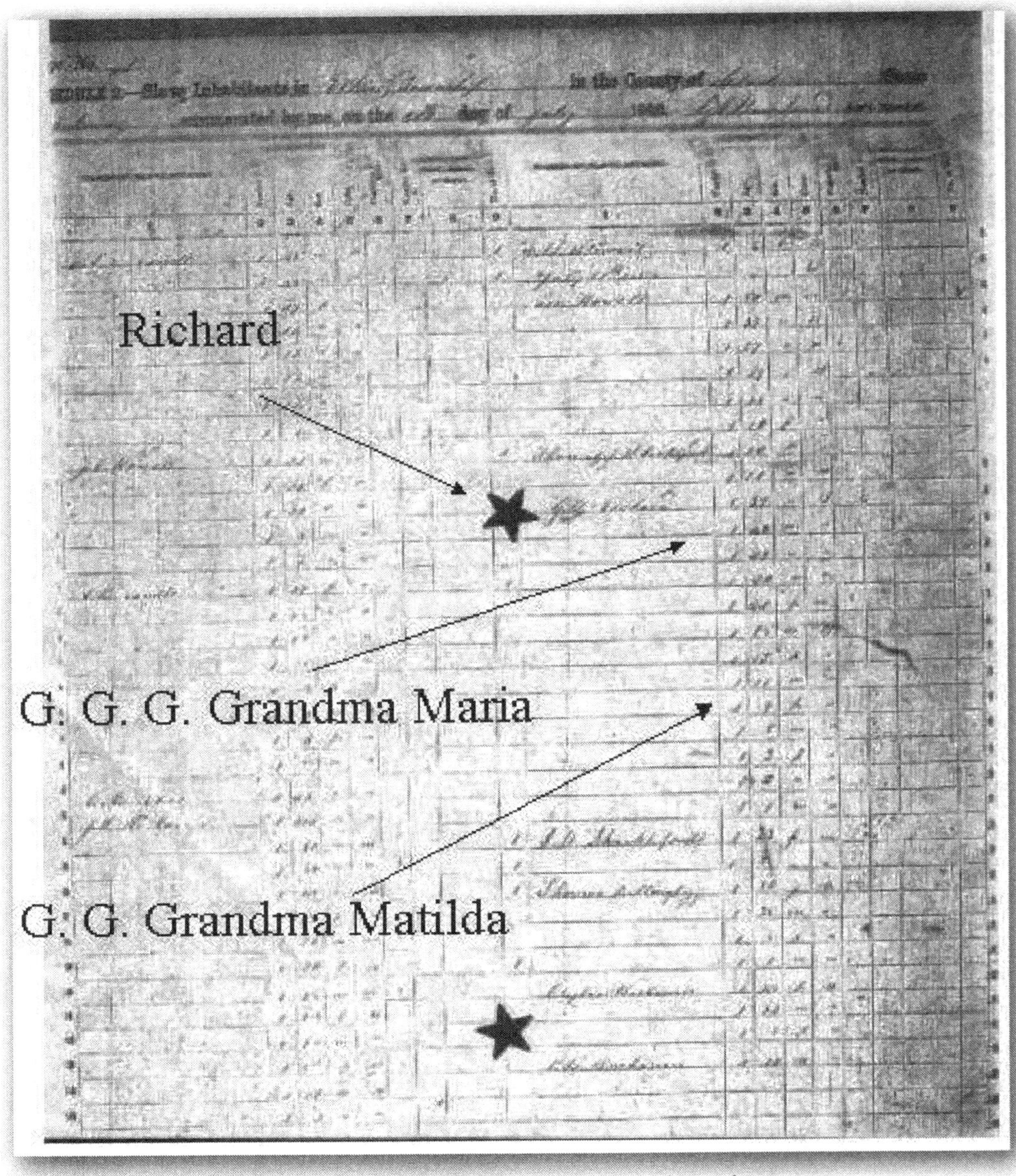

Fig. 36. 1860 Slave Schedule: Elkins Township Arkansas

During slavery days, Matilda; her sister Nancy; and her mother, Maria, are recorded in the 1860 Slave Schedule as nameless property. Only the age and sex are recorded in the slave schedules. The 1860 census recorded free Americans only. When we look at the 1870 census, we see that Great-Grandma Jane and her sister were both mulattos, but no father is present in the house. They had taken the last name of their previous owner, which was Richard. Most of the Richard family wealth was in their slaves so following slave liberation the Richard's were broke. The Richard's moved out of the area and my family remained in their slave cabins.

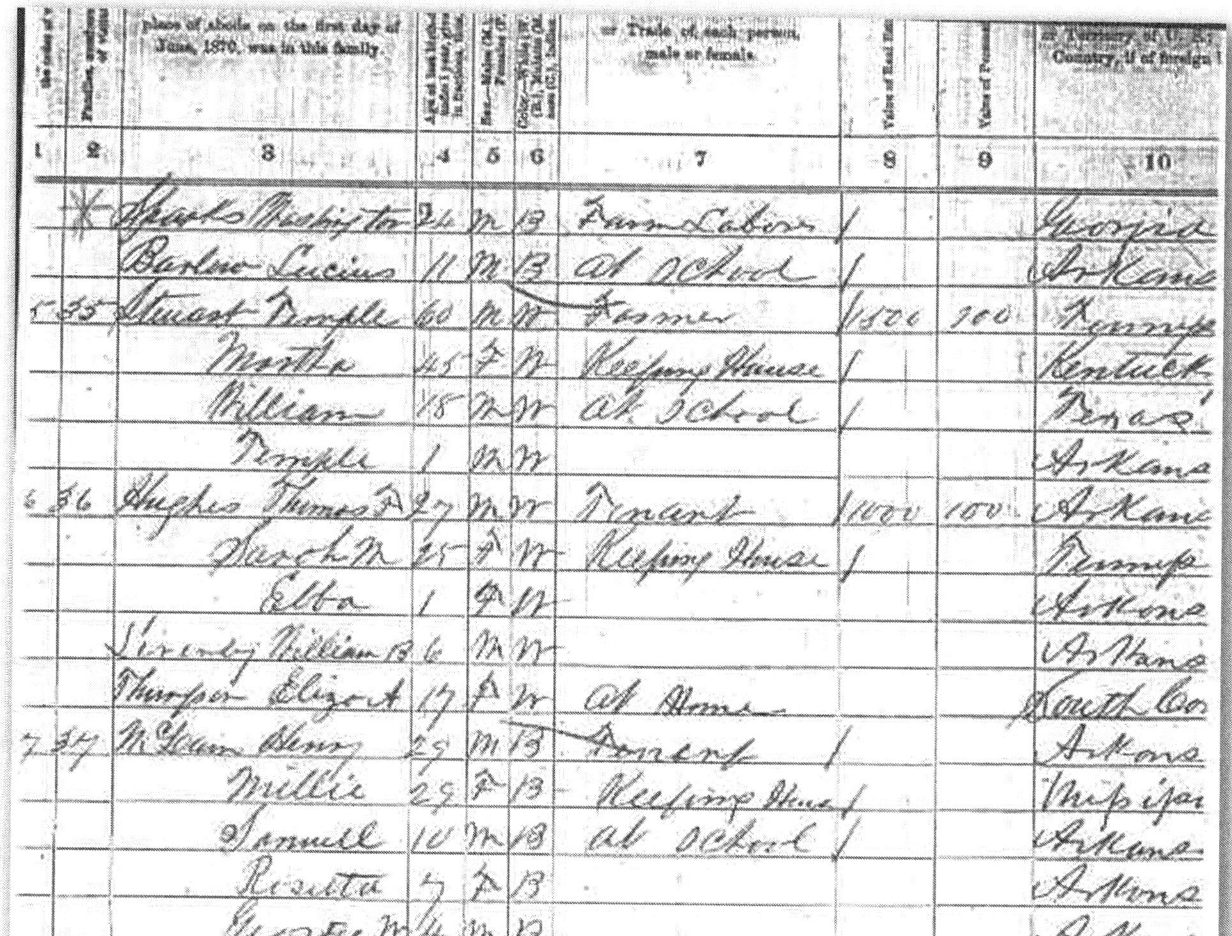

1	2	3 (place of abode on the first day of June, 1870, was in this family)	4	5	6	7 (or Trade of each person, male or female)	8	9	10 (or Territory of U.S.; or Country, if of foreign ...)
	*	Sparks Washington	24	M	B	Farm Laborer			Georgia
		Barlow Lucius	11	M	B	At School			Arkans
5	35	Stuart Temple	60	M	W	Farmer	1500	100	Tennesse
		Martha	45	F	W	Keeping House			Kentuck
		William	18	M	W	At School			Texas
		Temple	1	M	W				Arkans
6	36	Hughes Thomas F	27	M	W	Tenant	1000	100	Arkans
		Sarah M	25	F	W	Keeping House			Tennesse
		Elba	1	F	W				Arkans
		Tirenly William B	6	M	W				Arkans
		Thompson Eliza A	17	F	W	At Home			South Ca
7	37	McLean Henry	29	M	B	Tenant			Arkans
		Millie	29	F	B	Keeping House			Mississippi
		Samuel	10	M	B	At School			Arkans
		Rosetta	7	F	B				Arkans
		George W	4	M	B				Arkans
		Louis H	1	M	B				Arkans
8	38	Richard Nancy	25	F	B	Keeping House			Tennesse
		Mary	2	F	M				Arkans
		William	4/12	M	B				Arkans
9	39	Richard Matilda	15	F	B	Keeping House			Tennesse
		Luella	2	F	M				Arkans
		Maria E	1	F	M				Arkans
10	40	Richard Maria	48	F	B	Keeping House			Tennesse
		Pocahontas	11	F	B	At School			Arkans
		Cornelia	9	F	B	At School			Arkans
		Annis	6	F	B				Arkans
11	41	Welch Moses	27	M	B	Tenant			Arkans
		[illegible]	[illegible]	[illegible]	[illegible]	Keeping House			Arkans

Fig. 37. 1870 Clark County Arkansas Census
Genealogy Study performed by Sandra Craighead

Fig. 38. Clara White and My Great Grand Father Rev. Charley White, 1867-1934, holding his Bible.

My great-great-grandma Clara Taylor White was born a slave in Mobile Alabama. Her father was born in the District of Columbia and his name was Charles Taylor. Since both Grandma Clara and her dad were born in cities, they were probably house servants, since field slaves were born in rural areas. Grandma Clara was also a midwife. She would have been typical of the people interviewed for the slave narratives. She recalled that her father was sold to a nearby farm and they saw him on weekends. She also recalled that she admired her owners' furniture and dreaming of one day owning similar furniture.

Grandma Clara was liberated in Texas. She was married to George Sharp and their son was my great grandfather Charley Sharp. George Sharp died and Grandma Clara remarried in Arkansas. Grandpa Charley White took his last name from Clara's second husband Jerry White. We are fortunate to have a copy of her picture.

My family was deeply religious on both my mother's and father's sides. My mother's dad, Sam Bragg, was a minister of the Church of God. Sam's father was David Bragg who was born a slave on the Bragg farm in Ouachita County, Arkansas.

On my father's side, my great-grandfather Charley White, the son of Clara White, established a church in Holly Grove, Clark County, Arkansas. Grandpa Charley was a preacher, and his picture is shown with his Bible. My ancestors are buried in the cemetery across the street from the church. Following WWII there was a mass migration of people from rural places like Holly Grove to cities like Flint Michigan; however the love for their home was not forgotten. My father attended that church's annual homecoming as he aged well into his eighties.

Most African American families were liberated after the Civil War; however my wife Nancy's family was an exception. Nancy's great-great-great grandfather William Douglas was freed by a will fifty years prior to the Civil War.

132

Elizabeth Douglas willed William his freedom upon her death in 1809. She died at the age of 23 and had inherited her slaves a short time prior to her death. William was in trust to a free black lady before being freed. The remainder of Elizabeth's slaves was a family in trust to her brother. Her brother was in dept however and those slaves were never freed.

Elizabeth Douglas lived in Accomack, Virginia which was populated by 38% black of which 50% of them were free. Virginia however was not accommodating to free blacks. Virginia laws such as laws that prohibited black prayer meetings made Virginia inhospitable to free blacks. In 1820 William moved from Northumberland, Virginia to Aliceton, Kentucky in a wagon train of free blacks. Kentucky was one of two states that was not inhospitable to free blacks and had available land. Kentucky did not have laws restricting the education of blacks like that of Virginia and Ohio, the neighboring free state to the north of Kentucky. In 1820 William's son Wednesday was born. Wednesday's son Wallace Douglas became a member of the 114th United States Colored Troops at Camp Nelson Kentucky. William was also the name of Wallace's son which was my wife Nancy's grandfather.

Douglas family history is courtesy of Pat Spaulding.

Fig. 39. The Jubilee Singers (*The American Experience*, PBS Online)

The Fisk Jubilee Singers

The spirituals were first introduced outside of the African American community by the Fisk Jubilee Singers at Oberlin College. I had the opportunity to participate in an African American USCT Living History program at Oberlin College twenty years ago. Oberlin College is in northern Ohio in a small town of the same name. Oberlin was the home of Lewis Clarke, a former slave that inspired Harriet Beecher Stowe, who was the author of the book "Uncle Tom's Cabin." Oberlin College was the only college that admitted black students in the 1830's. The college was founded by two Presbyterian ministers and was against slavery

On November 16, 1871 a national convention of influential ministers was held at the college and the Fisk Jubilee Singers performed. The singers were trying to raise money for Fisk University. They wanted to build class rooms that could not be burned down by the KKK. They had sung common songs of the period for white audiences before but they were not inspirational and did not raise much money. They sang a couple of the contemporary ballads at Oberlin but results were again uninspiring. For the first time however, the singers started singing spirituals, the songs born during great tribulation. These were songs that were sung in secret prayer meetings in woods, fields and slave trading yards. They sang "Still Away to Jesus" and "All of a sudden, there was no talking," [174] says musicologist Horace Boyer. "They said you could hear the soft weeping . . . and I'm sure that the Jubilee Singers were joining them in tears, because sometimes when you think about what you are singing, particularly if you believe it, you can't help but be moved." Many people in the audience had been abolitionist that took a stand against slavery when their position was not popular. Many were criticized for being abolitionist but now they felt exonerated. They felt that Jesus did not support American slavery and they were now rewarded with this spiritual serenade.

Following their successful appearance at Oberlin College word spread and they were invited to other events. In December the Jubilee Singers appeared at Henry Ward Beecher's weekly prayer meeting at Brooklyn's Plymouth Church. Following that appearance demand for the singers surged. They would go on and sing for Mark Twain, President Ulysses S. Grant, congressmen and diplomats. They made spirituals such as "Swing Low, Sweet Chariot" and "This little light of mine," a permanent part of American heritage.

They toured Europe as well, performing for the royal families of Holland, Germany, and Britain. Queen Victoria wrote in her journal: "They are real Negroes," "They come from America and have been slaves. They sing extremely well together."

The Jubilee Singers returned to Fisk University after seven years of touring. They had raised enough money to complete Jubilee Hall and save the school from financial failure. As well as save the college the singers also saved souls and brought unbelievers closer to Jesus.

The spirituals united free blacks and slaves in their worship of God. The spirituals united people that were the descendents of many African tribes and gave them hope that carried them through the days of tribulation. The spirituals were translated into gospel music in the twentieth century and remained part of Africa American religious faith. However, many popular contemporary singers were trained in the church but altered their music for the large secular audience. Where spirituals focused on maintaining a relationship with God, secular music focused on maintain relationships with people. Relationships with God tend to substantially support human needs for security more than unpredictable relationships with people. The life of Whitney Houston is a good example. A great gospel voice was born in the church but ended tragedy by drugs in the secular world. This was a scenario repeated many times over by many singers and artist. The path to heaven revealed in the spirituals was replaced by drugs, the shortcut of the secular world to heaven.

Butler's Political Career

Butler switched from the conservative Democratic Party to the liberal Republican Party. He served in the US House of Representatives from 1867 to 1875. He drafted the initial version of the Civil Rights Act of 1871, called "The Ku Klux Klan Act." Butler tried to outlaw racial discrimination in public places, although it would not be until the Civil Rights Act of 1964 was passed that Butler's provisions would become law.

---

174 PBS Online, "The Jubilee Singers," *The American Experience*, http://www.pbs.org/wgbh/amex/singers/filmmore/description.html.

The film "Birth of a Nation" claimed that black troops protected newly won black voting rights during the initial phase of reconstruction. Blacks used the opportunity to elect black representatives to Congress who were not greeted with open arms except for Butler. Following the battle of New Market Heights Butler said "And, as I guided my horse this way and that way that his hoof might not profane their dead bodies, I swore to myself an oath, which I hope and believe I have kept sacredly, that they and their race should be cared for and protected by me to the extent of my power so long as I lived." Butler kept his promise, at a colored banquet in New Orleans, the master of ceremonies offered the toast: *"Here's to General Butler. He has a white face, but he has a black heart."* [175]

Butler was the governor of Massachusetts from 1883 to 1884, after which he ran for the presidency of the United States. In that short period as governor, he made several historic appointments. He was the first to appoint an African American (George Louis Ruffin) and an Irish American as judges. He was also was the first to appoint a woman to executive office. He appointed Clara Barton to head the Massachusetts Reformatory for Women (Wikipedia).

175 R. S. Holzman, *Stormy Ben Butler*, 205.

CHAPTER 15

Flawed History Is Flawed Identity

"The army wouldn't let us tell the truth about the black troops because the government figured they were expendable."

HISTORIANS FREQUENTLY CATER to their audience. Most Civil War battlefields are located in the South, and most southern Civil War history buffs support the Confederacy. African Americans have roots in the South, where people like Butler and John Brown are thought of as villains. Since Civil War historians cater to their audience, it is essential for African Americans to be part of that audience in order to be fairly represented in American history. History teaches us the importance of values that help us to be successful. If we don't understand how hard slaves fought to win their freedom, we may not recognize our obligation to do something to preserve our history and our culture. One thing we can do is make sure African American history is told completely and accurately, without omissions and exaggerations.

History is frequently taught through the media, and omitted history is flawed history. My father's experience illustrates my point. My father, John White Sr., was a sergeant in the 3,168th Quartermaster Service Company during World War II and landed on the beach of Normandy in the seventh wave on D-Day. One of their responsibilities was to bury the many dead American soldiers. They shared the hardships and casualties along with white troops. He never shared his war experience until I shared with him the hidden history of black Civil War soldiers. He started to understand that the lack of visibility of black World War II soldiers was not a reflection of their heroism, but a reflection of a desire for the American public to have their heroes look like themselves. Black and white worlds were segregated in those days, and blacks were very much a minority. He understood that the accomplishments of blacks might not be popular to the American public, but he was proud of what black soldiers accomplished. He made his opinion known to the *Flint Journal*, and they eagerly published his story on the front page of the Sunday edition (November 11, 2001). After all, Flint had a growing black public that was interested in black World War II heroes. He opened up and gave many speeches describing his D-Day experience.

The first movie that I saw that portrayed black World War II soldiers was called *Red Ball Express*. The Red Ball Express supplied General Patton's army as they marched toward Berlin, Germany. Blacks were featured unloading and loading the trucks, but the truck drivers were white. As they unloaded the trucks, they sang work songs, an old and forgot tradition. Work songs go back to Africa and were commonly song by African porters in *Tarzan* movies (my exposure to African American history). The songs were simple call and response, but they bound the men together so they worked in rhythm as one.

My uncle L. T. Wyatt (we called him Bredum), told me that he drove a truck during the war, so I told him about the movie. He told me that he was truck driver in the Red Ball Express, and everyone was black including the truck drivers. The movie was intended to give credit to black World War II soldiers, but compromises had to be made to

136

make it profitable. My uncle was shot twice in the side and wounded by shrapnel. The online encyclopedia Wikipedia describes the danger involved in the black unit:

> *"Director Budd Boetticher claimed that:*
> *The army wouldn't let us tell the truth about the black troops because the government figured they were expendable. Our government didn't want to admit they were kamikaze pilots. They figured if one out of ten trucks got through, they'd save Patton and his tanks."*[176]

Battle of New Market Heights Flawed Historical Record

General Butler was a visionary. He understood that blacks needed freedom but also needed respect to be equal American citizens. Respect had to be earned on the battlefield. Supporting African Americans damaged his reputation as a general due to the prejudice that existed against blacks. He was hated by his Union colleagues as well as his Confederate enemies. He felt that capturing New Market Heights would accomplish three goals. First, it would destroy General Lee's first line of defenses around Richmond and tighten Richmond's siege. Second, it would earn respect for black men, giving them the opportunity to liberate their own people and prove that all men are created equal. Many lives of white Union troops were lost in the Civil War and by 1864, Confederate troops were entrenched. Prove that black troops were capable and willing to drive the confederates from these trenches supported President Lincoln's 1864 reelection. Finally, it would demonstrate his competency and proof that he was a good general.

The Battle of New Market Heights was an enormous blow to the Confederacy. It was not only a military defeat but a psychological defeat as well. Recall that General Cobb said, "The day you make a soldier of them is the beginning of the end of the revolution. And if slaves seem good soldiers, then our whole theory of slavery is wrong. And was not that the theory the South fought for?" Black troops had destroyed the Confederate capital's outer defenses without firing a dozen shots and made them question what the South was fighting for.

Butler was successful at all three goals, but he lost the battle to historians over one hundred years later. Common knowledge of this history would have made segregation and African American persecution significantly more difficult. Americans would know nothing of the Battle of New Market Heights or the honors that black soldiers received. During the next century, the theory of slavery would live on. African Americans would carry the burden of the shame of slavery and endure segregation and discrimination.

Control of African American history and identity was maintained in many small, detailed ways. The history of the Battle of New Market Heights is a good example. Modern historians as well as the National Park Service have accepted a southern view of the Battle of New Market Heights that discredits the contribution of the black troops. This view says that the Confederate force held the black troops at New Market Heights in check until they were redeployed to Fort Harrison and the black troops overran empty Confederate trenches.

Modern historians use *Richmond Redeemed the Siege at Petersburg*, by Richard J. Sommers, as their major source for the history of the Battle of New Market Heights. Sommers discredited the achievement of black troops at the battle. He argued that the Confederates were not driven from their trenches at New Market Heights but were redeployed. The Union rally was the result of evacuated Confederate trenches. The *Flint Journal* published an article about a teacher that studied the battle.

---

176 Wikipedia, *Red Ball Express (film)*, http://en.wikipedia.org/wiki/Red_Ball_Express_(film).

"There is no question of the fact that the blacks were very brave," said Sommers. "(But) as far as I'm concerned, there is equally no question that it wasn't until the Confederates voluntarily abandoned their position that the blacks were able to move forward and occupy it. "[177]

No official Confederate records exist of the battle. The book *Hood's Texas Brigade*, by J. B. Polley, was used by Sommers as the primary source. Polley said the Texas Brigade, Arkansas Brigade, Benning's Brigade, and Gary's Cavalry were all at New Market Heights. Benning's Brigade plus the Texas Brigade alone consisted of eight hundred men. Gary's cavalry was composed of an additional eight hundred men, bringing the total Confederate force at New Market Heights to at least eighteen hundred men, counting Arkansas. Polley's overall description of the battle does not vary significantly from Union battle reports. The only exception is the so-called redeployment of the Texas Brigade during the charge of the colored troops. Recall that Polley wrote that "the firing had hardly ceased when word came that Gary's cavalry and Benning's brigade had been driven from their positions."[178]

Not comfortable with Polley's account of Gary's Cavalry and Benning's Brigade being driven from their trenches, modern historians imply that practically all of the Confederates were redeployed before black troops entered the trenches. This was done by first reducing Confederate troop strength at New Market Heights and second by redeploying Confederate troops during the battle. Wikipedia is a popular online encyclopedia with a reputation of having accurate information. Wikipedia describes the Battle of New Market Heights under the title of "Battle of Chaffin's Farm."[179] A map is included that resembles that made by Sommers. Wikipedia's battle map shows that Benning's Brigade of Confederate troops was missing from the battle, which deflates Confederate troop strength. Second, Wikipedia says Confederate General John Gregg redeployed all his troops from New Market Heights during the battle: "Word of Union success against Fort Harrison then reached Gregg, compelling him to pull Confederate troops back to Forts Gregg." This perspective is from Sommers as well and is widely accepted. The historian M. Gorman wrote on the US Park Service website that the black regiments attacking the trenches at New Market Heights: "found the Rebel works almost deserted. The few remaining Confederates either surrendered or fled."[180] The black troops therefore rallied against empty trenches, which was the only way they were able to capture New Market Heights.

This view contradicts Union battle reports as well as Polley's recollection, which is not even an official report. Polley said that only his Texas brigade was redeployed; the other Confederate regiments, which were Gary's Calvary and Benning's Brigade, were driven from their trenches by the charging black troops. The fact is that the Negro regiments drove all Confederates troops from their trenches at New Market Heights without firing a shot. As Polley put it, "Not a dozen shots in all were fired by the blacks."

Polley's book is the main source used by historians to diminish the accomplishment of the black troops at New Market Heights. However, Polley's credibility is questionable; he sought to please his proslavery audience, and he used typical stereotypical comments to accomplish this. For example, he professes that black troops would dare not attack their slave masters. He described a captured black soldier as saying, "Dar wahnt no way outer jinin', but fo' God, Marster, dis chile wouldn't nebbah un chawged you white folkses breas' wuks lack we did, eff der Yankkees hadn't er tole us day'd shoot us eff we didn't."[181] In no way should Polley's book trump official Union battle reports to discredit Congressional Medal of Honor winners.

---

177 Jonathan Tilove, "Hidden History Educator salutes black heroes who served in Civil War," Newhouse News Service, *Flint Journal*, Sunday, July 19, 1998.

178 Polley, *Hood's Texas Brigade*, 254.

179 Wikipedia, "Battle of Chaffin's Farm," http://en.wikipedia.org/wiki/Battle_of_Chaffin's_Farm.

180 Gorman, *The Union Perspective,* http://www.nps.gov/rich/historyculture/usct.htm.

181 Polley, J. B., *Hood's Texas Brigade*, p251

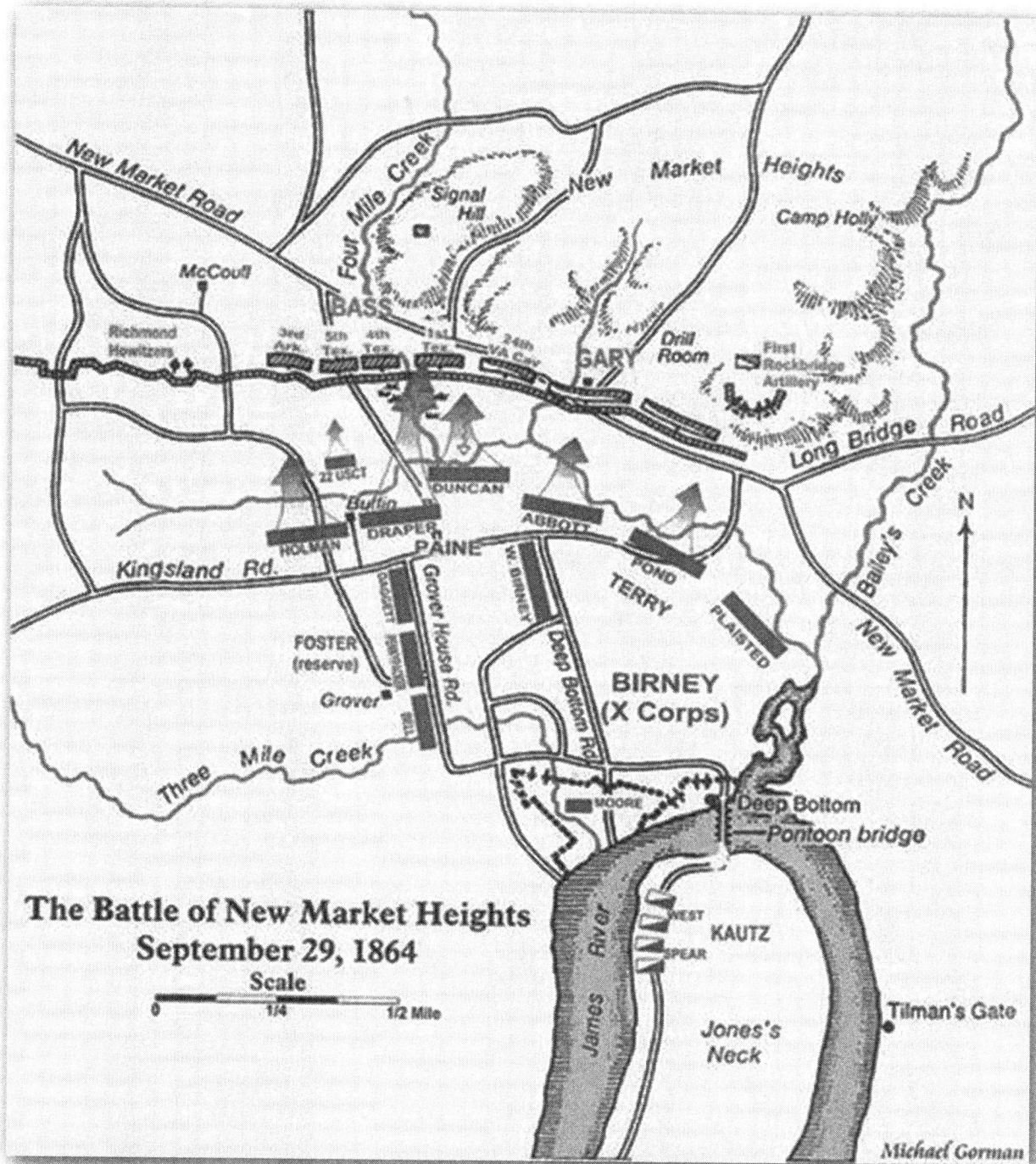

Fig. 40. Wikipedia, *Battle of Chaffin's Farm*

This was a case of historians rewriting history to sell books at the expense of the first black Congressional Medal of Honor winners. These Congressional Medals of Honor were not only the first given to African Americans but were also the greatest honor given to African Americans for an event in American history. To accept flawed history at New Market Heights is to devalue the honor bestowed on the event. Starting in April 2001, I worked with my congressman Dale Kildee to correct the National Park Service's history of the battle.

Although New Market Heights was not in his district, Kildee was a member of the *House Committee on Resources* and held a seat on the Subcommittee on National Parks and Public Lands. This subcommittee controls funding to the National Parks. Kildee had known my father since he was a junior congressman. Kildee was a catholic and committed to serving the poor, like my father. He complimented me by saying I was like my father. The NPS made significant improvements to its New Market Heights website, and I encourage the reader to visit the site: *http://www.nps.gov/rich/ historyculture/usct.htm*. The website is difficult to find from the battlefields home page, and a link should be installed by the Park Service.

New Market Heights, Virginia

The Battle of New Market Heights was marked with just a single roadside sign on New Market Road at the time of my visit during October 2011. There was no easy access to the sign; visitors had to find available parking and walk along the shoulder of the road to the sign's location. There were no available sidewalks or parking. This was not a reflection of the significance of the battle but more a reflection of a lack of attention given to the battle by American history. Since my 2011 visit, I participated in the 150th anniversary of the Battle of New Market Heights, hosted by Henrico County Virginia, September 27–28, 2014. The reenactment was outstanding. It was well organized by Henrico County and well attended by both Union and Confederate reenactors. The battle was reenacted historically correct. Henrico County also plans on improving the battle markers.

CHAPTER 16

My Remarks; Hunger and Thirst for Righteousness

MOST OF US are leader centered; we depend on leadership for guidance. This attribute is universal; however, it has its drawbacks. We assume that our leaders act in our best interests, but this is frequently not the case. Often leaders work in their own best interests. Leaders are often chosen by their courage at standing in front of a crowd and demanding attention; they are not necessarily chosen by their wisdom. During the early 1970s, I observed how a junior-college student-union leader initiated a race riot over a poor grade that he got on an English paper. I was historically a poor English student, but I received better English grades than he did.

A more recent example is the labeling of the LA Clippers basketball owner Donald Sterling as a racist. Comments were caught on tape that he did not want his young girlfriend fraternizing with black players. Black leadership on and off the court attacked Sterling, and the whole nation followed. Somehow Sterling became a symbol of a rich slave owner who used racism to dehumanize his slaves. Ironically, professional basketball players are wealthy. Racists believe in the superiority and inferiority of races. Racism was the core of slavery, the Civil War, and the fight for justice during the Civil Rights Movement. Labeling a jealous old man as a racist minimizes the history of the African American struggle for justice.

Racism is not very common; in fact, I have only run into one "card-carrying" racist. He argued that the differences between dog breeds and mixes served as an analogy for the inequality of the races. I was gentle with him because I wanted to get to know him, but he ran off. Racists depend on fear and ignorance to reinforce their wacky beliefs, and apparently I didn't have enough of either to hold his attention. Sterling's girlfriend was of mixed race (black and Mexican), which would be totally unacceptable to a true racist.

The church is the traditional source for moral leadership; however, John Brown questioned the churches support of slavery. The southern church was attached to the southern economy and benefited from the slavery system. John Brown refused to accept visits from the clergy before his execution. He felt that a slave and her child would be better company at his death than clergy that supported slavery.

An alternative to depending on leaders for guidance is to become principle centered. Principles such as truth are used for guidance, and we become our own moral compass. The problem here, however, is that one may find oneself separating from the group. This has been the theme throughout this book. Initially, I didn't believe that blacks fought in the Civil War because I shared the belief system of my friends. Many of us accepted our own inferiority—as sometimes happens when people like us have poor self-images—rather than embrace the truth alone. This is probably the point that motivated the Union army to select white USCT officers based on the results of an intelligence test. Intelligent people are more likely to be principle centered than unintelligent people, who rely on traditions, culture, and friends for guidance.

There are many cases, however, where very intelligent people follow idiots for various reasons. Although they are intelligent, they may lack inner strength or courage. Miss Sally was a perfect example of this dilemma. She chose to stand up to her father when she saw that he had lost his humanity. I believe that tenderhearted people experience peace and are reluctant to become dehumanized by dehumanizing others.

Prayer can be an important act that reinforces commitment to high ideals and principles. We are what we sing, chant, repeat, and believe. Sharing our desires with God is a way of committing ourselves to high ideals.

My Dad and the KKK

Here I would like to briefly digress and describe how the Ku Klux Klan touched my own family's life a hundred years after the Fort Pillow massacre. It is an account of how my father won a battle over the Ku Klux Klan by simply being fair.

My father grew up in the sticks of Arkansas under the stigma of racism. He fought in a segregated unit of the army in World War II and landed on Omaha Beach. He came up to Michigan after the war and went to work in the automotive plants in Flint, Michigan. He has told many stories of fighting racism in the automotive plants, but I found the following story to be the most meaningful, as it demonstrates how it is possible for one individual to have an influence that is the result of his or her character.

First, you must know my father; he was not able to attend high school, but he is very intelligent. Back in those days, the mid-1950s, management used fear to motivate workers. My father's foreman warned them to look busy whenever "big shots" were around. One day a big shot decided to make a surprise visit to my father's plant; his name was Mr. Mott. The name Mott is a giant in the automotive industry because the family was at the center of building General Motors. Mr. Mott was observed in the plant, so the word got out from line foremen to either look busy or hide. The production line had slowed down, so the workers in my father's area ran for cover—all except my father, that is. Mr. Mott saw him standing alone and went over to talk to him. He said to my father, "Why aren't you busy?"

My father replied, "The line is down." Then he said, "I have a question for you. Do you want me to be afraid of you and run when I see you coming?"

Mott said no.

"Well," my father said, "That is the way these plants are operating. They are putting on a show for you, and they go back to normal when you leave."

Mr. Mott thanked him and came back to visit my father whenever he visited that plant. Why? Because he knew he could get the truth from my father. My father was principle centered as opposed to being eager to please people with significant authority.

In those years there were many people from the South working in the automotive plants, and they brought their baggage with them. One piece of baggage was the Ku Klux Klan. Management's position was that Klan activities would not be tolerated. A young white worker was caught with Klan material, and the plant decided to make an example of him by firing him. The matter was brought to my father's attention by a group of white workers. They told him that the white kid was young, he did a stupid thing, and he had five kids who would suffer from his actions. They knew my father was fair and was well respected by management, going up to high levels.

My father agreed to help and spoke with the worker's managers. They told him that it was a done deal and that the white kid was history. My father did not like accepting no for an answer in this case. He decided that he needed to take the matter to a higher level. One day Mr. Mott was visiting my father's plant and was in a meeting with plant management. My father asked to be let into the meeting but was denied entry. Mr. Mott observed that it was my father and said, "Let him in." Again, my father requested that the white kid be given a second chance. Mr. Mott agreed, and the kid was given his job back. The tearful young man thanked my father and promised to avoid Klan activity. He stood by his agreement, and so did many other workers who dropped from the Klan. The Klan vanished at my father's plant.

Righteousness in a Jail Cell

How does it feel to be a slave? My answer would be it is humiliating, powerless and hopeless. Only those that have been incarcerated would know these feelings. One in every 10 black males is currently incarcerated and one of three will be incarcerated at least once during their life[182]. In 2013 there were 807,076 more black men under criminal justice supervision (1.68 million) than there were men enslaved in 1850[183] (before the Civil War). I was fortunate enough to experience these statistic first hand.

My father taught me to judge people by their character, not by the situation that they happen to be in. I taught this history in several Michigan prisons. Most of the inmates were black and had been incarcerated for drug-related crimes. I was never concerned about my safety, but eventually my material was considered to be too risky, so I was not allowed to continue teaching.

Ironically, the roles were reversed and I became a student of several inmates when I spent a night in a Flint, Michigan, jail cell. First, it was embarrassing to be there, but deep in my heart I knew it was Gods will and I must serve him. It was a very uncomfortable place. The holding room was about twenty feet wide and thirty feet long and held over thirty men. The ventilation was nonexistent, so the air quality was very poor, and breathing was difficult. I chatted with my fellow inmates, mostly about why we were there; charges ranged from defaulting on child support to armed robbery. (My offense was minor and later expunged.) A younger man passed out due to the bad air quality, and I was afraid I would be the next to drop, as I was an elder in the group. I thought that I could handle anything that these guys could tolerate, but I was straining to breathe. I was surprised when several inmates spoke up for me. They told the guard that I was not like them and I should not be there. They convinced the guard to let me sit on a bench outside of the cell where the air was fresh. As I sat there, I agreed with them; I was not like them. In my eyes, they were better people. I met my match in a jail cell. They were people who tried to help a stranger, even when they were at their lowest time, with nothing to gain. I promised them that I would never forget their kindness and I will speak up for them at any cost of my own prestige.

Why mention a Flint jail cell in a book about African American liberation? I have often wondered what possessed John Brown to ignite the Civil War. Lately, I noticed a healthy young black lady parking in a handicap parking space, then jogging into the store. We often judge a group of people based upon the actions of a few. I felt reluctant to help people that were self centered, but then I remembered the gentlemen in the Flint jail cell. I believe that some time

---

182 The Sentencing Project, *RACIAL DISPARITY,* http://www.sentencingproject.org/template/page.cfm?id=122

183 Politifact, *Brown U. student leader: More African-American men in prison system now than were enslaved in 1850,* http://www.politifact.com/rhode-island/statements/2014/dec/07/diego-arene-morley/brown-u-student-leader-more-african-american-men-p/

during John Brown's journey he met slaves like the Flint prisoners that I met; John Brown may have been repaying an act of kindness.

Affirmative Action; My Path to the Promised Land

As I write this conclusion on April 23, 2014, I have become aware of some disturbing news, Michigan's ban on racially based affirmative action has been upheld by the US Supreme Court. The decision is based upon the belief that all Americans have equal opportunity to be educated and no race should have preferential treatment.

Michigan's ban on affirmative action is the result of a voter initiative. The Supreme Court supported the University of Michigan's affirmative action program, so Michigan voters banned it. I know a little about the University of Michigan's affirmative action program, as I was a recipient, and both my sons graduated from the University of Michigan; however, my uncle did not. My uncle, Arthur Bragg (my mother's youngest brother), was the smartest man I had ever known. He was accepted to the University of Michigan's PhD program in mathematics in the 1950s and was among the first blacks to do so. I had a chance to view his grades; he had straight A's, and I examined his equations and proofs in awe. Unlike history, there is not much room for subjectivity in mathematics; there is usually only one answer to the problem that is correct. My uncle was a mathematical genius. He did not complete his PhD, however; his counselor died, and no one else would work with him on his thesis. Uncle Buck, as we called him, inspired all of his nephews and nieces; he shaped our identity. Many of us finished college and went on to have successful careers. He went on to teach at Delaware State University, where he was chairmen of the mathematics department until his retirement. He was also a colonel in the army reserves. He died of Parkinson's disease. When he was very ill, he would lie on his back and stare at the ceiling. I showed him my lithographs of black troops storming Fort Wagner and defeating Confederates at the Battle of Nashville. He perked up and became alert. It does not matter how smart we are or what we accomplish; all African Americans are affected by identity persecution and have that bond between us. This is because we are always viewed as black and carry the shame of slavery as viewed by those who do not know us personally.

I enrolled at the University Of Michigan College Of Engineering in 1970; it was the only college in the state that had an aeronautical engineering program. I learned about aeronautical engineering from watching a 1960s sitcom called *My Three Sons*. The comedy chronicled the life of a widower with three sons, and he happened to be an aeronautical engineer. One episode showed him working with jet-fighter aircraft that was malfunctioning. My dream was to design aircraft, and that's how I became acquainted with the occupation. I never met an engineer until I dated the daughter of one in college; her name was Lynn Geisert. Mr. Geisert would say to me, "Engineers can't write." The reader will be judge as to whether I was listening. I recall jogging with him, and he turned it on at the end to show me his speed; that was a race that I didn't mind losing. Their family was a lot like the white officers in the USCT, and I still love them today.

I was greeted at the U of M by a black grad student in charge of the new Office of Minority Student Affairs. White students welcomed me and ask me to sit on the engineering honor council. During my first meeting, I was met with silent stares from the white engineering students. I was sure they had discovered my deficiencies in thermodynamics, a course that I was struggling with. But to my surprise, they gave explanations as to why they did not participate in the U of M student class boycott. *What boycott?* I wondered. I had never heard of the strike, and I lived fifty miles away in Flint. They then went on to explain that no one explained the strike to them, and had they been aware of the reasons for the boycott, they would have joined the other schools in the strike. I accepted their apology and investigated the strike following the meeting. Apparently the U of M had a quota on how many blacks could go to the university. The students discovered the quota, and all of U of M's colleges went on strike except the engineering college. The quota was eliminated, and affirmative action was initiated.

I spent two years with U of M engineering students, and those guys were great. They were very smart but also very conservative. You could recognize the engineers one hundred yards away by their short haircuts and the slide rules worn on their hips. I wore the slide rule that my uncle Buck had given me. In this case, discrimination was documented as a quota, but discrimination is usually subjective.

In 1997 A white girl who lived near Flint Michigan initiated a lawsuit (*Gratz v. Bollinger*, 539 U.S. 244) against the University of Michigan's affirmative action program, and it was heard by the Supreme Court. The Supreme Court supported the University of Michigan's affirmative action program at the same time my son, Christopher White, was attending the U of M College of Engineering. My younger son, Sean, attended the Flint campus of the U of M with the financial aid that he received for his six years of service in the army reserves.

I understand the point of view that affirmative action is outdated, but this view does conflict with what I have said here. Recall that in my introduction, I described a Flint inner-city Sunday-school class composed of kids who identified themselves as "niggers." They may not have role models like my uncle Buck; their role models may call themselves "niggers." The Supreme Court's decision implies that these kids have the same opportunity as any other kids in the nation, although statistics would certainly not support that assumption. Most of the Supreme Court knows nothing of identity persecution. They have never read Mary Reynolds's narrative, nor do they know of the heroism at New Market Heights. The Supreme Court has been known to get it wrong, such as the *Dred Scott* case. I would, however, expect them to know law, such as *Brown v. the Board of Education*. It was revealed that black children did not see themselves as equal to white children and suffered from what I call identity persecution. Affirmative action may not be the answer to equal opportunity, but maybe equal opportunity is no longer an American value. This is where history plays a part in defining America's identity.

Conclusions

"The truth shall set you free"

AMERICA REMAINS HAUNTED by the N-word. Careers and lives have been significantly impacted by people accused of using the N-word. Generations of African American youth, however, have adopted the word and are reluctant to let it go. Prominent black activists have called for banning the word to improve the image of black youth. But when we examine the N-word, we discover that it simply means "black African American." The offensiveness of the word comes from the fact that African Americans experienced identity persecution to support slavery and post slavery discrimination. African American history that taught values such as valor, courage, and self-sacrifice was buried in past American history and replaced by mediocrity. The truth is that African American identity was persecuted but also resurrected by the adoption of a biblical identity. We also discovered that this biblical identity played a significant role in the African American struggle for freedom. It was not just a source of pride; the new identity brought hope and new responsibility. The power of God is often considered second to the power of arms. In the case of the slave, however, the power of God was the only power that existed. The biblical identity called for them to be slaves of God, but to serve God they had to be respected by men. Recall that a *New York Tribune* writer speaking of the Battle of Port Hudson wrote, "A race ready to die thus was never yet retained in bondage, and never can be." I have met black New Orleans tour guides who had never heard of the battle but were very knowledgeable of local history. If these events are lost from history, then the importance of African American sacrifices is lost, and a race may return to bondage. When history is lost, important lessons are lost, and repeating enslavement becomes possible.

African American identity was controlled by controlling African American history. Important lessons can be drawn from this. First, it is important to maintain one's accurate history. If people have no control of their history, they can be enslaved with a false history and made the prey of opportunists. Important ancestral teachings will be lost that may improve their lives. Second, the quote from Jesus, "The truth shall set you free" (John 8:32), is affirmed here. If false identity can enslave one, then discovering the truth about one's identity can set one free. Third, it is shown that a belief in the power of God can give hope where there is none, which can significantly improve our lives. Hope is a path out of depression and destruction. Finally, an accurate knowledge of one's identity can lead to more personal responsibility. Black troops proved at New Market Heights that all men are created equal. This could not be affirmed more by any other people at any other time in history. The belief that all men are equal benefits people around the world, not just African Americans. It is important to know one's true identity and accept the responsibility that comes with it. Personal responsibility is key to respecting one's identity. We will all experience loss and tragedy in our lives, but if we seek the power of God through prayer, we will find what we lost and much more.

The Park Service needs to correct the history "Black Soldiers on the Appomattox Campaign." This book will be published at the beginning of President Obama's last year of his presidency. President Obama is the first African American president of the United States. African Americans have carried the stigma of slavery for centuries. American history has supported the narrative that African American's were victims that did little to acquire their freedom. This narrative was used to support racism and is a detriment to African American identity. President Obama's support of accurate USCT history would correct this false narrative and add significantly to his legacy as president of the United States.

References

Abbot, Col. Joseph C. "7th New Hampshire Infantry." In *The War of the Rebellion: A Compilation of the Official Records of the Union and Confederate Armies*. Washington, DC: Government Printing Office, 1880–1901. No. 87: 702–03.

Atwell, Capt. Seager S. "7th Connecticut Infantry." In *The War of the Rebellion: A Compilation of the Official Records of the Union and Confederate Armies*. Washington, DC: Government Printing Office, 1880–1901. No. 87: 712–13.

Bennett Jr., Lerone, *Before the Mayflower*, New York: Penquin Group, 1984.

Berlin, Ira, ed. *Free At Last: A Documentary History of Slavery, Freedom, and the Civil War*. New York: New York Press, 1864.

*Brown, William Wells. *The Negro in the American Rebellion*. n.p.: Lee & Shepard, 1866.

*Butler, Benjamin F. *Butler's Book*. n.p.: A. M. Thayer & Co., n.d.

Chester, Thomas Morris. *Thomas Morris Chester: Black Civil War Correspondent, His Dispatches from the Virginia Front*. Edited by R. J. M. Blackett. Baton Rouge: Louisiana State Press, 1989.

*Douglass, Frederick. *Life and Writings of Frederick Douglass: Early Years, 1817–1849*.

Draper, Col. Alonzo. "36th US Colored Troops." In *The War of the Rebellion: A Compilation of the Official Records of the Union and Confederate Armies*. Washington, DC: Government Printing Office, 1880–1901. No. 87: 819–20.

Du Bois, William Edward Burghardt. *The Negro Church: Report of a Social Study Made Under the Direction of Atlanta University; Together with the Proceedings of the Eighth Conference for the Study of the Negro Problems, Held at Atlanta University, May 26th, 1903*. Atlanta: Atlanta University Press, 1903.

Glatthaar, Joseph T. *Forged in Battle: The Civil War Alliance of Black Soldiers and White Officers*. New York: Penguin Group, 1990.

Gorman, Michael D. "The Union Perspective of the Battle of New Market Heights." Richmond National Battlefield Park. http://www.nps.gov/rich/historyculture/union.htm.

Graham, Martin, and George Skoch. *Great Battles of the Civil War*. New York: Beekman House, 1990.

*Higginson, T. W. *Army Life in a Black Regiment*.

Holzman, R. S. *Stormy Ben Butler*. New York: Collier Books, 1961.

Janes, Capt. Albert. "22nd US Colored Troops." In *The War of the Rebellion: A Compilation of the Official Records of the Union and Confederate Armies*. Washington, DC: Government Printing Office, 1880–1901. No. 87: 817.

McPherson, James M. *Battle Cry of Freedom: A Complete History of the Civil War*. New York: Oxford University Press, 1988.

Mellon, James, ed. *Bullwhip Days: The Slaves Remember: An Oral History*. New York: Grove Press, 1988.

*Parton, James. *General Butler in New Orleans*. n.p.: Mason Brothers, 1864.

Pleasants, Henry. *Inferno at Petersburg*. Philadelphia: Chilton Book Co., 1961.

*Polley, Joseph B. *Hood's Texas Brigade: Its Marches, Its Battles, Its Achievements*. n.p.: The Neale Publishing Company, 1910.

*Pollock, John. *Amazing Grace*.

Raboteau, Albert J. *Slave Religion: The "Invisible Institution" in the Antebellum South.* Oxford University Press, 1978.

Redkey Edwin S., ed. *A Grand Army of Black Men: Letters from African-American Soldiers in the Union Army, 1861–1865.* Cambridge Studies in American Literature and Culture 63. New York: Cambridge University Press, 1993.

*Sobel, Mechal. *Trabelin' on the Slave Journey to an Afro-Baptist Faith.*

Stedman, John Gabriel. *Narrative of a Five Year Expedition against the Revolted Negroes, of Surinam in Guiana on the Wild Coast of South America from the years 1772 to 1777.* Vol. 1. London, 1796.

Walker, David. *Appeal.* Boston, 1829.

Ward, Geoffrey C. *The Civil War: An Illustrated History.* Based on the PBS documentary by G. C. Ward, R. Burns, and K. Burns. New York: Alfred A. Knopf, 1992.

*Williams, George W. *Negro Troops in the Rebellion, 1861–1865.* n.p.: Harper & Brothers, 1887.

www.ingramcontent.com/pod-product-compliance
Lightning Source LLC
Chambersburg PA
CBHW081146040426

42445CB00015B/1787